Frank Jacob (ed.)
Wallerstein 2.0

Sociology

Frank Jacob, born in 1984, is a professor of global history at Nord Universitet, Norway. He received his PhD in Japanese studies from Friedrich-Alexander-Universität Erlangen-Nürnberg in 2012 and held positions at Julius-Maximilians-Universität Würzburg and The City University of New York before moving to Norway in 2018. His research interests include transnational anarchism and revolution theory.

Frank Jacob (ed.)
Wallerstein 2.0
Thinking and Applying World-Systems Theory in the 21st Century

[transcript]

Published in Open Access thanks to the financial support from Nord Universitet

Bibliographic information published by the Deutsche Nationalbibliothek
The Deutsche Nationalbibliothek lists this publication in the Deutsche Nationalbibliografie; detailed bibliographic data are available in the Internet at http://dnb.d-nb.de

This work is licensed under the Creative Commons Attribution-Non Commercial 4.0 (BY-NC) license, which means that the text may be may be remixed, build upon and be distributed, provided credit is given to the author, but may not be used for commercial purposes.
To create an adaptation, translation, or derivative of the original work, further permission is required and can be obtained by contacting rights@transcript-publishing.com
Creative Commons license terms for re-use do not apply to any content (such as graphs, figures, photos, excerpts, etc.) not original to the Open Access publication and further permission may be required from the rights holder. The obligation to research and clear permission lies solely with the party re-using the material.

First published in 2023 by transcript Verlag, Bielefeld
© Frank Jacob (ed.)

Cover layout: Maria Arndt, Bielefeld
Printed by: Majuskel Medienproduktion GmbH, Wetzlar
https://doi.org/10.14361/9783839460443
Print-ISBN: 978-3-8376-6044-9
PDF-ISBN: 978-3-8394-6044-3
ISSN of series: 2703-1691
eISSN of series: 2747-3007

Printed on permanent acid-free text paper.

Contents

1. **Wallerstein 2.0**
   Thinking and Applying World-Systems Theory in the 21st Century
   Frank Jacob 7

2. **Global History, World History, and Wallerstein's World-Systems Theory as Definitional Caesuras**
   Frank Jacob 33

3. **Zemiperiphery Matters**
   Immigration, Culture, and the Capitalist World-System
   Stephen Shapiro 49

4. **Semiosphere and World-System**
   A Semiotic Reflection on Migration and Nationalism within the World-System
   Giuditta Bassano 73

5. **An Ongoing Paradox in the World-System of Migration**
   The EU's Response to the Migration Crises, Rising Nationalism, and its Treatment of Greece
   James Horncastle 99

6. **Wallerstein's World-Systems Theory and the Role of Revolutions**
   Frank Jacob 121

7. **Nationalist New Education**
   A Wallersteinian Approach to Education in the World-System
   Sebastian Engelmann 155

8. **Contributors** 177

1. Wallerstein 2.0
Thinking and Applying World-Systems Theory in the 21st Century

Frank Jacob

Introduction

> "My intellectual biography is one long quest
> for an adequate explanation of contemporary reality
> that I and others might act upon."[1]

Immanuel Wallerstein is often named "the master of the field"[2] when scholars discuss world-systems theory, and while there are others whose works paved the way for this kind of analysis,[3] it is true that the former had a prominent position within the field he helped to create. Wallerstein, however, would not only be perceived as a "worldwide renowned and influential sociologist and economic historian, interdisciplinary researcher of the emergence, functioning and structural crisis of the polarised world system of capitalist economy, as well as radical intellectual who closely related scientific analysis and political action of antisystemic movements,"[4] but also as a "prolific writer and forceful

---

1   Immanuel Wallerstein, *The Essential Wallerstein* (New York: The New Press, 2000), 15.
2   William G. Martin, "Still Partners and Still Dissident after All These Years? Wallerstein, World Revolutions and the World-Systems Perspective," *Journal of World-Systems Research* 11, no. 2 (2000): 235.
3   For a broader survey of the field and relevant works see Salvatore J. Babones and Christopher Chase-Dunn, eds., *Routledge Handbook of World-Systems Analysis* (London/New York: Routledge, 2012).
4   Vera A. Vratuša Žunjić, "In Memoriam: Scientific and Political Legacy of Immanuel Wallerstein (1930–2019)," *Sociološki pregled / Sociological Review* 53, no. 4 (2019): 1339.

polemicist on a wide range of topics from contemporary Africa to social theory.[5] Considering both of these sides of Wallerstein's voluminous œuvre, it is safe to agree with Christopher Chase-Dunn, Jackie Smith, Patrick Manning, and Andrej Grubačić, who described Wallerstein as "an intrepid protagonist of human equality and an innovative and influential social scientist who led a scholarly movement to build a coherent framework for understanding the emergence and development of global capitalism."[6] Wallerstein was searching for theoretical answers to historical problems[7] as well as a way to "translate the lessons from [world-systems] analyses into action aimed at transforming this indisputably unjust system."[8] Indeed, Wallerstein and his colleagues opened a path for a specific look at the history and the current state of the globalized world, and world-systems theory became an essential part of the analysis of capitalist modernity. Despite often being criticized and probably never truly en vogue for a majority of scholars in the humanities and social sciences, world-systems theory can offer more than is frequently anticipated.[9] Before these aspects are taken into closer consideration, a closer look at Wallerstein's life and work and the elements or events that influenced them seems to be in order to see how his conceptualization of what would later be termed "world-systems theory" or "world-systems analysis" was, in a certain way, just a consequence of his personal experiences.

---

5   Robert S. DuPlessis, "Wallerstein, World Systems Analysis, and Early Modern European History," *The History Teacher* 21, no. 2 (1988): 221.

6   Christopher Chase-Dunn, Jackie Smith, Patrick Manning, and Andrej Grubačić, "Remembering Immanuel Wallerstein," *Journal of World-Systems Research* 26, no. 1 (2020): 5.

7   Robert A. Denemark and Barry K. Gills, "World-System History: Challenging Eurocentric Knowledge," in *Routledge Handbook of World-Systems Analysis*, eds. Salvatore J. Babones and Christopher Chase-Dunn (London/New York: Routledge, 2012), 163–171.

8   Chase-Dunn, Smith, Manning, and Grubačić, "Remembering Immanuel Wallerstein," 6.

9   Walter L. Goldfrank, "Wallerstein's World-System: Roots and Contributions," in *Routledge Handbook of World-Systems Analysis*, eds. Salvatore J. Babones and Christopher Chase-Dunn (London/New York: Routledge, 2012), 97–103. See also the recently published anthology on the "critical juncture" of world-systems analysis: Corey Payne, Roberto Patricio Korzeniewicz, and Beverly J. Silver, eds., *World-Systems Analysis at a Critical Juncture* (London/New York: Routledge, 2022).

Wallerstein's Life and Work

I believe that I have been fairly consistent in my views over the time I have been writing. Still, I have to acknowledge that there were three turning points in my political and intellectual development. The first, as I have already indicated, was my struggle with the issues that have plagued the left for most of its organizational history-the rift between the Second and Third Internationals. The second was my encounter with Africa and with national liberation movements. This enabled me to put the debates of the Internationals into their proper context, as essentially European debates that ignored the fundamental and ongoing polarization of the capitalist world-economy. And the third was the world revolution of 1968, which I experienced directly at Columbia University, and which helped expunge from my thinking both the lingering illusions of liberalism and a rosy view of the antisystemic movements. It sobered me up.[10]

Wallerstein, born in 1930 as a child of a "German Jewish immigrant family" in New York City, grew up in an international metropolis until he went to study sociology at Columbia University in 1947.[11] He chose this subject due to the "freedom offered by this then young discipline, whose boundaries were not rigid," and when one considers the broad diversity of topics Wallerstein worked on during his career, he probably continued to appreciate the freedom sociology as a discipline offered him.[12] Early on, Wallerstein grew up with a political conscience that was stimulated by his family and the possibilities provided by the metropolis, which acted as "both a haven for refugee intellectuals and the prime vantage point for seeing the world as a whole."[13] Wallerstein himself said that his

> family was politically conscious, and world affairs were always discussed in our home. The fight against Nazism and fascism was of primary concern to us long before Pearl Harbor. We were also very conscious of the great split in

---

10 Wallerstein, *The Essential Wallerstein*, xxi-xxii.
11 Stéphane Dufoix and Yves-David Hugot, "Le système-monde Wallerstein," *Socio* 15 (2021): 9-19.
12 Ibid.
13 Walter L. Goldfrank, "Paradigm Regained? The Rules of Wallerstein's World System Method," *Journal of World-Systems Research* 11, no. 2 (2000): 153.

the global left at the time, that between the Second and Third Internationals. Even in the muted atmosphere of wartime unity, the issues that divided the two Internationals were salient, and they were reflected for me at a local level by the political differences between New York's Liberal and American Labor parties. When I entered Columbia College in 1947, the most vibrant political organization on campus during my freshman year was the American Veterans Committee (AVC). Although I was too young to have been a veteran, I attended the public meetings of the AVC, and saw it torn apart (and destroyed) by this same split.[14]

This political split within the Internationals and the struggle or divide between communism and social democracy would have a long-term impact on the thoughts of Wallerstein.[15]

Wallerstein was a student at Columbia University until 1957. He turned out to be an Africanist first and foremost, and he later became the president of the American Association of Africanists in 1973.[16] After a Master's thesis on McCarthyism, Wallerstein focused on Africa for his PhD thesis, which compared the nationalist movements in two African states: the Ivory Coast and Ghana.[17] Although Wallerstein studied continuously at Columbia, he also took opportunities to study abroad, e.g., in Paris, where his "experience gave him access to a rich and proud scholarly tradition which could reinforce his New Yorker's disdain for conventional U.S. social science, a tradition which was furthermore free from the rigidities of pre-New Left Marxism."[18]

Wallerstein's dissertation-related fieldwork also led him into the so-called Third World, where he could gain first-hand impressions of the consequences of Western imperialism at a time in which those scholars whose work focused

---

14 Wallerstein, *The Essential Wallerstein*, xv.
15 Ibid. Wallerstein argues in this regard: "Politically, this created dilemmas with which I have had to wrestle ever since. Intellectually, it turned me to a set of questions that I have developed in my writings over the years: the nature of what I came to call the antisystemic movements, and how their activities were structured by systemic constraints from which they were never able fully to release themselves."
16 Dufoix and Hugot, "Le système-monde Wallerstein."
17 Immanuel Wallerstein, *The Road to Independence: Ghana and the Ivory Coast* (Paris: Mouton, 1964). The book was described as "unremarkable in theory or method but notable for the high degree of personal involvement in the research." Goldfrank, "Paradigm Regained?" 156.
18 Goldfrank, "Paradigm Regained?" 155.

on Africa could not yet claim to be part of a specific disciplinary field but who would ultimately help to forge one.[19]

Besides his PhD thesis, which was later published as a book as well, Wallerstein wrote "two influential books"[20] on Africa: *Africa: The Politics of Independence* (1961) and *Africa: The Politics of Unity* (1967).[21] While working on topics related to African history and politics, "Wallerstein's early career and thinking was profoundly impacted by his friendship with Frantz Fanon, whose thinking remained among the most important influences on Wallerstein's work."[22] Fanon's critical works about colonialism and imperialist exploitation influenced Wallerstein's critical thought about questions related to the capitalist world-system that he later formulated through his own theoretical reflections.[23] Wallerstein's reading of Walter Rodney's work about the intentional underdevelopment of Africa[24] to serve European capitalism and expansionism may have been similarly important, although the former did not consider parts of the work "very satisfying."[25] However, Wallerstein later invited Rodney to work with him and used the latter's considerations as a basis for his own critical approach toward a better understanding of Africa:

> To understand Africa, we must reconceptualize world history. And for the scholarly world to effectuate such reconceptualization, we as Africanists must do our share by doing our work within such a perspective. I am not calling for intellectual supermen. I am merely asking that we concentrate on grinding a new pair of glasses, and that we wear these new glasses in the very process of grinding them. This is a hard task, but not a new one, since this is the only way in which man has ever invented the new truths

---

19 Immanuel Wallerstein, "Africa in a Capitalist World," *Issue: A Journal of Opinion* 10, no. 1/2 (1980): 21.
20 Vratuša Žunjić, "In Memoriam," 1340.
21 Immanuel Wallerstein, *Africa: The Politics of Independence* (New York: Vintage Books, 1961); Immanuel Wallerstein, *Africa: The Politics of Unity* (New York: Random House, 1967).
22 Chase-Dunn, Smith, Manning, and Grubačić, "Remembering Immanuel Wallerstein," 6.
23 Frantz Fanon, *Les damnés de la terre*, with a preface by Jean-Paul Sartre (Paris: Maspero, 1961).
24 Walter Rodney, *How Europe Underdeveloped Africa* (London: Bogle-L'Ouverture, 1972).
25 Wallerstein, "Africa in a Capitalist World," 25.

that caught up his new realities and yet simultaneously criticized these new realities in the light of human potentialities.[26]

Although Wallerstein's research focus eventually drifted away from Africa, he was well aware of the role it had played in his own scientific formation: "I credit my African studies with opening my eyes both to the burning political issues of the contemporary world and to the scholarly questions of how to analyze the history of the modern world-system. It was Africa that was responsible for challenging the more stultifying parts of my education."[27]

Another experience that tremendously impacted Wallerstein's life and intellectual development was the global revolution of 1968. The events and experiences in this year seem to have given more focus to Wallerstein's thoughts about the world-system, which until then had been more confused. His writings of the early 1960s dealt with numerous elements of his world-systems theory, but the trigger to bring them together into one larger theoretical framework must have been this year of global revolutionary developments.[28]

However, Wallerstein's theoretical transition was not only related to his observation of the global protests of 1968, as the young sociologist was actually quite involved in the political struggles that accompanied or expressed this "global revolution" in its US context. His involvement seemed to weaken his academic position at Columbia University in the early 1970s, which is why he left for McGill University in 1971, while his colleague Terence Hopkins[29] moved on to SUNY Binghamton, where both would work together again from 1976. There were consequently also personal changes that might have stimulated Wallerstein's reorientation with regard to his research, although, as Gregory

---

26   Ibid., 25–26.
27   Wallerstein, *The Essential Wallerstein*, xvii.
28   Chase-Dunn, Smith, Manning, and Grubačić, "Remembering Immanuel Wallerstein," 5; Gregory P. Williams, *Contesting the Global Order: The Radical Political Economy of Perry Anderson and Immanuel Wallerstein* (Albany, NY: State University of New York Press, 2020), 91.
29   Terence Hopkins (1928–1997) was an American sociologist who was important for the study of world-systems theory at Binghamton, where he founded the graduate program in sociology. He worked closely with Wallerstein, and together they published, among other works: Terence K. Hopkins and Immanuel Wallerstein, eds., *Processes of the World-System* (Beverly Hills, CA: Sage Publications, 1980); Terence Hopkins and Immanuel Wallerstein, *World-Systems Analysis: Theory and Methodology* (Beverly Hills, CA: Sage Publications, 1982). See also Immanuel Wallerstein, "Terence K. Hopkins (11/20/1928 – 1/3/1997)," *Review* (Fernand Braudel Center) 39, no. 1/4 (2016): n.p.

P. Williams remarked, "[t]he transition Wallerstein underwent from 1967 to 1973 was not in research topic, but rather in historical imagination and measurement."[30] The student protests in New York City "pushed him further to the left politically," a fact that partially influenced Wallerstein's decision to leave Columbia University, "impelling him further towards a kind of sublimated revenge against the academic establishment."[31] The protesters in New York City expressed their voices against the war in Vietnam in solidarity with the civil rights movement and, at the same time, demanded more political rights for students. In this situation, Wallerstein was among those faculty members who were solidaric with the students and supported their demands. He was "one of ... very few white professors trusted by the black students in the undergraduate college, and took a leading role in drafting the left faculty's proposed reforms."[32] He also documented the crisis of the university system in a later publication.[33]

It was in the 1970s that Wallerstein, mainly due to his recent experiences, began to take a different look at the world and began to coin "world-systems analysis," a process based for him on "major intellectual decisions. [One, and probably the most important,] was that the choice of the 'unit of analysis' was crucial, and that the only plausible unit of analysis was a 'world system,' or more generally, an 'historical social system.'"[34] Eventually, Wallerstein's changed perspective was, as Walter L. Goldfrank described it, "a formidable synthesis of continental historicism, 'Third World' radicalism, and Marxism."[35] His former research on Africa stimulated this intellectual transformation, especially considering the fact, outlined by American sociologists Daniel Chirot and Thomas D. Hall, that "[w]orld-system theory is a highly political approach to the problem of economic development in the Third World. It was created by policy-oriented intellectuals in countries at a medium level of development to account for their societies' demonstrable inability to catch up to the rich countries."[36] Within American sociology, world-systems theory was perceived "as a direct

---

30   Williams, *Contesting the Global Order*, 93.
31   Goldfrank, "Paradigm Regained?" 157–158.
32   Ibid., 158.
33   Immanuel Wallerstein, *University in Turmoil: The Politics of Change* (New York: Atheneum, 1969).
34   Wallerstein, *The Essential Wallerstein*, xvii.
35   Goldfrank, "Paradigm Regained?" 150.
36   Daniel Chirot and Thomas D. Hall, "World-System Theory," *Annual Review of Sociology* 8 (1982): 81.

attack against the version of development theory that had prevailed in the 1950s and 1960s"[37] and therefore, in a way, expressed a generational struggle within the discipline as such. The idea to apply world-systems analysis would change the way modernization and development were to be understood and thereby also challenged previous theoretical reflections about these processes.

While Walt W. Rostow, an American economist, argued for a "uniform evolutionary theory of development,"[38] this only considered developing societies to move in one direction through the following stages: "traditional economies, the transition to take-off (the adoption of scientific methods of technology), the take-off (rapid capital accumulation and early industrialization), the drive to maturity (high industrialization in which the standard of living of the masses remains low), and the age of high consumption."[39] In contrast to many who shared Rostow's ideas about the flow of development from one stage to another and who next expected a post-industrial stage,[40] those who believed the world-system to be a better or more suitable analytical unit countered such considerations. The latter group included the German-American sociologist and economic historian Andre Gunder Frank,[41] whom Wallerstein referred to as "one of the major figures of world anti-Establishment thought in the twentieth century"[42] and probably "one of the most polemical and simplistic of the world-system theorists, but one of the most intellectually influential."[43]

Ultimately, however, it was Wallerstein "who brought world-system theory (including the name itself) into the sociological limelight in the 1970s."[44] In 1976, Wallerstein took the chance to join Hopkins at Binghamton, where they would work together closely and found the Fernand Braudel Center.[45] Their

---

37   Ibid.
38   Ibid., 82.
39   Ibid. For his full theoretical approach, see Walt W. Rostow, *The Stages of Economic Growth: A Non-Communist Manifesto* (Cambridge: Cambridge University Press, 1960).
40   Daniel Bell, *The Coming of Post-Industrial Society: A Venture in Social Forecasting* (New York: Basic Books, 1973).
41   Frank's works include, among others, *The Development of Underdevelopment* (New York: Monthly Review Press, 1966) and *Dependent Accumulation and Underdevelopment* (New York: Monthly Review Press, 1978).
42   Immanuel Wallerstein, "Remembering Andre Gunder Frank," *History Workshop Journal* 61 (2006): 305.
43   Chirot and Hall, "World-System Theory," 83.
44   Ibid., 84.
45   The center unfortunately closed in June 2020.

research challenged "classical ideas" about development,[46] and his theoretical approach to history, namely the study and analysis of world-systems, would make Wallerstein well-known beyond his original field of research and expertise. In addition, his position as Distinguished Professor and Chair provided Wallerstein with some advantages. For example, in addition to directing the new center, he could bring in new faculty members and hire some foreign visiting professors as adjuncts. The center also published the newly established journal *Review*, which would have a particular impact on world-systems studies in the following decades.[47]

With such a secure position, Wallerstein could safely pursue his academic endeavors, and it was he, together with Frank, Samir Amin, and Giovanni Arrighi (the so-called "Gang of Four"), who continued to stress the importance of the world-system as an analytical category to better understand the world.[48] Wallerstein later stated that they "agreed on at least eighty per cent of the analysis of the modern world. As for those issues about which we disagreed, there was no pattern to the alliances among us. But it was the areas of accord that were the most important to us."[49]

Wallerstein's ideas and others' criticism of them shall be briefly summarized in the next section to illuminate the intellectual impact world-systems theory has had within numerous fields of research.

World-Systems Theory

> World-systems analysis ... is not a theory but a protest against neglected issues and deceptive epistemologies. It is a call for intellectual change ... It is an intellectual task that is and has to be a political task as well.[50]

Wallerstein's world-systems theory is well-known and probably does not need a substantial introduction.[51] However, Walter L. Goldfrank's well-worded sum-

---

46 Terence K. Hopkins and Immanuel Wallerstein, "Patterns of Development of the Modern World-System," *Review* (Fernand Braudel Center) 39, no. 1/4 (2016): 83–128.
47 Goldfrank, "Paradigm Regained?" 158; Williams, *Contesting the Global Order*, 2.
48 Samir Amin, Giovanni Arrighi, Andre Gunder Frank, and Immanuel Wallerstein, *The Dynamics of Global Crisis* (New York: Monthly Review Press, 1982).
49 Wallerstein, "Remembering Andre Gunder Frank," 306.
50 Wallerstein, *The Essential Wallerstein*, xxii.
51 For a short and concise introduction, see Goldfrank, "Paradigm Regained?" 177–182.

mary will be reproduced here to provide a short evaluation of his theory and its impact within different disciplines:

> Wallerstein's method of reconceptualization and reinterpretation has regenerated many long-standing controversies in social science. To some extent, this is due to the confusing disjuncture between general concepts and explanatory building blocks. To some extent, it is due to the difficulty of giving new technical meanings to familiar words, such as "world" (as applying to anything less than the globe), "empire" (as applied in the usage "world-empire" to redistributive totalities), and "capitalism" ("capitalist" accumulation plus "primitive" accumulation within a system of unequally strong, competitive states). But if some of the contributions to these controversies are old songs sung by new voices, most seem to be sophisticated and useful in advancing both theoretical and substantive work on questions of large-scale, long-term change. The work of Wallerstein and his collaborators, while still unfinished, has provided a major push to historical social analysis, including historical analysis of the present.[52]

Andrew B. Appleby has emphasized the value of Wallerstein's theoretical approach for historical research in particular, as the latter showed and emphasized the necessity to apply better theoretical toolsets to avoid historians "drowning in their own data" and keep them from ending up in "the dust bins of antiquarianism."[53] In contrast to history as a field, sociology, particularly in the US context, "has been marked by an almost pervasive disinterest in history as an element of explanation of present and future social relations."[54] This made Wallerstein's approach quite unconventional for sociologists there, to say the least. Wallerstein consequently also revived an interest in historical studies, especially since his considerations demanded a longer time span to explain social change and the state of the current world. *The Modern World-*

---

52   Goldfrank, "Paradigm Regained?" 193.
53   Andrew B. Appleby, "Review of Immanuel Wallerstein. The Modern World-System: Capitalist Agriculture and the Origins of the European World-Economy in the Sixteenth Century," *The American Historical Review* 80, no. 5 (1975): 1323–1324, cited in DuPlessis, "Wallerstein," 222.
54   Stanley Aronowitz, "A Metatheoretical Critique of Immanuel Wallerstein's 'The Modern World System'," *Theory and Society* 10, no. 4 (1981): 503.

System thus changed perceptions of social change as such, something a single scholarly work had not been able to achieve for a long time.[55]

In the first volume of *The Modern World-System*, Wallerstein explained how the modern capitalist world-system had been created since the beginning of the 16th century and in which ways "[t]his complementary and interlocking structure of labor delivered to the states and privileged classes of the core the chief benefits of capital accumulation in the world-system as a whole."[56] The latter, by these processes, is eventually divided into core, semi-periphery, and periphery. Although Wallerstein continues to describe its development in the following volumes on the world-system, including cyclical trends, the main theoretical frame had been laid out in the first volume. All in all, it is "[t]he boldness of his approach, his capacity to combine close attention to a specific period with a theory of historical transformation," that, according to Stanley Aronowitz, offers "a kind of model of historical sociology."[57] Wallerstein's "central idea" challenged existent thoughts about history and development, arguing that "the modern global system has an evolving hierarchy based on institutionalized exploitation."[58] What is probably more significant, and also makes Wallerstein's world-systems theory an important analytical tool in different disciplinary contexts, is the fact that "the *whole system* was the proper unit of analysis, not national societies, and that development and underdevelopment had been structured by the long history of global power relations, shaped over centuries."[59] His analysis in this regard also surpassed the nation-state or national society as an analytical boundary and offered a truly global and more comparative approach to the understanding of the maturation and the current state of the world.[60] American sociologist Philip McMichael called this approach an "incorporated comparison,"[61] as it compares the de-

---

55   Ibid. Aronowitz compares the impact of *The Modern World-System* with Karl Polanyi's *The Great Transformation* (New York: Farrar & Rinehart, 1944).
56   Steve J. Stern, "Feudalism, Capitalism, and the World-System in the Perspective of Latin America and the Caribbean," *The American Historical Review* 93, no. 4 (1988): 830.
57   Aronowitz, "A Metatheoretical Critique," 503.
58   Chase-Dunn, Smith, Manning, and Grubačić, "Remembering Immanuel Wallerstein," 5.
59   Ibid.
60   Philip McMichael, "Incorporating Comparison within a World-Historical Perspective: An Alternative Comparative Method," *American Sociological Review* 55, no. 3 (1990): 385–386.
61   Ibid., 386.

velopments or states of different parts of the world system within the latter's wholeness.[62] This, in a way, also secures a more critical and, probably more importantly, flexible approach with regard to the analytical units, as "[t]he whole ... does not exist independent of its parts. Whether considering nation-states or a singular world system, neither whole nor parts are permanent categories or units of analysis."[63] In contrast to previous analytical units, for Wallerstein, the world-system offered "a self-contained entity based on a geographically differentiated division of labor and bound together by the world market and the international system of national states,"[64] and it could be "used to describe the difficulties of change within advanced industrial societies."[65]

Wallerstein intended to change the way we look at the world when we try to understand it. Regardless of the criticism his theoretical approach may have caused, he was relatively successful in this because many scholars have since begun to study the modern world-system and applied his theoretical reflections to the point that world-systems analysis developed its own disciplinary frame. Wallerstein later reflected on his analytical approach as follows:

> World-systems analysis allowed me to range widely in terms of concrete issues, but always in such a way that the pieces might fit together at the end of the exercise. It is not that world-systems analysis enabled me to "discover the truth." It is rather that it enabled me to make what I considered to be plausible interpretations of social reality in ways that I believe are more useful for all of us in making political and moral decisions.[66]

The modern world-system, or, as Wallerstein insisted, "a capitalist world-economy,"[67] and its formation or establishment determined the course of human history and the development of human societies, creating "five major cleavages of our modern world: race, nation, class, ethnicity, and gender."[68] Wallerstein not only wanted to explain the creation of the modern world-system but also,

---

62 Immanuel Wallerstein, *Welt-System-Analyse: Eine Einführung* (Wiesbaden: VS Verlag für Sozialwissenschaften, 2019), 22.
63 McMichael, "Incorporating Comparison," 386.
64 Chase-Dunn, Smith, Manning, and Grubačić, "Remembering Immanuel Wallerstein," 5.
65 Williams, *Contesting the Global Order*, 94.
66 Wallerstein, *The Essential Wallerstein*, xviii.
67 Ibid., xix.
68 Ibid.

in a way, to decode it: "It seems to me that it is the duty of the scholar to be subversive of received truths, and that this subversion can be socially useful only if it reflects a serious attempt to engage with and understand the real world as best we can."[69] World-systems analysis thereby allows a focus on a space-time context that passes through multiple political and cultural units, although the overall system follows a particular set of rules.[70] In this regard, Wallerstein applied ideas previously expressed by the French historian Fernand Braudel, especially concerning the multiplicity of social times and the *longue durée*.[71] The latter, as Wallerstein emphasized, was the lifetime of a particular world-system that would be analyzed.[72]

As a result of his bold ideas, Wallerstein was criticized from all sides, be it Marxists, who argued that world-systems analysis would "neglect the productionist basis of surplus value and the class struggle between bourgeoisie and proletariat as a central variable of social change,"[73] or the defenders of state autonomy, who criticized the economic dependency of the world-system.[74] Other critics tried to emphasize that world-systems theory would be Eurocentric in its historical approach and interpretation due to its lack of a stronger focus on culture.[75] Considering that Wallerstein tried to foster a broad analytical framework, he was naturally in danger of certain shortcomings that would open the door to critical remarks: "When one is dealing with a complex, continuously evolving, large-scale historical system, concepts that are used as shorthand descriptions for structural patterns are only useful to the degree one clearly

---

69 Ibid., xxi.
70 Wallerstein, *Welt-System-Analyse*, 22.
71 Fernand Braudel, "Histoire et Sciences sociales: La longue durée," *Annales* 13, no. 4 (1958): 725–753.
72 Wallerstein, *Welt-System-Analyse*, 24.
73 Ibid., 26. See also Robert A. Denemark and Kenneth P. Thomas, "The Brenner-Wallerstein Debate," *International Studies Quarterly* 32, no. 1 (1988): 47. Robert Brenner was one of Wallerstein's harshest critics, and as Denemark and Thomas point out, "[f]or Brenner, the nation-state is the proper level of analysis, and the proper unit of analysis is the class. For Wallerstein, in contrast, the world-system is the proper level of analysis, and there are a number of units of analysis of interest, including classes and states." Ibid., 48. Brenner was later also criticized by Theda Skocpol. Daniel Garst, "Wallerstein and His Critics," *Theory and Society* 14, no. 4 (1985): 469–470.
74 Wallerstein, *Welt-System-Analyse*, 26. See also Aristide Zolberg, "Origins of the Modern World System: A Missing Link," *World Politics* 33, no. 2 (1981): 255.
75 Ibid., 27.

lays out their purpose, circumscribes their applicability, and specifies the theoretical framework they presuppose and advance."[76] Wallerstein intended to investigate the structures of the modern world-system that "manifest themselves in cyclical rhythms, that is, mechanisms which reflect and ensure repetitious patterns. But insofar as this system is historical, no rhythmic movement ever returns the system to an equilibrium point but instead moves the system along various continua which may be called the secular trends of this system."[77] The world-system's existence and functioning also impacted cultural developments, especially since it was used to distinguish the different spheres and groups within the world-economy.[78]

While world-systems analysis was initiated in the 1970s by people for whom it "was an attempt to combine coherently concern with the unit of analysis, concern with social temporalities, and concern with the barriers that had been erected between different social science disciplines,"[79] its impact went much further than this. Economic historian Eric Vanhaute correctly emphasized that "nowadays world and global history would be in a different shape without Wallerstein's work," because the latter "has triggered a wide array of research, including different topics and questions, different research strategies, different scopes, scales and units of analysis."[80] Furthermore, to quote Vanhaute once more, "world-systems analysis has avoided the sharp categorical distinctions central to other approaches within modernization and globalization studies. It suggests the possibility of concurrent but divergent paths of development and stresses continuous rather than dichotomous processes."[81] It can also help to explain global protest movements as they occurred in the first decades of the 20th century—often in waves and even in the core

---

76   Wallerstein, *The Essential Wallerstein*, 253.
77   Ibid., 253–254.
78   Ibid., 265–268.
79   Wallerstein, *Welt-System-Analyse*, 22.
80   Eric Vanhaute, "Immanuel Wallerstein's Lasting Impact on the Field of World History: A Historian's View," *Socio* 15 (2021): 93–103.
81   Ibid.

regions[82]—as an expression of unrest within the existent world-system.[83] Hence, due to its relation with the end of the Cold War—a process that led some to believe history had ended with the victory of US-led liberalism—the world-system seemed to change once more.[84] From Wallerstein's perspective, the 21st century marked a caesura for the world-system and its state:

> We are at a triple turning-point. World capitalism is facing a long-term structural squeeze on profits, and its major institutional prop, the modern state, is under severe attack. The structure of knowledge that has been produced in this capitalist world-system and has served as its intellectual underpinnings is also under severe attack. And the interstate container of the system is going through one of its periodic restructurings, but this time it is as likely to decenter the system as to hold it together.[85]

Regardless of these restructurings, the state, as Wallerstein emphasized, was still a capitalist necessity; thus, while the "players" within the world-system may be the same, their position within it was contested—particularly in the post-Cold War era—as the system did not collapse but began to shift again, a process that might not even yet be fully concluded.[86]

Naturally, Wallerstein's systematization of historical processes and the current state of societies was not generally greeted with support and understanding. Very often, his work became the target of harsh criticism, further stimulating the circulation of the debate about world-systems analysis. The theoretical approaches Wallerstein proposed aroused some enthusiasm in the US, Latin America, and some European countries but not in others; for example, in France, world-systems analysis was not embraced enthusiastically by

---

82   For a detailed discussion of one such global wave in relation to the First World War, see Marcel Bois, "1916–1921: Ein globaler Aufruhr," in *Zeiten des Aufruhrs (1916–1921): Globale Proteste, Streiks und Revolutionen gegen den Ersten Weltkrieg und seine Auswirkungen*, eds. Marcel Bois and Frank Jacob (Berlin: Metropol, 2020), 13–57.

83   Minqi Li, "The End of the 'End of History': The Structural Crisis of Capitalism and the Fate of Humanity," *Science & Society* 74, no. 3 (2010): 292.

84   Immanuel Wallerstein, "Islam in the Modern World-System," *Sociologisk Forskning* 43, no. 4 (2006): 68. For the most influential exponent of this view, see Francis Fukuyama, *The End of History and the Last Man* (New York: The Free Press, 1992).

85   Immanuel Wallerstein, "Contemporary Capitalist Dilemmas, the Social Sciences, and the Geopolitics of the Twenty-First Century," *The Canadian Journal of Sociology / Cahiers canadiens de sociologie* 23, no. 2/3 (1998): 141.

86   Ibid., 142.

French academia.[87] However, Wallerstein faced more than enthusiasm regarding the reception of his attempt to change the way we look at and understand the world. Indeed, numerous reviews expressed harsh criticism.[88]

This, however, is only one side of the story. Many understood the value of Wallerstein's ideas, which had often been presented too simplistically,[89] and Theda Skocpol provided a more nuanced reading of Wallerstein's work, particularly *The Modern World-System*. According to the well-known US sociologist, the book "aims to achieve a clean conceptual break with theories of 'modernization' and thus provide a new theoretical paradigm to guide our investigations of the emergence and development of capitalism, industrialism, and national states. This splendid undertaking could hardly be more appropriately timed and aimed."[90] Skocpol appreciated Wallerstein's ambition to avoid an "intellectual dead-end of ahistorical model-building"[91] and critically and ambivalently argued that

> *The Modern World-System* is a theoretically ambitious work that deserves to be critically analyzed as such. And, as I shall attempt to show, Wallerstein's arguments are too misleading theoretically and historically to be accepted at face value. Because *The Modern World-System* does suffer from inadequacies of reasoning and evidence, there may be hypercritical reviews that will use the book's weaknesses as an excuse for dismissing out of hand any such world-historical or Marxist-oriented approach. With such an evaluation I have no sympathy. Like many other important pioneering works, Wallerstein's *Modern World-System* overreaches itself and falls short of its aims. It is therefore incumbent especially upon those of us who are sympathetic to its aims to subject this work to rigorous critical scrutiny. For the true contribution of *The Modern World-System* will lie, not in the proliferation of empirical

---

87 Dufoix and Hugot, "Le système-monde Wallerstein."
88 For a summary of the negative criticism Wallerstein received, see DuPlessis, "Wallerstein." See also Denemark and Thomas, "The Brenner-Wallerstein Debate," 47.
89 Garst, "Wallerstein and His Critics," 470. For a supportive argument see Christopher Chase-Dunn and Joan Sokolovsky, "Interstate System and Capitalist World Economy: A Response to Thompson," *International Studies Quarterly* 27, no. 3 (1983): 357–367
90 Theda Skocpol, "Wallerstein's World Capitalist System: A Theoretical and Historical Critique," *American Journal of Sociology* 82, no. 5 (1977): 1075.
91 Immanuel Wallerstein, "The Rise and Future Demise of the World Capitalist System: Concepts for Comparative Analysis," *Comparative Studies in Society and History* 16, no. 4 (1974): 388.

research based uncritically upon it, but in the theoretical controversies and advances it can spark among its friends.[92]

Skocpol therefore emphasized the value of Wallerstein's work without omitting some of its shortcomings. She criticized a deficiency in the description of the world-system's dynamics that Wallerstein often mentions—although limited to the "market processes: commercial growth, worldwide recessions, and the spread of trade in necessities to new regions of the globe"—but fails to explain in a theoretically clear way.[93] Skocpol also points out that "Wallerstein treats 'labor control' primarily as a market-optimizing strategy of the dominant class alone" and thereby omits important elements, e.g., "the sociological key to the functioning and development of any economic system."[94] One of Skopcol's main points of criticism is Wallerstein's limitation to economic conditions as an explanation for the world-system and the nation-state structures within it.[95] Her final evaluation therefore emphasizes a "teleological assertion"[96] in Wallerstein's methodological approach toward the world-system and argues for more research that would enhance his ideas: "Perhaps we still sense that Wallerstein's vision of an enduring, exploitative division of labor is correct, but in that case the theoretical reasons why it is correct must be found elsewhere than in the market economics and the economic-reductionist political sociology of Wallerstein's own model of the world capitalist system."[97] Wallerstein's work eventually provided a particular stimulus toward more comparative approaches in historical and sociological studies, and broader comparative studies that tried to analyze larger historical processes and phenomena were written partly as a consequence of the debate his work on the world-system triggered.[98] That Wallerstein's theoretical ideas can still be useful in many different ways is probably the main argument of the present volume,

---

92 Skocpol, "Wallerstein's World Capitalist System," 1076.
93 Ibid., 1078.
94 Ibid., 1079.
95 Ibid., 1080.
96 Ibid., 1088.
97 Ibid., 1087.
98 Charles C. Ragin, *The Comparative Method: Moving Beyond Qualitative and Quantitative Methods* (Berkeley, CA: University of California Press, 1987); Theda Skocpol, "Emerging Agendas and Recurrent Strategies in Historical Sociology," in *Vision and Method in Historical Sociology*, ed. Theda Skocpol (New York: Cambridge University Press, 1984), 356–391; Charles Tilly, *Big Structures, Large Processes, Huge Comparisons* (New York: Russell Sage, 1984); Wallerstein, "The Rise and Future Demise."

which intends to show different ways of reading and applying world-systems theory in areas not limited to historical and sociological studies.

Wallerstein 2.0

> "I think of world-systems analysis as a perspective and not as a theory."[99]

Since 1974, as Binghamton sociologist William G. Martin described it, "world-systems scholarship has ... thrived in book series, journals, universities and professional organizations—creating in the process a world-systems diaspora scattered around the planet."[100] However, Martin also emphasizes that "[f]or many, particularly sociologists, the world-systems perspective is the victim of its own success. For as 'globalization' has been accepted within and across the social sciences and the humanities, world-systems work has, from this point of view, lost its distinctiveness through the acceptance of its globalizing premise."[101] In contrast to sociology, as American historian Bruce Mazlish remarked, "[t]he historical profession has been slow to appreciate the importance of globalization,"[102] although global and transnational approaches have since gained influence. In fact, world-systems theory can still offer, not only to the historian, an analytical tool that might help as some kind of historical caesura. Beyond showing how "the modern commercial and capitalist world came into existence,"[103] Wallerstein's world-systems theory offers a way to focus on dependencies beyond the economic sector and can even be applied to look at specific historical problems determined by the dynamics of a world-

---

99 Wallerstein, *The Essential Wallerstein*, 129.
100 Martin, "Still Partners," 234.
101 Ibid., 235. See also Charles Tilly, "Macrosociology, Past and Future," *Newsletter of the Comparative and Historical Sociology Section of the American Sociological Association* 8, no. 1/2 (1995): 1–4; Giovanni Arrighi, "Globalization and Historical Macrosociology," in *Sociology for the Twenty-First Century: Continuities and Cutting Edges*, ed. Janet Abu-Lughod (Chicago: Chicago University Press, 2000), 117–133.
102 Bruce Mazlish, "Comparing Global History to World History," *The Journal of Interdisciplinary History* 28, no. 3 (1998): 385. See also Craig A. Lockard, "Global History, Modernization and the World-System Approach: A Critique," *The History Teacher* 14, no. 4 (1981): 491.
103 Ibid., 387.

system that may differ from Wallerstein's.[104] This does not mean that one can easily omit national histories because "[t]he dynamism of the world economy and state system depend greatly on the absence of centralized world authority (a world state or empire), and global culture is essentially a by-product of hegemony with no causal significance in its own right."[105] In this regard, world-systems analysis would, in a way, fulfill a central demand of global history, as "[i]ts core concerns are with mobility and exchange, with processes that transcend borders and boundaries. It takes the interconnected world as its point of departure, and the circulation and exchange of things, people, ideas, and institutions are among its key subjects."[106]

Due to an increased interest in globalization and its accompanying changes and processes, interest in world-systems analysis seems to have gained interest again, although it is still far from the scientific mainstream.[107] National and regional histories can hardly be written, and the respective societies hardly be fully understood, "without reference to these universalizing and globalizing forces"[108] stimulated by transitions or transformations within the world-system. Although there are "limits of Wallerstein's world-system interpretation"[109] in some particular regional contexts, the theoretical approach he suggested can, as some of the contributions of this volume will show, be used beyond the classical macro- and micro-perspectives related to larger systems or nation-states, respectively. The core-semiperiphery-periphery complex—or zemiperiphery, as Stephen Shapiro puts it in his chapter—can be used as an analytical frame that goes beyond historical and sociological understandings of the world. Moreover, it can be used interdisciplinarily to find answers related to all kinds of dynamics and divisions that exist on smaller and larger scales—on this, see Giuditta Bassano's and Sebastian Engelmann's

---

104 See, for example, Janet L. Abu-Lughod, *Before European Hegemony: The World System A.D. 1250–1350* (New York: Oxford University Press, 1989).
105 John W. Meyer, John Boli, George M. Thomas, and Francisco O. Ramirez, "World Society and the Nation-State," *American Journal of Sociology* 103, no. 1 (1997): 147.
106 Sebastian Conrad, *What is Global History?* (Princeton, NJ: Princeton University Press, 2016), 5.
107 Thomas Clayton, "'Competing Conceptions of Globalization' Revisited: Relocating the Tension between World-Systems Analysis and Globalization Analysis," *Comparative Education Review* 48, no. 3 (2004): 274.
108 David Washbrook, "South Asia, the World System, and World Capitalism," *The Journal of Asian Studies* 49, no. 3 (1990): 482.
109 Stern, "Feudalism, Capitalism, and the World-System," 831.

contributions in particular. Cultural systems, even on regional and national scales, might show divisions that match Wallerstein's division of the world-system—for instance, James Horncastle's contribution relates to a world-system of migration. It consequently seems important to identify these divisions, although they might overlap or even replicate the larger divisions within an existent world-system.

Although, as Thomas Clayton argued, "[t]he recent excitement about globalization in the scholarly community and the general acceptance of globalization as an orienting concept for studies in myriad domains could be seen as an important validation for that group of scholars who have for decades recognized the existence of an integrated world-economy operated by a single division of labor and who have worked diligently to understand how multiple phenomena both effect and are affected by this formation,"[110] world-systems analysis is often limited in the sense that it is often applied to explain economic development and dynamics, e.g., an "endless commodification,"[111] while "certain globalization scholars have carefully positioned world-systems analysis as fundamentally different from, and therefore not affirmable by, their own approach."[112] Regardless of the fact that "transnational corporations are maintaining today the same structural stance vis-à-vis the states as did all their global predecessors, from the Fuggers to the Dutch East India Company to nineteenth-century Manchester manufacturers"[113] and that, as a consequence, the world-system dynamics Wallerstein described are still at play, the theoretical use of world-systems-analysis, as mentioned before, could and should go much further.

Wallerstein himself emphasized that "[w]orld-systems analysis is not a theory about the social world, or about part of it. It is a protest against the ways in which social scientific inquiry was structured for all of us at its inception in the middle of the nineteenth century."[114] Furthermore, it "was born as a moral,

---

110 Clayton, "'Competing Conceptions of Globalization' Revisited," 276.
111 Jason W. Moore, "Ecology, Capital, and the Nature of Our Times: Accumulation and Crisis in the Capitalist World-Ecology," *Journal of World-Systems Research* 17, no. 1 (2011): 107–146.
112 Clayton, "'Competing Conceptions of Globalization' Revisited," 276. See also Leslie Sklair, "Competing Conceptions of Globalization," *Journal of World-Systems Research* 5, no. 2 (1999): 143–162.
113 Immanuel Wallerstein, "Response: Declining States, Declining Rights?" *International Labor and Working-Class History* 47 (1995): 24.
114 Wallerstein, *The Essential Wallerstein*, 129.

and in its broadest sense, political protest,"[115] and its "basic logic is that the accumulated surplus is distributed unequally in favour of those able to achieve various kinds of temporary monopolies in the market networks."[116] Wallerstein attempted to explain inequality and provide a theoretical analysis that would make us understand the roots of such existent inequalities around the globe. For him, "the 'modern world-system' was born out of the consolidation of a world economy. Hence it had time to achieve its full development as a capitalist system. By *its* inner logic, this capitalist world economy then expanded to cover the entire globe, absorbing in the process all existing mini-systems and world empires."[117] In this regard, I would argue, he was successful, and many studies have shown how globalization, accompanied by an accumulation of capital and an exploitation of diverse peripheries (geographical and otherwise), shaped the inequalities we still face today. Wallerstein's theoretical approach also allows an understanding of global problems from a broader and transnational perspective, offering a wider focus for a critical analysis of the world as a whole.[118]

Regardless of this wider analytical perspective, world-systems theory does not neglect regional or national developments: "global comparisons do not erase regional frames, they reinvent them."[119] In fact, there is all the more reason to apply world-systems analysis further because "[s]ocial science is a product of the modern world-system, and Eurocentrism is constitutive of the geoculture of the modem world."[120] For the "godfather" of world-systems theory, it was obvious that "if social science is to make any progress in the 21st century, it must overcome the Eurocentric heritage which has distorted its analyses and its capacity to deal with the problems of the contemporary world."[121] At the same time, world-systems theory should be decentralized, meaning that one should apply it as a theoretical frame to questions of human societies beyond a purely economic perspective. There are other cores, semiperipheries, and peripheries beyond the world-systems and nation-states that have been debated before, and in addition to thinking about Wallerstein's

---

115 Ibid.
116 Ibid., 139–140.
117 Ibid., 140.
118 Aronowitz, "A Metatheoretical Critique," 504; Vratuša Žunjić, "In Memoriam," 1340.
119 Vanhaute, "Immanuel Wallerstein's Lasting Impact."
120 Immanuel Wallerstein, "Eurocentrism and Its Avatars: The Dilemmas of Social Science," *Sociological Bulletin* 46, no. 1 (1997): 21.
121 Ibid., 22.

theory along geographical lines, it probably also makes sense to open the framework to other approaches. The 21st century is a globalized one, yet it is no less complex than the 20th century with regard to the functionality of its world-system(s). Wallerstein's quest will consequently continue through further widening his perspectives to find new ways to apply his thoughts. The contributions in this volume try to show how this endeavor can be undertaken in different fields and with interesting new foci. If we intend to better understand the world, we should not stop with Wallerstein but continue the path he tried to pave with his ideas.

Works Cited

Abu-Lughod, Janet L. *Before European Hegemony: The World System A.D. 1250–1350*. New York: Oxford University Press, 1989.
Amin, Samir, Giovanni Arrighi, Andre Gunder Frank, and Immanuel Wallerstein. *The Dynamics of Global Crisis*. New York: Monthly Review Press, 1982.
Appleby, Andrew B. "Review of Immanuel Wallerstein. The Modern World-System: Capitalist Agriculture and the Origins of the European World-Economy in the Sixteenth Century." *The American Historical Review* 80, no. 5 (1975): 1323–1324.
Aronowitz, Stanley. "A Metatheoretical Critique of Immanuel Wallerstein's 'The Modern World System'." *Theory and Society* 10, no. 4 (1981): 503–520.
Arrighi, Giovanni. "Globalization and Historical Macrosociology." In *Sociology for the Twenty-First Century: Continuities and Cutting Edges*, edited by Janet Abu-Lughod, 117–133. Chicago: Chicago University Press, 2000.
Arrighi, Giovanni, Terrence Hopkins, and Immanuel Wallerstein. "1968: The Great Rehearsal." In *Revolution in the World-System*, edited by Terry Boswell, 19–31. New York: Greenwood Press, 1989.
Babones, Salvatore J. and Christopher Chase-Dunn, eds. *Routledge Handbook of World-Systems Analysis*. London/New York: Routledge, 2012.
Bell, Daniel. *The Coming of Post-Industrial Society: A Venture in Social Forecasting*. New York: Basic Books, 1973.
Bois, Marcel. "1916–1921: Ein globaler Aufruhr." In *Zeiten des Aufruhrs (1916–1921): Globale Proteste, Streiks und Revolutionen gegen den Ersten Weltkrieg und seine Auswirkungen*, edited by Marcel Bois and Frank Jacob, 13–57. Berlin: Metropol, 2020.

Braudel, Fernand. "Histoire et Sciences sociales: La longue durée." *Annales* 13, no. 4 (1958): 725–753.
Chase-Dunn, Christopher and Joan Sokolovsky. "Interstate System and Capitalist World Economy: A Response to Thompson." *International Studies Quarterly* 27, no. 3 (1983): 357–367.
Chase-Dunn, Christopher, Jackie Smith, Patrick Manning, and Andrej Grubačić. "Remembering Immanuel Wallerstein." *Journal of World-Systems Research* 26, no. 1 (2020): 5–8.
Chirot, Daniel and Thomas D. Hall. "World-System Theory." *Annual Review of Sociology* 8 (1982): 81–106.
Clayton, Thomas. "'Competing Conceptions of Globalization' Revisited: Relocating the Tension between World-Systems Analysis and Globalization Analysis." *Comparative Education Review* 48, no. 3 (2004): 274–294.
Conrad, Sebastian. *What is Global History?* Princeton, NJ: Princeton University Press, 2016.
Denemark, Robert A. and Kenneth P. Thomas. "The Brenner-Wallerstein Debate." *International Studies Quarterly* 32, no. 1 (1988): 47–65.
Denemark, Robert A. and Barry K. Gills. "World-System History: Challenging Eurocentric Knowledge." In *Routledge Handbook of World-Systems Analysis*, edited by Salvatore J. Babones and Christopher Chase-Dunn, 163–171. London/New York: Routledge, 2012.
Dufoix, Stéphane and Yves-David Hugot. "Le système-monde Wallerstein." *Socio* 15 (2021): 9–19.
DuPlessis, Robert S. "Wallerstein, World Systems Analysis, and Early Modern European History." *The History Teacher* 21, no. 2 (1988): 221–232.
Fanon, Frantz. *Les damnés de la terre*, with a preface by Jean-Paul Sartre. Paris: Maspero, 1961.
Frank, Andre Gunder. *The Development of Underdevelopment*. New York: Monthly Review Press, 1966.
Frank, Andre Gunder. *Dependent Accumulation and Underdevelopment*. New York: Monthly Review Press, 1978.
Fukuyama, Francis. *The End of History and the Last Man*. New York: The Free Press, 1992.
Garst, Daniel. "Wallerstein and His Critics." *Theory and Society* 14, no. 4 (1985): 469–495.
Goldfrank, Walter L. "Wallerstein's World-System: Roots and Contributions." In *Routledge Handbook of World-Systems Analysis*, edited by Salvatore J. Babo-

nes and Christopher Chase-Dunn, 97–103. London/New York: Routledge, 2012.

Goldfrank, Walter L. "Paradigm Regained? The Rules of Wallerstein's World System Method." *Journal of World-Systems Research* 11, no. 2 (2000): 150–195.

Hopkins, Terence K. and Immanuel Wallerstein. "Patterns of Development of the Modern World-System." *Review* (Fernand Braudel Center) 39, no. 1/4 (2016): 83–128.

Hopkins, Terence K. and Immanuel Wallerstein, eds. *Processes of the World-System*. Beverly Hills, CA: Sage Publications, 1980.

Hopkins, Terence and Immanuel Wallerstein. *World-Systems Analysis: Theory and Methodology*. Beverly Hills, CA: Sage Publications, 1982.

Li, Minqi. "The End of the 'End of History': The Structural Crisis of Capitalism and the Fate of Humanity." *Science & Society* 74, no. 3 (2010): 290–305.

Lockard, Craig A. "Global History, Modernization and the World-System Approach: A Critique." *The History Teacher* 14, no. 4 (1981): 489–515.

Martin, William G. "Still Partners and Still Dissident after All These Years? Wallerstein, World Revolutions and the World-Systems Perspective." *Journal of World-Systems Research* 11, no. 2 (2000): 234–263.

Mazlish, Bruce. "Comparing Global History to World History." *The Journal of Interdisciplinary History* 28, no. 3 (1998): 385–395.

McMichael, Philip. "Incorporating Comparison within a World-Historical Perspective: An Alternative Comparative Method." *American Sociological Review* 55, no. 3 (1990): 385–397.

Meyer, John W., John Boli, George M. Thomas and Francisco O. Ramirez. "World Society and the Nation-State." *American Journal of Sociology* 103, no. 1 (1997): 144–181.

Moore, Jason W. "Ecology, Capital, and the Nature of Our Times: Accumulation and Crisis in the Capitalist World-Ecology." *Journal of World-Systems Research* 17, no. 1 (2011): 107–146.

Payne, Corey, Roberto Patricio Korzeniewicz, and Beverly J. Silver, eds. *World-Systems Analysis at a Critical Juncture*. London/New York: Routledge, 2022.

Polanyi, Karl. *The Great Transformation*. New York: Farrar & Rinehart, 1944.

Ragin, Charles C. *The Comparative Method: Moving Beyond Qualitative and Quantitative Methods*. Berkeley, CA: University of California Press, 1987.

Rodney, Walter. *How Europe Underdeveloped Africa*. London: Bogle-L'Ouverture, 1972.

Rostow, Walt W. *The Stages of Economic Growth: A Non-Communist Manifesto*. Cambridge: Cambridge University Press, 1960.

Sklair, Leslie. "Competing Conceptions of Globalization." *Journal of World-Systems Research* 5, no. 2 (1999): 143–162.

Skocpol, Theda. "Emerging Agendas and Recurrent Strategies in Historical Sociology." In *Vision and Method in Historical Sociology*, edited by Theda Skocpol, 356–391. New York: Cambridge University Press, 1984.

Skocpol, Theda. "Wallerstein's World Capitalist System: A Theoretical and Historical Critique." *American Journal of Sociology* 82, no. 5 (1977): 1075–1090.

Stern, Steve J. "Feudalism, Capitalism, and the World-System in the Perspective of Latin America and the Caribbean." *The American Historical Review* 93, no. 4 (1988): 829–872.

Tilly, Charles. *Big Structures, Large Processes, Huge Comparisons*. New York: Russell Sage, 1984.

Tilly, Charles. "Macrosociology, Past and Future." *Newsletter of the Comparative and Historical Sociology Section of the American Sociological Association* 8, no. 1/2 (1995): 1–4.

Vanhaute, Eric. "Immanuel Wallerstein's Lasting Impact on the Field of World History: A Historian's View." *Socio* 15 (2021): 93–103.

Vratuša Žunjić, Vera A. "In Memoriam: Scientific and Political Legacy of Immanuel Wallerstein (1930–2019)." *Sociološki pregled / Sociological Review* 53, no. 4 (2019): 1339–1349.

Wallerstein, Immanuel. "Africa in a Capitalist World." *Issue: A Journal of Opinion* 10, no. 1/2 (1980): 21–31.

Wallerstein, Immanuel. *Africa: The Politics of Independence*. New York: Vintage Books, 1961.

Wallerstein, Immanuel. *Africa: The Politics of Unity*. New York: Random House, 1967.

Wallerstein, Immanuel. "Contemporary Capitalist Dilemmas, the Social Sciences, and the Geopolitics of the Twenty-First Century." *The Canadian Journal of Sociology / Cahiers canadiens de sociologie* 23, no. 2/3 (1998): 141–158.

Wallerstein, Immanuel. "Eurocentrism and Its Avatars: The Dilemmas of Social Science." *Sociological Bulletin* 46, no. 1 (1997): 21–39.

Wallerstein, Immanuel. "Islam in the Modern World-System." *Sociologisk Forskning* 43, no. 4 (2006): 66–74.

Wallerstein, Immanuel. "Remembering Andre Gunder Frank." *History Workshop Journal* 61 (2006): 305–306.

Wallerstein, Immanuel. "Response: Declining States, Declining Rights?" *International Labor and Working-Class History* 47 (1995): 24–27.

Wallerstein, Immanuel. "Terence K. Hopkins (11/20/1928 – 1/3/1997)." *Review (Fernand Braudel Center)* 39, no. 1/4 (2016): n.p.
Wallerstein, Immanuel. *The Essential Wallerstein*. New York: The New Press, 2000.
Wallerstein, Immanuel. *The Road to Independence: Ghana and the Ivory Coast*. Paris: Mouton, 1964.
Wallerstein, Immanuel. "The Rise and Future Demise of the World Capitalist System: Concepts for Comparative Analysis." *Comparative Studies in Society and History* 16, no. 4 (1974): 387–415.
Wallerstein, Immanuel. *University in Turmoil: The Politics of Change*. New York: Atheneum, 1969.
Wallerstein, Immanuel. *Welt-System-Analyse: Eine Einführung*. Wiesbaden: VS Verlag für Sozialwissenschaften, 2019.
Washbrook, David. "South Asia, the World System, and World Capitalism." *The Journal of Asian Studies* 49, no. 3 (1990): 479–508.
Williams, Gregory P. *Contesting the Global Order: The Radical Political Economy of Perry Anderson and Immanuel Wallerstein*. Albany, NY: State University of New York Press, 2020.
Zolberg, Aristide. "Origins of the Modern World System: A Missing Link." *World Politics* 33, no. 2 (1981): 253–281.

2. Global History, World History, and Wallerstein's World-Systems Theory as Definitional Caesuras

Frank Jacob

World and global history are often used interchangeably, and a concrete definition is usually lacking. The use of Wallerstein's world-systems theory could, however, help provide clearer definitional categories for the two historical subdisciplines or theoretical approaches toward the study of pre-world-system and post-world-system history. In 2021, Norwegian historians Leidulf Melve and Eivind Heldaas Seland published *What is Global History?* (*Hva er globalhistorie*), in which they provide a short introduction to this field and discuss the question of what global history actually is.[1] While the book is particularly beneficial for students approaching the subfield of global history for the first time, some of its theoretical aspects deserve more discussion. Melve and Seeland correctly argue that "we are living in a global age, and it is important to understand the past as well as the present from a global vantage point"[2] when we discuss history, which, as a scientific discipline, has often served national demands since the 19th century.[3] When the two authors therefore argue that "we shall return to global narratives,"[4] they seem to refer to an older historiographic tradition that, for a long time, considered larger parts of the world or even the whole world at once.[5] Regardless of these claims, there are still some issues concerning the definition of global history, even though it has been discussed

---

1   Leidulf Melve and Eivind Heldaas Seland, *Hva er globalhistorie* (Oslo: Universitetsforlag, 2021).
2   Ibid., 8–9.
3   For a Norwegian perspective, see Steinar Aas, "Nationalism, Populism, and Norwegian Historiography," in *Nationalism and Populism: Expressions of Fear or Political Strategies?* eds. Carsten Schapkow and Frank Jacob (Berlin: De Gruyter, 2022), 191–210.
4   Melve and Seland, *Hva er globalhistorie*, 14.
5   Daniel Woolf, *A Global History of History* (Cambridge: Cambridge University Press, 2011), 233–280. See also Matthias Middell, *Weltgeschichtsschreibung im Zeitalter der*

in numerous volumes.[6] Melve and Seeland state that global history is a form of "transcending history" not only with regard to "national and chronological boundaries, but also theoretical and methodological [ones]."[7] What they do not provide, however, is a clear definition of world history in abstraction to global history. For the two authors, the former is "essentially a teaching subject."[8] This statement needs more refinement and better definitions of world, global, and transnational history, and in this regard, Wallerstein's world-system can help to provide a theoretical framework that allows clearer and probably more accurate definitions of world and global history alike. This chapter will try to provide these necessary definitions and intends to show 1) that world history is more than just a "teaching subject," although world history has been a prominent teaching subject for decades now, 2) that global history is modern and transnational in nature and has to be studied accordingly, and 3) that transnational history exists within regional and global realms, although not before the existence of Wallerstein's capitalist world-system and/or the modern nation-state, which determine the limits this particular kind of history needs to transcend. The chapter should therefore not be considered overly critical of Melve and Seland, whose work in a way stimulated the following thoughts; instead, it intends to offer theoretical reflections that add to their perspective. Furthermore, it aims to stimulate further discussion about global history and the disciplinary implications this field of study possesses for the historical discipline at large and Wallerstein's world-systems theory in particular.

World History, World-Systems Theory, and the World before the Global Age

World history is *not* global history, although the two terms are often and falsely used interchangeably without a distinction being made between the two. Some scholars speak of global history in time periods, during which the globe as such

---

Verfachlichung und Professionalisierung: Das Leipziger Institut für Kultur- und Universalgeschichte 1890–1990, 3 vols. (Leipzig: Leipziger Universitätsverlag, 2005).
6   Sebastian Conrad, *Globalgeschichte: Eine Einführung* (Munich: C.H. Beck, 2013); Sebastian Conrad, *What is Global History?* (Princeton, NJ: Princeton University Press, 2016).
7   Melve and Seland, *Hva er globalhistorie*, 12.
8   Ibid., 9.

existed but was neither fully explored and connected nor imagined in its actual form.[9] However, world history is much more than a name for educational courses that have gained popularity in US curricula and, as a consequence, in other parts of global academia. Despite this trend, world history is not global history, although it leads toward the possibility of studying the latter. To put it quite frankly: There is no global history without world history; the latter is the *conditio sine qua non* to reach a global world that can be studied along the theoretical lines of global history.

This relationship should be explained in more detail. Regardless of the fact, to quote American historian Bruce Mazlish, that "the implication seems to be that world history is 'the whole history of the whole world,' thus offering no obvious principle of selection,"[10] one of the shared assumptions about it appears to emphasize that "interactions between peoples participating in large-scale historical processes to be one of the principal concerns of world history."[11] World history itself should be understood in abstraction from global history, and the caesura between the two approaches toward the study of a globalizing world and a globalized world was marked by the establishment of Wallerstein's capitalist world-system. According to this view, world history is understood, as mentioned before, as the necessary precondition for global history, meaning that the global system, which should be understood along the lines of Wallerstein's capitalist world-system, is established through the steady connection of regions through trade and other forms of cultural exchange. However, a global system has not been fully established. Global history is therefore only a possible result of worldwide developments that world history should be inclined to study. Eric Vanhaute argued with regard to this twofold perspective on Wallerstein's world-systems theory and the study of world and global history that

---

9   Dawid W. Del Testa, ed., *Global History: Cultural Encounters from Antiquity to the Present*, vol. 1 (London: Routledge, 2003); Michael Scott, *Ancient Worlds: A Global History of Antiquity* (New York: Basic Books, 2016).

10 Bruce Mazlish, "Comparing Global History to World History," *The Journal of Interdisciplinary History* 28, no. 3 (1998): 385. Sometimes histories that cover historical events in all parts of the world during the same or multiple time periods are referred to or refer to themselves as global history. See, for example, Francis D. K. Ching, Mark Jarzombek,and Vikramaditya Prakash, *A Global History of Architecture*, 3rd ed. (Hoboken, NJ: Wiley, 2017).

11 Jerry Bentley, review of Bruce Mazlish and Ralph Buultjens, eds., *Conceptualizing Global History* (Boulder, CO, 1993), cited in Mazlish, "Comparing Global History to World History," 385.

"[w]orld and global history [on the one hand] deconstruct world-making processes and construct new world-making narratives [on the other]."[12] If we connect world and global history to world-systems theory, this would mean that the establishment of the system that consists of core, periphery, and semiperiphery is studied as world history,[13] while its eventual existence and functionality are understood as global history.[14] For example, during the expansion and exploration of trade networks, the world was steadily globalized, yet trade was based on short-distance and mid-distance trade routes, e.g., the tea, horse, and silver[15] trade from and to Yunnan Province in medieval and early modern China,[16] or the early trade in Manila that connected mid-distance trade routes from China, Japan, and Spanish America with long-distance trade routes to Europe.[17] It was, in addition, not impossible that trade goods from East Asia,

---

12 Eric Vanhaute, "Immanuel Wallerstein's Lasting Impact on the Field of World History: A Historian's View," *Socio* 15 (2021): 93–103.

13 Immanuel Wallerstein, "From Feudalism to Capitalism: Transition or Transitions?" *Social Forces* 55, no. 2 (1976): 273–283. Nevertheless, there have also been debates among world-system scholars about chronological periodization. See, for example, Andre Gunder Frank and Barry K. Gills, eds., *The World System: Five Hundred Years or Five Thousand?* (New York: Routledge, 1992).

14 For an introduction to Wallerstein's world-systems analysis, see Immanuel Wallerstein, *Welt-System-Analyse: Eine Einführung* (Wiesbaden: VS Verlag für Sozialwissenschaften, 2019). On the functionalities or positions of specific regions that could be compared within the theoretical frame of the fully established capitalist world-system, see Immanuel Wallerstein, "Africa in a Capitalist World," *Issue: A Journal of Opinion* 10, no. 1/2 (1980): 21–31; Immanuel Wallerstein, "The Rise and Future Demise of the World Capitalist System: Concepts for Comparative Analysis," *Comparative Studies in Society and History* 16, no. 4 (1974): 387–415.

15 Chinese traders were often referred to in European sources as "dear friends of silver." Juan de Medina, *Historia de los Sucesos de la Orden de N. Gran P. S. Agustín de Estas Islas Filipinas, Desde Que se Descubrieron y no Poblaron por los Españoles: Con las Noticias Momorables (1630)* (Manila: Tipo-Litografía de Chofré y Comp, 1893), 69.

16 Bin Yang, "Horses, Silver, and Cowries: Yunnan in Global Perspective," *Journal of World History* 15, no. 3 (2004): 281–322.

17 Birgit Tremml-Werner, *Spain, China, and Japan in Manila, 1571–1644: Local Comparisons and Global Connections* (Amsterdam: Amsterdam University Press, 2015). For contemporary reports about the Manila trade, see Pedro Chirino, SJ, *Relación de las Islas Filipinas i de lo que en ellas an trabaiado los padres de la Compañía de Iesus* (Rome: Esteban Paulino, 1604); Diego de Aduarte, *Historia de la Provincia del Santo Rosario de Filipinas, Japón y China del Sagrado Orden de Predicadores*, vol. 1 (Manila: Colegio de Santo Tomás, por Luís Beltrán, 1640).

e.g., silk, would reach the Roman Empire or even Scandinavia in antiquity or later time periods.[18] However, this was more related to an insecure connection of many trade possibilities that sometimes only came into existence or could solely be facilitated through the movement of pastoralist societies that connected the geographical edges of such trade routes with each other.[19] Direct trade connections based on existent, known, and actively used long-distance trade routes, e.g., the Silk Road(s), "the long and middle-distance land routes by which goods, ideas, and people were exchanged between major regions of Afro-Eurasia,"[20] did not cover the globe before the formation of Wallerstein's world-system theory had been completed. Connections and economic and cultural exchanges before the existence of a clear image and a solid interconnectedness of most parts of the globe would therefore be studied as world history or pre-world-system history. That said, this would also mean limiting the study periods of interest for world history mostly until the saddle time (*Sattelzeit*) that marked the transition between the early modern and modern periods.[21]

Of course, this would lead to a conceptional problem and possible debates, as global history could no longer be used as a concept or theoretical approach

---

18 Berit Hildebrandt, ed., *Silk: Trade and Exchange Along the Silk Roads Between Rome and China in Antiquity* (Oxford: Oxbow Books, 2016); Hyun Jin Kim, Samuel N. C. Lieu, and Raoul McLaughlin, eds., *Rome and China: Points of Contact* (London: Routledge, 2021); Samuel N.C. Lieu and Gunner B. Mikkelsen, eds., *Between Rome and China: History, Religions and Material Culture of the Silk Road* (Turnhout: Brepols, 2015); Raoul McLaughlin, *The Roman Empire and the Silk Routes: The Ancient World Economy & the Empires of Parthia, Central Asia & Han China* (Barnsley: Pen & Sword, 2016); Marianne Vedeler, *Silk for the Vikings* (Oxford: Oxbow Books, 2014); Marianne Vedeler, "Silk Trade to Scandinavia in the Viking Age," in *Textiles and the Medieval Economy: Production, Trade, and Consumption of Textiles, 8th-16th Centuries*, eds. Angela Ling Huang and Carsten Jahnke (Oxford: Oxbow Books, 2015), 78–85.
19 David Christian, "Silk Roads or Steppe Roads? The Silk Roads in World History," *Journal of World History* 11, no. 1 (2000): 1–26.
20 Ibid., 3.
21 Reinhart Koselleck, "Einleitung," in *Geschichtliche Grundbegriffe*, vol. 1, eds. Otto Brunner, Werner Conze and Reinahrt Koselleck (Stuttgart: Klett-Cotta, 1979), xv. One could argue about this temporal separation between the two disciplinary approaches, especially since the exploration and expansion of some parts of the world has continued in the modern period. Naturally, one would therefore speak of an overlap, especially with regard to the parts of the world that have not yet been fully integrated into the existent global world-system.

for those who study ancient, medieval, or (early) modern history, as these periods had not yet witnessed a fully globalized world. Regardless of this dilemma, historians with a research focus on these periods have done significant work in the field of world history, helping to explain how the world became connected by more and more transregional and long-distance networks of exchange, be they cultural, economic, political, or social. At the same time, however, such a clear demarcation between world and global history would allow the understanding of the two theoretical approaches and frameworks to be less confusing, which could help with the additional necessary definitions within the field. Wallerstein's theoretical considerations about the world-system could consequently mark a watershed within the historical process.

Global History: An Explanation of Modernity and the Functionality of the Modern World-System

Global history, in relation to the world-system, is supposed to explain the latter's functionality, although different aims and perspectives have been discussed with regard to its interpretation. The existence of the world-system seems to be the essential precondition for any process, network-building, exchange of ideas, etc. to be considered global in nature in the first place. Regardless of this consideration, global history has been widely understood as either a "history of everything," the history of exchange between networks and the history of transregional (in the modern context, transnational) connections, or an integrative approach that embeds national histories into their global context.[22] However, the systematized connections and dependencies that cause or impact the course of history in the modern period are especially relevant for the study of and research approaches related to global history. These connections and dependencies are nevertheless created by the formation of a capitalist world-system.[23] Wallerstein defined such a system as

---

22 Conrad, *What is Global History?* 6–11.
23 Immanuel Wallerstein, "Dependence in an Interdependent World: The Limited Possibilities of Transformation within the Capitalist World Economy," *African Studies Review* 17, no. 1 (1974): 1–26. See also Immanuel Wallerstein, "Development: Lodestar or Illusion?" *Economic and Political Weekly* 23, no. 39 (1988): 2017–2019 and 2021–2023. Another scholar who emphasized the role of European expansion to create dependencies through underdevlopment was Walter Rodney. See Walter Rodney, *How Europe Underdeveloped Africa* (London: Bogle-L'Ouverture, 1972). Rodney's book can be used for stud-

a concrete singular historical system which I shall call the 'capitalist world-economy,' whose temporal boundaries go from the long sixteenth century to the present. Its spatial boundaries originally included Europe (or most of it) plus Iberian America but they subsequently expanded to cover the entire globe. I assume this totality is a *system*, that is, that it has been relatively autonomous of external forces; or to put it another way, that its patterns are explicable largely in terms of its internal dynamics.[24]

Once the expansion and establishment of the global world-system are completed, it can only be studied within its global context, analyzing the relationships between the core, the periphery, and the intermediate sphere between the two: the semiperiphery. As all three spheres are closely linked to each other—core exploits periphery, periphery intends to become semiperiphery, semiperiphery struggles to become core and avoid falling back to the periphery—their relationships must be at the center of the study of global history. Of course, there have been different opinions since a truly global world existed. To name just one example, Hans Kohn argued in *The Age of Nationalism: The First Era of Global History* (1962)[25] that the first global age was achieved in the mid-20th century. Others disagreed with this evaluation and instead, as Wallerstein suggested, put it in the 16th century. Ultimately, however, it is hard to define a clear moment in time, especially one that would be universally fitting with regard to the variety of topics and regions that need to be included to reach a "universal global age."

In 1991, Nathan Douthit tried to shed some light on the problems of nomenclature related to global history, stating that

> There seem to be two current definitions of global history. One treats global history as synonymous with world history, a history that encompasses all

---

ies of world and global history alike, since he describes Africa before and after the establishment of the world-system. The pan-African scholar also had the chance to exchange ideas with Wallerstein at Binghamton University, where he was invited to serve as visiting professor after he was denied a position in Guyana. On Rodney's work and impact, see Frank Jacob, *Walter Rodney: Black Power and Revolution* (Marburg: Büchner, 2022).

24　Immanuel Wallerstein, "The Three Instances of Hegemony in the History of the Capitalist World-Economy," in Immanuel Wallerstein, *The Essential Wallerstein* (New York: The New Press, 2000), 253.

25　Hans Kohn, *The Age of Nationalism: The First Era of Global History* (New York: Harper, 1962).

the major civilizations and their interactions. Let's call this the general definition of global history. However, if one refers to "the era of global history," then one means the recent period of intensified global interconnections which has followed western expansion since 1500. Let's call this the special definition of global history.[26]

Douthit's attempt shows that what global history meant and how it should be approached by or incorporated into the traditional discipline of historical research remained relatively vague for a long time. If one applied Wallerstein's world-system as a factor that, in a way, created a chronological caesura, global history would follow the mentioned special definition, albeit with a later time frame, and demand a genuine interest in the system's totality, i.e., the functionality and impact of its existence.

Such an approach matched the global historian Sebastian Conrad's statement that "[t]he case for global history is thus also a plea to overcome such fragmentation, and to arrive at a more comprehensive understanding of the interactions and connections that have made the modern world."[27] The "core concerns" of global history are, according to Conrad, "mobility and exchange, ... processes that transcend borders and boundaries. It takes the interconnected world as its point of departure, and the circulation and exchange of things, people, ideas, and institutions are among its key subjects."[28] The latter often represent transnational elements, i.e., people and ideas that cross borders and become influential in different regions of the world, and were studied from a global perspective. Consequently, global intellectual histories,[29] and global bi-

---

26   Nathan Douthit, "The Dialectical Commons of Western Civilization and Global/World History," *The History Teacher* 24, no. 3 (1991): 296.

27   Conrad, *What is Global History?* 5. I agree with Conrad here, yet I would rather use "determined" instead of "made," since the creational perspective is related to world history if one applies the theoretical approach this article advocates.

28   Ibid. The "interconnected world" is one in which a world-system has already been established, while the "circulation and exchange of things" refers to the networks that link core to semiperiphery and periphery.

29   Some recent exemplary studies include Johannes Feichtinger, Jan Surmann, and Franz L. Fillafer, eds., *The Worlds of Positivism: A Global Intellectual History, 1770–1930* (London: Palgrave Macmillan, 2018); Eric Heillener, *The Neomercantilists: A Global Intellectual History* (Ithaca, NY: Cornell University Press, 2021). For a discussion of theoretical approaches toward a global intellectual history, see Samuel Moyn and Andrew Sartori, eds., *Global Intellectual History* (New York: Columbia University Press, 2013).

ographies[30] in particular, seem to provide insight into the history of the world's connectedness in times when such exchanges could take place on a broader scale.[31]

Eventually, the nation—as something particularly modern and, first and foremost, related to the world-system's core, where it stimulated imperialism, and to its semiperiphery, where it stimulated revolutionary processes[32]—added another modern aspect to the world-system and helped to characterize global history as something that, with regard to its functionality and impact, transcends national borders.[33] However, the relationship between global and transnational history should also be taken into more detailed consideration.[34]

---

30 Laura Almagor, Haakon Ikonomou, and Gunvor Simonsen, eds., *Global Biographies: Lived History as Method* (Manchester: Manchester University Press, 2022).
31 This exchange could take place in different forms and could be stimulated by a physical border crossing, the permanent migration of people, or the exchange of published books, journals or newspapers, to name just a few aspects that have been studied with regard to global networks, e.g., anarchist or socialist networks. Relevant works to the latter include, among others, Constance Bantman, "Internationalism without an International? Cross-Channel Anarchist Networks, 1880–1914," *Revue belge de philologie et d'histoire*, 84, no. 4 (2006): 961–981; Constance Bantman and Bert Altena, "Introduction: Problematizing Scales of Analysis in Network-Based Social Movements," in *Reassessing the Transnational Turn: Scales of Analysis in Anarchist and Syndicalist Studies*, eds. Constance Bantman and Bert Altena (London/New York: Routledge, 2014), 3–22; Constance Bantman, "The Dangerous Liaisons of Belle Epoque Anarchists: Internationalism, Transnationalism, and Nationalism in the French Anarchist Movement (1880–1914)," in *Reassessing the Transnational Turn: Scales of Analysis in Anarchist and Syndicalist Studies*, eds. Constance Bantman and Bert Altena (London/New York: Routledge, 2014), 174–192; Frank Jacob and Mario Keßler, "Transatlantic Radicalism: A Short Introduction," in *Transatlantic Radicalism: Socialist and Anarchist Exchanges in the 19th and 20th Centuries*, eds. Frank Jacob and Mario Keßler (Liverpool: Liverpool University Press, 2021), 1–20; James Michael Yeoman, *Print Culture and the Formation of the Anarchist Movement in Spain, 1890–1915* (Edinburgh: AK Press, 2022).
32 See Frank Jacob's chapter on revolutions and the world-system in this volume.
33 David Washbrook, "South Asia, the World System, and World Capitalism," *The Journal of Asian Studies* 49, no. 3 (1990): 481.
34 For a broader analysis see Akira Iriye, *Global and Transnational History: The Past, Present, and Future* (London: Palgrave Macmillan, 2013).

Global and Transnational History: Only Sometimes Related

World history is without any doubt transregional, as basic forms of expansion[35] usually cause some form of intrusion into one so far relatively unknown spatial realm and thereby begin the process that ultimately leads to the establishment of a world-system. Empire-building wars of expansion, total migration as a consequence of wars or natural catastrophes, mass migration by individuals who decide to seek better living opportunities or freedom from political or religious oppression, steady border colonization, settler colonialism, or base networking that connects important geostrategic trade or military cities to each other all expand the existent spatial environment of those who move and integrate different parts of the world into a realm that will eventually turn into a global world-system. Therefore, world history is and always must be transregional in nature, although it is not yet transnational – the latter needs the nation-state as a categorial base. Global history, on the other hand, can be transregional if the nation-state does not yet fully exist as a spatial determination, but it will become transnational once the latter has been established. Ernest Renan emphasized that the nation is something modern because it is based on a shared history and its peoples' consensus to live together within a union in the present and future.[36] Mazlish, therefore, correctly emphasized with regard to the relation of global history to the nation that

> [a]lthough global history is mainly transnational in its object of study, it would be a grave error to neglect the study of the nation as well. National history merits reexamination in light of how the forces of globalization have affected the nation-state and vice-versa. Nations will not be going away. They are still the preferred settings for large numbers of people to organize in behalf of common ends – protection of territory and property, economic production, and, last but not least, group identity.[37]

Regardless of this emphasis, the nation is often nothing more than the starting point for transnational studies, which are often comparative in nature

---

35 Jürgen Osterhammel, *Kolonialismus: Geschichte, Formen, Folgen*, 5th ed. (Munich: C.H. Beck, 2006), 8–15.
36 Ernest Renan, "A Lecture Delivered at the Sorbonne, 11 March 1882: 'Qu'est-ce qu'une nation'," in *Oeuvres Completes*, vol. 1 (Paris: Calmann-Lévy, 1947), 887–907.
37 Mazlish, "Comparing Global History to World History," 393.

and search for the effects and impacts of transnational events on the national level or global similarities in certain situations occurring in culturally and geographically different regions, depending on the format of the comparative study.[38] The latter can search analytically for similarities but is not bound to such an approach and might sometimes look for the exact opposite. Differences might actually be more interesting and offer possibilities for de-nationalized – which often means non-Eurocentric – reflections about historical developments on a global scale.[39]

Global history is consequently always transnational in nature, especially since the nation-state is as much a modern study unit as the globalized world-system; transnational history, on the other hand, does not have to be global but can be limited to regional studies, e.g., the role or impact of specific historical events in a closely connected region. The comparative case study must consequently be transnational and transregional alike to be able to be considered fully global. Ideally, one would suggest a comparison of historically and culturally different regions, especially if one is interested, beyond any Eurocentric bias in particular, to see if reactions towards a certain transnational phenomenon are generically similar, regardless of the historical or cultural determination of the cases taken into consideration. The determination of whether something is both transnational and global needs to be taken into careful consideration when thinking about possible study approaches in the theoretical realm related to global history. Not everything transnational is automatically qualified to be considered global history, but any study related to global history in the modern period must be transnational as a precondition to fall into this category.

---

38   On the historical comparison, see Hartmut Kaelble, *Der historische Vergleich: Eine Einführung zum 19. und 20. Jahrhundert* (Frankfurt am Main/New York: Campus, 1999); Hartmut Kaelble and Jürgen Schriewer, eds., *Vergleich und Transfer: Komparatistik in den Sozial-, Geschichts- und Kulturwissenschaften* (Frankfurt am Main/New York: Campus, 2003).

39   Jürgen Osterhammel, "Sozialgeschichte im Zivilisationsvergleich: Zu künftigen Möglichkeiten komparativer Geschichtswissenschaft," *Geschichte und Gesellschaft* 22, no. 2 (1996): 143–164.

Concluding Remarks

To sum up the previous reflections, one can apply the following basic considerations to answer the initial question about the nature of global history in relation to world-systems theory. If, as suggested here, one uses Wallerstein's world-system as a chronological caesura between a period studied according to the theoretical approaches or conceptual frame of world history and one studied as global history, it makes sense to categorize them as follows:

1. World history is interested in a pre-world-system analysis of the expansion or growing of the global connectedness between core, periphery, and semiperiphery. It is, therefore, necessarily transregional in nature but not yet transnational.
2. Global history is interested in a post-world-system analysis of the connectedness and functionality of historical processes within an existent capitalist world-system that shapes the interactions between core, periphery, and semiperiphery. It is, therefore, necessarily transregional in nature and is, due to its modern existence, very often transnational as well.
3. Consequently, transnational history cannot be a form of analysis related to world history but only to global history; however, if it is not transregional, it would not qualify as a suitable approach for a study in the field of global history either.

If these aspects are seriously considered for the future designation of global history, it would also mean that global history as a discipline could only be located in space-time continuums that were considered to be modern in the sense that a world-system, as described by Wallerstein and others, had been fully established. Ancient, medieval, and (early) modern histories would consequently still have global perspectives to study, although the latter would be expressed first and foremost through the study of pre-modern world history.

Works Cited

Aas, Steinar. "Nationalism, Populism, and Norwegian Historiography." In *Nationalism and Populism: Expressions of Fear or Political Strategies?*, edited by Carsten Schapkow and Frank Jacob, 191–210. Berlin: De Gruyter, 2022.

Aduarte, Diego de. *Historia de la Provincia del Santo Rosario de Filipinas, Japón y China del Sagrado Orden de Predicadores*, vol. 1. Manila: Colegio de Santo Tomás, por Luís Beltrán, 1640.
Almagor, Laura, Haakon Ikonomou, and Gunvor Simonsen, eds. *Global Biographies: Lived History as Method*. Manchester: Manchester University Press, 2022.
Bantman, Constance. "Internationalism without an International? Cross-Channel Anarchist Networks, 1880–1914." *Revue belge de philologie et d'histoire*, 84, no. 4 (2006): 961–981.
Bantman, Constance and Bert Altena. "Introduction: Problematizing Scales of Analysis in Network-Based Social Movements." In *Reassessing the Transnational Turn: Scales of Analysis in Anarchist and Syndicalist Studies*, edited by Constance Bantman and Bert Altena, 3–22. London/New York: Routledge, 2014.
Bantman, Constance. "The Dangerous Liaisons of Belle Epoque Anarchists: Internationalism, Transnationalism, and Nationalism in the French Anarchist Movement (1880–1914)." In *Reassessing the Transnational Turn: Scales of Analysis in Anarchist and Syndicalist Studies*, edited by Constance Bantman and Bert Altena, 174–192. London/New York: Routledge, 2014.
Ching, Francis D. K. Mark Jarzombek, and Vikramaditya Prakash. *A Global History of Architecture*. 3rd ed. Hoboken, NJ: Wiley, 2017.
Chirino, Pedro, SJ. *Relación de las Islas Filipinas i de lo que en ellas an trabaiado los padres de la Compañía de Iesvs*. Rome: Esteban Paulino, 1604.
Christian, David. "Silk Roads or Steppe Roads? The Silk Roads in World History." *Journal of World History* 11, no. 1 (2000): 1–26.
Conrad, Sebastian. *Globalgeschichte: Eine Einführung*. Munich: C.H. Beck, 2013.
Conrad, Sebastian. *What is Global History?* Princeton, NJ: Princeton University Press, 2016.
Del Testa, Dawid W. ed. *Global History: Cultural Encounters from Antiquity to the Present*, vol. 1. London: Routledge, 2003.
Douthit, Nathan. "The Dialectical Commons of Western Civilization and Global/World History." *The History Teacher* 24, no. 3 (1991): 293–305.
Feichtinger, Johannes, Jan Surmann, and Franz L. Fillafer, eds. *The Worlds of Positivism: A Global Intellectual History, 1770–1930*. London: Palgrave Macmillan, 2018.
Frank, Andre Gunder and Barry K. Gills, eds. *The World System: Five Hundred Years or Five Thousand?* New York: Routledge, 1992.

Heillener, Eric. *The Neomercantilists: A Global Intellectual History*. Ithaca, NY: Cornell University Press, 2021.

Hildebrandt, Berit, ed. *Silk: Trade and Exchange Along the Silk Roads Between Rome and China in Antiquity*. Oxford: Oxbow Books, 2016.

Iriye, Akira. *Global and Transnational History: The Past, Present, and Future*. London: Palgrave Macmillan, 2013.

Jacob, Frank. *Walter Rodney: Black Power and Revolution*. Marburg: Büchner, 2022.

Jacob, Frank and Mario Keßler. "Transatlantic Radicalism: A Short Introduction." In *Transatlantic Radicalism: Socialist and Anarchist Exchanges in the 19th and 20th Centuries*, edited by Frank Jacob and Mario Keßler, 1–20. Liverpool: Liverpool University Press, 2021.

Kaelble, Hartmut. *Der historische Vergleich: Eine Einführung zum 19. und 20. Jahrhundert*. Frankfurt am Main/New York: Campus, 1999.

Kaelble, Hartmut and Jürgen Schriewer, eds. *Vergleich und Transfer: Komparatistik in den Sozial-, Geschichts- und Kulturwissenschaften*. Frankfurt am Main/New York: Campus, 2003.

Kim, Hyun Jin, Samuel N. C. Lieu, and Raoul McLaughlin, eds. *Rome and China: Points of Contact*. London: Routledge, 2021.

Kohn, Hans. *The Age of Nationalism: The First Era of Global History*. New York: Harper, 1962.

Koselleck, Reinhart. "Einleitung." In *Geschichtliche Grundbegriffe*, vol. 1, edited by Otto Brunner, Werner Conze, and Reinahrt Koselleck, xiii-xxvii. Stuttgart: Klett-Cotta, 1979.

Lieu, Samuel N.C. and Gunner B. Mikkelsen, eds. *Between Rome and China: History, Religions and Material Culture of the Silk Road*. Turnhout: Brepols, 2015.

Mazlish, Bruce. "Comparing Global History to World History." *The Journal of Interdisciplinary History* 28, no. 3 (1998): 385–395.

McLaughlin, Raoul. *The Roman Empire and the Silk Routes: The Ancient World Economy & the Empires of Parthia, Central Asia & Han China*. Barnsley: Pen & Sword, 2016.

Medina, Juan de. *Historia de los Sucesos de la Orden de N. Gran P. S. Agustín de Estas Islas Filipinas, Desde Que se Descubrieron y no Poblaron por los Españoles: Con las Noticias Momorables (1630)*. Manila: Tipo-Litografía de Chofré y Comp, 1893.

Melve, Leidulf and Eivind Heldaas Seland. *Hva er globalhistorie*. Oslo: Universitetsforlag, 2021.

Middell, Matthias. *Weltgeschichtsschreibung im Zeitalter der Verfachlichung und Professionalisierung: Das Leipziger Institut für Kultur- und Universalgeschichte 1890–1990*, 3 vols. Leipzig: Leipziger Universitätsverlag, 2005.

Moyn, Samuel and Andrew Sartori, eds. *Global Intellectual History*. New York: Columbia University Press, 2013.

Osterhammel, Jürgen. *Kolonialismus: Geschichte, Formen, Folgen*. 5th ed. Munich: C.H. Beck, 2006.

Osterhammel, Jürgen. "Sozialgeschichte im Zivilisationsvergleich: Zu künftigen Möglichkeiten komparativer Geschichtswissenschaft." *Geschichte und Gesellschaft* 22, no. 2 (1996): 143–164.

Renan, Ernest. "A Lecture Delivered at the Sorbonne, 11 March 1882: 'Qu'est-ce qu'une nation'." In *Oeuvres Completes*, vol. 1, 887–907. Paris: Calmann-Lévy, 1947.

Rodney, Walter. *How Europe Underdeveloped Africa*. London: Bogle-L'Ouverture, 1972.

Scott, Michael. *Ancient Worlds: A Global History of Antiquity*. New York: Basic Books, 2016.

Tremml-Werner, Birgit. *Spain, China, and Japan in Manila, 1571–1644: Local Comparisons and Global Connections*. Amsterdam: Amsterdam University Press, 2015.

Vanhaute, Eric. "Immanuel Wallerstein's Lasting Impact on the Field of World History: A Historian's View." *Socio* 15 (2021): 93–103.

Vedeler, Marianne. *Silk for the Vikings*. Oxford: Oxbow Books, 2014.

Vedeler, Marianne. "Silk Trade to Scandinavia in the Viking Age." In *Textiles and the Medieval Economy: Production, Trade, and Consumption of Textiles, 8th-16th Centuries*, edited by Angela Ling Huang and Carsten Jahnke, 78–85. Oxford: Oxbow Books, 2015.

Wallerstein, Immanuel. "Africa in a Capitalist World." *Issue: A Journal of Opinion* 10, no. 1/2 (1980): 21–31.

Wallerstein, Immanuel. "Dependence in an Interdependent World: The Limited Possibilities of Transformation within the Capitalist World Economy." *African Studies Review* 17, no. 1 (1974): 1–26.

Wallerstein, Immanuel. "Development: Lodestar or Illusion?" *Economic and Political Weekly* 23, no. 39 (1988): 2017–2019 and 2021–2023.

Wallerstein, Immanuel. "From Feudalism to Capitalism: Transition or Transitions?" *Social Forces* 55, no. 2 (1976): 273–283.

Wallerstein, Immanuel. "The Rise and Future Demise of the World Capitalist System: Concepts for Comparative Analysis." *Comparative Studies in Society and History* 16, no. 4 (1974): 387–415.

Wallerstein, Immanuel. "The Three Instances of Hegemony in the History of the Capitalist World-Economy." In Immanuel Wallerstein, *The Essential Wallerstein*, 253–263. New York: The New Press, 2000.

Wallerstein, Immanuel. *Welt-System-Analyse: Eine Einführung*. Wiesbaden: VS Verlag für Sozialwissenschaften, 2019.

Washbrook, David. "South Asia, the World System, and World Capitalism." *The Journal of Asian Studies* 49, no. 3 (1990): 479–508.

Woolf, Daniel. *A Global History of History*. Cambridge: Cambridge University Press, 2011.

Yang, Bin. "Horses, Silver, and Cowries: Yunnan in Global Perspective." *Journal of World History* 15, no. 3 (2004): 281–322.

Yeoman, James Michael. *Print Culture and the Formation of the Anarchist Movement in Spain, 1890–1915*. Edinburgh: AK Press, 2022.

3. Zemiperiphery Matters
Immigration, Culture, and the Capitalist World-System

Stephen Shapiro

A lot of people are off the mark about world-system analysis because they haven't bothered to read it. The theory's broad enough to give you the space to do a lot of creative things, and it's also a perspective that's open to change because it's politically oriented, and it's changed a lot with time. Wallerstein's gotten criticism about neglecting things like culture. Well, culture's integrated now and gender's integrated now. It doesn't mean it's perfectly done, but I know of lot of theoretical perspectives that never change.[1]

Introduction

Anxious that world-systems analyses should not fall into the trap of rigid and aggressively-guarded orthodoxies, Immanuel Wallerstein shifted from calling these a perspective (rather than a theory) and began speaking about a world-systems knowledge movement.[2] The change in keyword emphasis was driven by a desire to both empower younger scholars who wished to continue unthinking prior orthodoxies and as a reply to an emerging reaction or resistance to world-systems' decolonial and emancipatory motivation. Those interested in exploring and utilizing world-systems approaches, especially those colleagues who are institutionally located within the social sciences, often encounter resistance that seeks to pigeonhole world-systems as an old, and thus super-

---

1 Wilma A. Dunaway, "Revisionist with a Cause: Interview with Wilma Dunaway," *Appalachian Journal* 31, no. 2 (2004): 176.
2 Immanuel Wallerstein, "World-System Analysis as a Knowledge Movement," in *Routledge Handbook of World-Systems Analysis*, eds. Christopher Chase-Dunn and Salvatore Babones (London: Routledge, 2012), 515–521.

seded, intervention. By no means! World-systems viewpoints are currently experiencing a renewal, beyond the circles of scholars whose names are known as having made key contributions alongside Wallerstein. Within this resurgence, topics that were previously little treated are now being considered through a world-systems optic, and the familiar terms of earlier efforts are being tested and applied in experimental ways to see how they might generate new research directions.

In this light, I wish to make five main claims about using world-systems approaches as a way of considering questions about immigration (transhumance). First, while the concept of the semiperiphery (from here on called the *zemiperiphery*, for reasons explained below) has been one of the signal contributions of a world-systems approach, it still needs to be expanded beyond an application that works only at the level of an integral nation-state or its borders. Second, while the zemiperiphery was initially conceptualized as lacking distinctive features of production, these regions are not simply ones of regulatory transit but are also places of tremendous social and cultural innovation, often creating and registering new lifeworld relations in advance of the core.

Third, the zemiperipheries' social and cultural production emerges from the particular presence and role of semiproletarianized (and, likewise with the above, now called *zemiproletarian*) labor, which is not fully waged, and households. As these features are highly dependent on the factors of gendered and ethno-racialized labor, the zemiperipheries are sites where status identities become incorporated within class ones. The social reproduction of class relations is often grounded on status distinctions, which becomes the avenue toward the social realization of capitalist accumulation. Fourth, the zemiperipheries are not merely unilinear way stations between the core and the peripheries. They also function as a circulatory realm linking one zemiperiphery to another. Rather than one zemiperipheral space existing in separation from another, as midpoints between core and periphery, they are also entangled and co-constitutive with each other. This knotting together of the zemiperipheries as their own realm means that they operate as a particularly apt site to gain insight into the capitalist world-system as a whole, especially as they record its temblors of crisis.

Lastly, by examining two different visual representations of women, Christian Petzold's *Gespenster* (Ghosts, 2005) and a set of 1930s and '40s images by or about Frida Kahlo, I seek to highlight different registrations of the zemiperiphery as a non-binary arena. My intention here is not to insist on identical responses but to sketch out a spectrum of concerns, or set of different aesthetic strategies, that might otherwise be imperceptible from the window of either the core or the peripheries. These illustrations seek, in turn, to suggest new themes in migration studies.

Zemiperiphery Matters

One challenge for migration studies is to shift focus away from the alpha and omega of transhumance – origin and intended destination – and not consider intermediate locations as either inconsequential or sites of incompleteness and blockage. This simplifying opposition endures partly because there is a truth in its framework, often even within the narratives by human agents about their migration and, of course, State legislation that frequently conceptualizes the regulation of immigration in terms of national origin and sought-for place of settlement. Here I want to explore an alternative view of migration, one that does not consider "incomplete" movement as outlier data or a lived experience of failure. The motivation for this turn is two-fold. First, to reconsider the discussion of migration towards the telos of citizenship, as that which is meant to erase the prior (traumatic) experiences and lifeworlds of human subjects. The category of the citizen as a legitimate and incorporated actor of a nation-state has haunted the discussion of migration. While citizenship has been involved as the civil therapeutic solution to the perceived social disability of foreignness, the unremarkable equivalence of the citizen makes its own structure of inequality. What was once used in radical and social circles as a non-hierarchical and internationally inclusive term – "To citizen Maurice la Chaitre" writes the now London-based Marx to the Parisian publisher of the French edition of *Capital* – became a key instrument to manage the tempo of historical transformation and the inevitable rise of popular governance ("democracy") by the swiftly dominant form of centrist liberalism. As Wallerstein argues:

> When inequality was the norm, there was no need to make any further distinction than that between those of different rank, generically between noble and commoner. But when equality became the official norm, then it was suddenly crucial to know who was in fact included in the "all" who have equal rights, that is, who are the "active" citizens. The more equality was proclaimed as a moral principle, the more obstacles – juridical, political, economic, and cultural –were instituted to prevent its realization. The

concept, citizen, forced the crystallization and rigidification – both intellectual and legal – of a long list of binary distinctions which have formed the cultural underpinnings of the capitalist world-economy in the nineteenth and twentieth centuries: bourgeois and proletarian, man and woman, adult and minor, breadwinner and housewife, majority and minority, White and Black, European and non-European, educated and ignorant, skilled and unskilled, specialist and amateur, scientist and layman, high culture and low culture, heterosexual and homosexual, normal and abnormal, able-bodied and disabled, and of course the ur-category which all of these others imply – civilized and barbarian.

To be sure, the concept of citizenship was meant to be liberating, and it did indeed liberate us all from the dead weight of received hierarchies claiming divine or natural ordination. But the liberation was only a partial liberation from the disabilities, and the new inclusions made sharper and more apparent the continuing (and new) exclusions. Universal rights turned out in actual practice to be somewhat of a linguistic mirage, an oxymoron. The republic of virtuous equals turned out to require the rejection of the non-virtuous.[3]

As these binary distinctions link to other ones forged by liberalism, not least of which are the public/private sphere distinctions that E.T.A. Hoffmann (*The Golden Pot* – Der goldne Topf) and Marx ("On the Jewish Question" – "Zur Judenfrage") critiqued from their respective Romantic and radical perspectives,[4] what might an alternative categorical framework be to evade the trap of liberal citizenship?

My second motivation is to propose denizenship as an alternative category of access to resources of social dignity based on physical presence without regard to natal origin, State recognition, or work status. In other words, *les misérables*. The project of a theoretical alternative to debates around citizenship is grounded in the urgency for all those "interrupted" in the transit stations that are neither ones of origin or ideal destination – such as Calais, Lampedusa, and the ones alongside the US-Mexican border. Marc Augé introduced

---

3   Immannuel Wallerstein, "Citizens All? Citizens Some! The Making of the Citizen," *Comparative Studies in Society and History* 45, no. 4 (2003): 652.
4   E.T.A. Hoffmann, *The Golden Pot and Other Tales* (Oxford: Oxford University Press, 1992); Karl Marx, "On the Jewish Question," in Karl Marx, *Early Writings* (New York: Vintage, 1975), 211–241.

the notion of "non-places" to describe the similar presence of locales, such as the ATM machine, that are simultaneously ubiquitous and nowhere, since their deterritorialized voids are based on the capitalist practices of creating spatialized equivalences, much as money-form operates.[5] Though Augé's description of these hollowed-out realms was not meant to consider "incomplete migration," the metaphor captures both the zones of precarious encampment found throughout the capitalist world-system and the emptying out of political and cultural representation for those subjects in these realms. By failing to develop a better terminology and framework for life in these camps, other than through slogans of necrotic bare life, we perpetuate an un-knowledge that reinforces the prior denial of these human subjects' existence. The concept of denizenship thus means to cement rights for those *in situ*, but not within State recognition, be they in quasi-detention camps or living without papers within the core nations.

An initial alternative may be that provided by the world-systems knowledge movement and its geography of the capitalist world-system: core, periphery, and zemiperiphery. World-systems perspectives are most closely associated with Immanuel Wallerstein's historical sociology, but this touchstone often obscures the valuable and varied uses of world-systems by Wallerstein's associates and later inheritors. Initiated as a way to counter developmental theories from post-war centrist liberal political economy as well as stage theories from party-affiliated Marxism, world-systems analyses seek to break free from 19th-century social science paradigms, which buttressed the separation of academic disciplines in ways that often endorsed Eurocentric versions of cultural superiority. An initial move in what today we might call decolonizing our knowledge formations (Wallerstein called this move "unthinking" the assumptions) was a world-systems approaches' use of core-periphery distinctions taken from South American theorists like Raúl Prebisch and Andre Gunder Frank ("the development of underdevelopment"),[6] who initially argued against Ricardo's notion of comparative advantage among nations by indicating that non-industrialized States remain structurally disempowered

---

5 Marc Augé, *Non-places: Introduction to an Anthropology of Supermodernity* (London: Verso, 1995).
6 Immanuel Wallerstein, *Unthinking Social Science: Limits of Nineteenth-Century Paradigms* (Philadelphia: Temple University Press, 2001); Walter L. Goldfrank, "Paradigm Regained? The Rules of Wallerstein's World-System Method," *Journal of World-Systems Research* 6, no. 2 (2000): 150–195.

even after titular decolonization. The notion of a core and periphery was used to highlight continuing inequality within the global marketplace.

The difference between the core and its peripheries is easily said. The world-systems core is composed of stable nation-states who recognize each other's sovereignty and control of tax and security borders. They are typified by having a greater proportion of their workforce in higher-waged labor, which is often composed of the secondary processing of commodities or in consumer services, including domestic logistics. Core regions have a heterogeneous palette of production processes and multiple industrial sectors, which may co-exist in various states of expansion or decline in ways that allow for overall systemic stability, despite declines in one industry. Peripheral regions typically have weak State functions, especially with regard to civil society aspects that do not explicitly depend on police intimidation or military force. Laborers in the peripheries are usually tasked with lower-waged work that is frequently unwaged and involves greater personal risk and industrial accidents. Unlike the varied kinds of commodities exchanged in the core, the peripheral zones have sectors treating a smaller range of commodities, and their labor markets are often dominated by extractive industries or monocultural crop production. Peripheral regions often lack free choice in accessing the global market as they face pre-established constraints to trade in ways that usually direct their markets to their former colonizing power so as to continue their historic subordination and dependence.

A world-systems approach differs from older "development of underdevelopment" models with its contribution of the category, the semiperiphery/semiperipheries. As Wallerstein conveyed it, semiperipheries are often states that seek entry into core-status while also fearing their decline into the rank of the peripheries.[7] The move from a binary core/periphery model to the tripartite core/zemiperiphery/periphery one is one of the signal accomplishments of a world-systems analysis as it allows for a greater degree of analytical options so as to avoid debates over what category different places are to be shoe-horned into and to allow for a historical transformation of nations in ways that does not assume consequential primacy. The core-periphery model flattens out time and space, as it does not easily allow for an analysis of competitive hierarchies among nation-states outside of the core and depends on assumptions that each nation-state is homogeneous in nature. Here a world-

---

7   Immanuel Wallerstein, *World-Systems Analysis: An Introduction* (Durham, NC: Duke University Press, 2004), 28–30.

systems approach incorporates the core/periphery framework but escapes its rigidities by introducing the concept of the zemiperiphery.

Yet even this move has often still remained caught within the legacy undertow of the older political sociology that it otherwise seeks to avoid. For example, Wallerstein insisted that there was no distinctive semiperipheral mode of production, unlike the core or the periphery. The zemiperipheries were regions that simply mixed production aspects of the core and the periphery together so that their function in the world-system was presented as sub-imperialist, where they enact policies and policing on the peripheries that the core did not wish to engage in directly, much as a manager controls employees for the sake of their distant, corporate owners.

If the zemiperipheries are presented as absent of unique economic processes and known more in terms of political processes that are supplemental to the core and the peripheries, they might seem to be analogous to the spheres of distribution in the total circuit of capital that are considered "unproductive" of surplus-value and thus ignorable. Rather than consider capital in the keywords of spheres of value's production and spheres of circulation, it is better conceptually to speak of capital's spheres of value's production and its realization, or manifestation, to underscore the systemic necessity for the presence of the spheres not strictly listed as ones of production, especially as these spheres of circulation are the ones where multiple commodity chains become entangled in ways that change each individual one's shape and produce a new aggregate compound of social relations. Similarly, when people move from the hinterland or periphery in order to seek access to the core, they must move into or stay within the zemiperiphery, such as when South and Central Americans looking to the United States do so through the Mexican zemiperiphery. Within these zemiperipheries, however, the lifeworld of those in migration alters culture in ways that create a new social compound.

In this spirit, the zemiperipheries act in ways that are greater than simply being a baffling corridor between the core and the periphery. As I have previously argued, these are the zones that enable the systematicity of the world-system.

> Because the social action of the core region is too incommensurate with that of the periphery, the world-system requires a calibrating zone that can mediate and "translate" the cultural and commodity economies of each sphere to one another. It receives, monetizes, and forwards two kinds of commodities: the core's "fictional" ones of credit, insurance, and contractual prop-

erty and intellectual rights and the periphery's labor-power and natural resources. As the "transistor" space where two different segments of a commodity chain become articulated and receive their first pricing, the semiperiphery is the contact zone that makes it possible for the core and periphery to transmit value to each other, especially as both the rural dispossessed of the hinterlands and the factors of the core's jobbing interests congregate there, one to commodify their labor and the other to finance and insure the material apparatuses that will consume this labor-power.[8]

Yet the zemiperipheries are not only zones that react to pressures between the core and periphery, they are also the spheres that are highly *productive* of new social and cultural phenomena that often occur *in advance* of either the core or the periphery. These are the locations

> where political economy receives its greatest cultural inflection and amplification, the semiperipheries are the sites where the experience of trauma by peripheral peoples and the speculative entrepreneurship of the core collide to produce new forms of representation, especially as it receives both the oral, folk beliefs of the periphery and the core's printed matter and institutionally consecrated notations, objects, and behavioral performances. ... As semiperipheries mediate the experience of violence and coercion in the periphery and in the core's institutions of cultural valorization, ... [they stand] as the locale of a heightened globalizing structure of feeling, producing affects and artifacts often in advance of these experiences' concrete articulation by agents at either end of the system.[9]

Hence, "if the semiperiphery is the zone of transculturation and transvaluation, then it stands as a privileged region for registering the sociocultural formations of each phase in the world-system."[10] As Chase-Dunn notes, the semiperipheries stand as a "fertile ground for social, organization, and technical innovation," and "the most interesting thing about semiperipheries is that interesting political movements are more likely to emerge in them."[11] For instance, Wallerstein argued that Tsarist Russia was zemiperipheral, and he

---

8   Stephen Shapiro, *The Culture and Commerce of the Early American Novel: Reading the Atlantic World-System*. University Park, PA: Pennsylvania State University Press, 2008), 37,
9   Ibid., 37–38,
10 Ibid.
11 Christopher Chase-Dunn, "Comparing World Systems: Toward a Theory of Semipheral Development," *Comparative Civilizations Review* 19, no. 19 (1988): 31; Christopher Chase-

endorsed Trotsky's analysis that combined and uneven development was a leading factor in catalyzing the Russian Revolution: "A Leninist strategy could succeed only in a semiperipheral country" because while they might not have strong capitalist-proletarian confrontations, they do have strong instances of combined and uneven development involving the collision of peripheral lifeworlds with core technologies and capitalist maneuvers.[12] In this way, world-systems approaches revise 19th-century Marxist claims that the core, urban centers of the industrialized West (England, Germany) would be the places of capital's greatest contradiction and, consequently, the catalyzing sites of revolution. Instead, it may be more accurate to say that it is within the zemiperiphery's tangles that we may best find the emergence of cultural and political opposition to the capitalist world-system.

Furthermore, these new cultural productions are not only transferred between the core and the periphery but are also laterally transmitted elsewhere to other zemiperipheries. In this way, the zemiperiphery also functions as

> the world-system's internal arterial matrix: the geocultural "system form" of the world-system. Since the world-system lacks a centralized point of regulation and command, it requires a circulatory system that allows all the world-system's regions to communicate with each other. As the zones of transmission where peripheral goods and peoples enter one node of the semiperipheral network to be translocated to another one closer to the core, the semiperipheral nodes also form a coherent matrix unto themselves, a realm with distinctive features shared among all the other semiperipheral templates.[13]

Yet changes in the organization of the world-system cannot be seen simply through a flat, two-dimensional map of nation-states, since the zemiperiphery is more akin to a multi-dimensional matrix. A better understanding of the zemiperiphery's topography comes as Christopher Chase-Dunn explains that the world-system is nested, so that "the core/periphery hierarchy is a system-wide dimension of structured inequality, but at the same time it is also a re-

---

Dunn, *Global Formation: Structures of the World-Economy* (London: Basil Blackwell, 1989), 213.

12   Immanuel Wallerstein, *Geopolitics and Geoculture: Essays on the Changing World-System* (Cambridge: Cambridge University Press, 1991), 88.

13   Shapiro, *Culture and Commerce of the Early American Novel*, 38–39.

gionally nested hierarchy."[14] Nation-states are not "internally homogeneous," and "many of the developments which we study at the level of the world-system also occur within countries."[15] Additionally, some of these strata operate even without reference to the nation-state but in a relationship with other analogous nodes, such as with Saskia Sassen's claim for a world-systemic network of cities and financial markets that have a dynamic that exceeds the nation-state. I have previously argued that

> the difference between periphery and core should not be conceptualized as simply between static boundaries, since these terms represent spatialized relations more than geographic demarcations. Each spatial level (area, national, regional, urban, familial) contains its own core-periphery differences. Individual nation-states have their own internal corelike and peripheral zones (north/south and urban/agrarian divisions), and they often have a "city-system," where some cities dominate others. Cities likewise have their own "Manchester-effect" of class-differentiated regions, such as the core sectors where elites live and work and the peripheral slums housing the manual labor force. The patriarchal family or a racialized society can also be conceptualized as having white men as its core and women and nonwhites as peripheral actors. None of these levels is either wholly independent of the others or mechanistically determined by them. They often intersect each other in unpredictable ways because the relations of one level are not necessarily analogous or contiguous to each other.[16]

The zemiperipheral sites of combined and uneven development are also ones where zemiproletarianized labor is more prevalent, along with their increased presence of and reliance on household structures. For Wallerstein,

> a typical household consists of three to ten persons who, over a long period (say thirty years or so), pool multiple sources of income in order to survive collectively. Households are not usually egalitarian structures internally nor are they unchanging structures (persons are born and die, enter or leave households, and in any case grow older and thus tend to alter their economic role). What distinguishes a household structure is some form of

---

14 Chase-Dunn, *Global Formation*, 209.
15 Ibid.
16 Shapiro, *Culture and Commerce of the Early American Novel*, 33–34.

obligation to provide income for the group and to share in the consumption resulting from this income. Households are quite different from clans or tribes or other quite large and extended entities, which often share obligations of mutual security and identity but do not regularly share income. Or if there exist such large entities which are income-pooling, they are dysfunctional for the capitalist system.[17]

Within these, there are five kinds of income: wage-income, subsistence activity, petty production, rent, and (generational or interfamilial) transfer payments. Hence the zemiperipheries increased variation of income inputs consequently means that much of their labor is defined as female (or ethno-racial).

In the current moment, migration studies should especially incorporate zemiperipheral matters for several reasons. As urbanization has increased throughout the world, it magnifies zemiperipheral experience, whether or not this transhumance crosses national boundary lines. Second, the downward B-phase of an on-going Kondratieff wave in conjunction with rapidly increasing ecological destruction means that attempted migration from peripheries to the core nation is increasing. Yet given that many, and perhaps most, origin-destination migrations remain "incomplete," migration studies needs to acknowledge the constitutive significance of the movement into the zemiperipheries, whether these result eventually result in arrival in the core or not.

If the world-system's zemiperipheries are increasing in size and the composition of the zemiperipheries foregrounds "women's work" in both un- or weakly-waged labor, then, consequently migration studies need to take seriously the role of gender-sex, as well as ethno-racial distinctions. Furthermore, if the zemiperipheries form as a means of cultural production and communication amongst other zemiperipheries, then rather than consider migration as a feature of older, male attainment, we need to perceive how a world-systems culture of migration emerges from feminized, ethno-racialized, and younger generational households. From this perspective, the (modernizing) experience of "contemporary" is not simply to be found in the core metropoles and core institutions of these metropoles but in spaces and forms previously discounted as "semi" or developmentally indistinct.

Consequently, in order to avoid the developmental connotations of "semi-," I propose calling the semiperipheries, the *zemiperipheries*, to highlight their su-

---

17   Wallerstein, *World-Systems Analysis*, 32.

turing of the world-system's locations, as well as their increased presence and role of households in labor economies. In this sense, the zemiperipheral matrix is the one that is most apt for discussions of migration as it can provide an analytical mechanism to consider both the para-urban worlds of what Mike Davis has called "the planet of slums": the barrios, favelas, bidonvilles, shantytowns, and slab-cities, be they in either the peripheries or the cores in zones of immigrant arrival as well as the camps of migration for those without papers.[18]

Here I want to take up the challenge of this project less from the vantage point of quantitative social sciences and more from the cultural side of non-literary media to suggest a set of formal registrations of zemiperipheral experience. To sketch out this initial question, I want to take what may initially seem as a paradoxical or catachrestic pair, Berlin-based German filmmaker Christian Petzold's *Gespenster*,[19] the second in his so-called *Gespenster* trilogy of films about transient women, alongside paintings by and a photograph of Frida Kahlo treating the artist's place in the United States. The goal here will be to use a limited set of evidentiary material to consider registrations of the zemiperiphery as a means of modeling one way that the world-systems knowledge movement may take further steps forward.

Petzold's Ghosts

At first glance, Christian Petzold's cinema seems mismatched to any consideration of zemiperipheral cultural production. Even in an age of European cross-funding, Petzold's work remains resolutely German in its artistic lineage, geography, and casting. A leading exemplar of the so-called Berlin School of post-Wall filmmakers, the (West) German-born and Berlin-trained Petzold has a body of work that seems to follow the prior generational one of Wim Wenders, as both share a dedication to slow-paced "road movies" that scenify existential tristesse. Yet perhaps due to Petzold's lifelong collaboration with his former teacher, Harun Farocki, his work is more intentionally politicized than Wenders's and socially critical, primarily of post-Wall Germany's embrace of bourgeois self-satisfaction in the aftermath of the Cold War. Here his work links more loosely to the male theatrical lineage of Brecht, Heiner Müller, and Thomas Ostermeier. However, Petzold can be criticized for depicting an almost

---

18   Mike Davis, *Planet of Slums* (London: Verso, 2006).
19   Christian Petzold, dir., *Gespenster* (Berlin: Schramm Film Koerner & Weber, 2005).

entirely white Germany, one absent of multicultural presences. The ethnically diverse world depicted in director Fatih Akin's Hamburg seems entirely distant from Petzold's Berlinscapes.

Petzold's thematic pursuits often combine the genres of crime procedural and road movie to convey how the contemporary German experience-system is caught in a listless stasis because of its continuing amnesia about various past historical thresholds. This failure of *Vergangenheitsbewältigung* results in the return to bourgeois pettiness, the meanness and willingness to sacrifice those not willing to adapt to and seek the comforts of normativity within dominant middle-class society. What makes Petzold distinctive in this critique is that his tales are ones usually centered on female trauma where women's anguish embodies the faults of a collective history.

Over the course of his career, Petzold has developed a visual syntax to convey these concerns. Foregoing complicated trick shots or expensive crane work, his films usually depend on a limited cast, few locations, and rarely exceed the 90 minutes that stand as the typical limit for films to be seen on German television. Nearly all of his films are plotted through scenes set in mixed public/private realms of nowhereness, tables in outside cafes or hotel lobbies. They convey the disempowerment of indeterminate location by frequently using use over the shoulder shots of someone driving along anonymous motorways or walking down mundane footpaths or empty streets as well as instances of a voyeuristic gaze, either with police-like grainy CCTV video or a quarter-angle noir-film downwards view. The films have slow dialogue that is voided by gaps of silence, a loss of expression that is often compensated for by scenes of the characters turning on sound-producing instruments to introduce diegetic music, usually pre-rock and roll American soul or early jazz standards, as a nod perhaps to the Allied reconstruction of postwar Germany.

These formal elements are used to convey a zemiperipheral structure of feeling, as seen in *Gespenster*, a film within Petzold's so-called Ghost trilogy about women whose liminal or spectral place in society is exemplified by their wandering through life with little direction or social cohesion. Like Wenders's *Himmel über Berlin/Wings of Desire* (1987), *Gespenster* places nearly all of its action within a tight perimeter around Berlin's Potsdamer Platz and the Tiergarten, in order to indicate that its events are entangled within the undertow of German reunification. The movie begins with Nina, a young woman wearing a hi-vis jacket, who is seen picking up trash from the Tiergarten's grass as part of some (coerced) youth program. Seeing a woman being chased, Nina slowly follows, but not before she picks up a dropped earing. She then sees a half-undressed woman, Toni, being punched by men who flee the scene once they notice Nina watching them. Whether Nina has just seen a mugging or a sexual assault is not clear to the viewers. After giving Toni one of the two t-shirts she is wearing, Nina watches her walk away. Nina is then yelled at by the youth crew's older manager, who accuses her of lying about working by filling her mandatory collection bag with trash from the waste bins. Emptying Nina's bag on the grass, he tells her to pick up the trash for real this time.

The suggestion here is that the newly re-unified Berlin has cut corners to achieve its "park" beauty, its "poor but sexy" allure, and that it has not really done the work of picking up its trash of history, or that the city's authorities have forced this labor onto populations who are themselves considered disposable, such as the State institutionalized Nina, housed in something like a borstal or youth supervisory hostel. Nina's depicted aimlessness and frequent mute refusal to respond to accusations of insubordination suggests that she is without narrative agency, unable to express herself in the language of the core's dominant society.

As a result of exclusion from these privileges, Nina becomes the target of two other female desires that seek to define her in a particular way. On the one hand, there is Francoise's pursuit of Nina. Francoise is an older and very wealthy French woman visiting Berlin, who says that she believes that Nina is her long-lost child abducted while she had left her infant untended in a shopping cart. Francoise pursues Nina and encourages Nina to identify or reveal herself as that child. On the other hand, the itinerant, and more street-smart, Toni sees Nina as a means of gaining money from others. Here Nina is caught in a vortex. She is uncertain whether to believe Francoise and thus join a narrative about a fragmented family that might be regrouped and reconstructed. This fantasy can be seen as an allegory about the two German nations' reconnection and return to the embrace of a more amicable European Union.

On the other hand, Nina is persistently attracted to Toni. When Toni wants to be cast in a movie called female friends [*Freundinnen*], she brings Nina to the casting call and tells her to fabricate an origin story about the two women's friendship. Nina remains silent until she is directly asked to speak by the male director, and then hesitatingly speaks about having dreamt beforehand of Toni being stripped naked and raped while Nina stands watching. The viewer is left uncertain about whether this is a fair account of what had actually happened off-screen in the park at the film's beginning, or if it is a fabrication by Nina. Regardless of what happened or not, Nina has finally spoken a truth about her actual erotic desire for Toni. For all her prior affectless brooding can retrospectively be seen as her struggle to articulate and make public her sexual preference identity.

In this sense, her social ghostliness represents LGBTQ existence in heteronormative society. On the other hand, an inter-textual reference exists in Petzold's casting of Julia Hummer for the role of Nina. Hummer had previously worked for Petzold in his *Die Innere Sicherheit* (The State I'm In),[20] where Hummer plays the daughter of a former RAF couple on the run. That film ends with Hummer's character being the only family survivor of a car crash. Is Nina, as a ward of the State and bearing a jagged scar on her leg, the daughter from *Die Innere Sicherheit*? Is she also the female embodiment of the defeat of 68-er alternatives as a result of reunification, a loss represented by Nina's slumping posture as an anti-*Siegessäule* (the gold Berlin statue to military victory seen fleetingly in *Gespenter*)?

Nina is thus caught then between a desire for a core bourgeois happy end, a national allegory represented by reintegration within a wealthy family, and one for erotic connection with a member of the precarious, floating, and peripheral underclass. In the end, both choices are denied her. Toni abandons Nina after they have slept together, and Francoise is taken away by her husband after he reveals that she repeatedly enacts a delusion about finding her abducted child as an older woman, even while she also knows, in fact, that her child had died as an infant.

The film ends with Nina walking back to the park trash bin where Toni had previously thrown Francoise's wallet that she had stolen from her. Nina sees there a picture of Francoise's lost child on a long strip of paper folded over into quarter sections. When Nina expands the turned-over units, like a film reel's movement, it reveals frames of the dead child's possible development, leading to an illustration that looks like Nina, who stares at these images and then angrily throws them back in the rubbish. The film ends with a static camera recording her walking away on a park path.

One reading of the scene is that Nina remains caught in directionless movement, as she is literally not able to "see" herself as belonging to any sequential history, thus not being able to imagine herself represented in any narrative form. Neither allowed the comfort of the core, nor willing to sink back into the periphery, Nina's tale is a zemiperipheral one, a tale that is highly

---

20 Christian Petzold, dir., *Die Innere Sicherheit* (Berlin: Schramm Film, Hessischer Rundfunk, and ARTE, 2000).

gendered and weakly-waged, as her compulsory labor seems to be more disciplinary than vocational. Despite Petzold's lack of ethnic characters, Nina's position mimics that of a migrant or "guest-worker."

Fig. 1: Nina examines her imagined development in Petzold's Gespenster

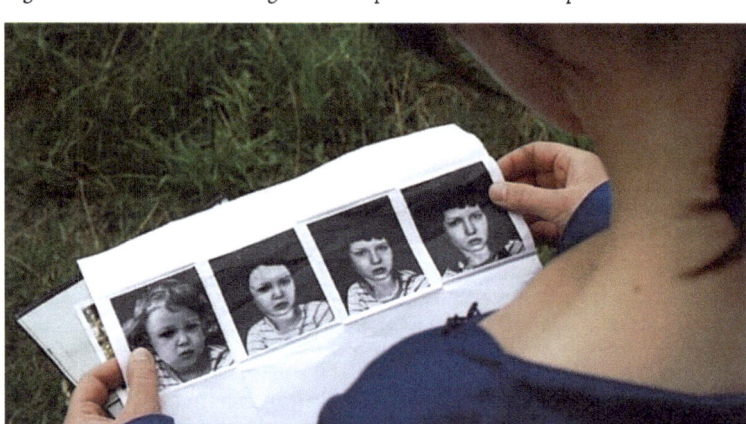

Here Petzold's cinema upholds a familiar tale told about the zemiperiphery as a place lacking significance or meaning and one that is incapable of unique self-identification. An entirely different strategy, however, is seen in the earlier work by, and about, Frida Kahlo, daughter of a German immigrant to Mexico.

Frida Kahlo's America

Kahlo might best be viewed as a zemiperipheral Mexico City – rather than simply peripheral Mexican – artist who resists core North Americanism and the European high art tradition by schooling herself in the patterns and palette of regional Mexican vernaculars that she herself does not know and must learn since she belongs to a metropolitanized formation and not a hinterland peasant one.

Kahlo's consciously world-system work begins with a pair of 1930s canvasses that directly address the relation between Mexico and the United States as existing in a core-periphery opposition. Kahlo's *Self-Portrait on the Borderline*

Between Mexico and the United States positions her on a podium between two national spaces, one configured as a brown-tinge and underdeveloped Mexico whose glory days have receded and the other as a metallic and industrial USA.[21] Given that the podium is off-centered and closer to the American side, the canvas is guardedly optimistic about immigration, with its suggestion that for all its seeming mechanical coldness, the USA stands as a modernizing freedom from the nightmare of peripheral obsolescence. The USA-space is composed of vertical skyscrapers and vaguely anthropomorphic metal vents. The lower field of the American side has womblike speakers and machinery with sun ray-like lines that seem to be the emissions of sound or electricity. Despite her recent miscarriage, Kahlo presents the USA as a place of large-scale productivity, not entirely barren of vibrant life, since the pastel coloring of the buildings matches that of her pink, stiff dress. The American side's serial smokestacks each have a letter that, taken together, spell out "Ford." But as smoke plumes from these towers uphold an American flag in the sky like a baby, the industry is presented as fertile. While Kahlo paints her self-representation in a guarded fashion, with her arms crossed protectively over her lower abdomen, perhaps as one might hold a wounded place, the cigarette she holds in the hand on the American side links its smoke to that of the factories in ways that present the manufacturing metropolis as a place of personal fulfillment, erotic satisfaction, and the possibility of renewed biological and artistic creation.

Conversely, the Mexican side, registered by a draping flag held in her other hand, has darker shades, and its field is strewn with obsolete detritus from the Mayan or Aztec eras. The American skyscrapers' verticality is contrasted by the Mexican's horizontal and squat temple that is supervised by a drooping quarter moon and demonic sun, depicted with downward flames. The only color is provided by a jumble of plants with visible deep roots, which cross over to the American side in order to link to its energetic machinery. Kahlo seems to be suggesting that the promise of peripheral beauty may only flower and be realized in the North's opportunity and modern promise. Here the movement of the individual from the periphery to the core is idealized, not entirely unlike many immigration dreams that arrival in the core can valorize the periphery's agents.

---

21 Detroit Institute of Arts, "Self-Portrait on the Borderline Between Mexico and the United States, Frida Kahlo, 1932," *Google Arts & Culture*, https://artsandculture.google.com/asset/self-portrait-on-the-borderline-between-mexico-and-the-united-states-frida-kahlo/JwHDw-_2L73Nzw.

Fig. 2: Frida Kahlo, Self-Portrait on the Borderline Between Mexico and the United States (1932)

Within only a year, *My Dress Hangs There* has lost this optimism.[22] In this painting, Kahlo draws no representation of her own body, which is indicated only by the outline of a dress hanging out to dry. As the garment's colors are those of the Mexican flag, the peripheral subject is presented only as an absence, a body lost and seen only by the traces of a worn dress left dangling within a degraded world of the core's trash and commercialized gaudiness.

The North of the United States is pictured by neoclassical architecture, with two columns upholding objects, an open toilet and an over-glorious trophy, as though to say that the idealized American republic has only delivered waste and cheap self-glorification. In this canvas, only the dress's lower green half is lively, since even the Hudson River's water is colored as dark and seemingly polluted. The perspective of Liberty Island and Manhattan is skewed to make them seem equal, but the Statue of Liberty is covered by soot, and its base is

---

22   Fridakahlo.org, "My Dress Hangs There, 1933 by Frida Kahlo," *fridakahlo.org*, https://www.fridakahlo.org/my-dress-hangs-there.jsp.

made to look carceral in ways that suggest free and mobile spirits being imprisoned. The canvas is frankly dystopian. The towers and metallic body-shapes of the prior canvas appear, but they are squeezed into a vanishing corner, as if to suggest the modernizing ideals associated with them are being squeezed out and expunged from the frame of vision. The dreams about the American promise as delivering personal fulfillment seen in Kahlo's painting in the prior year are extinguished.

Fig. 3: My Dress Hangs There (1933)

The spirit of failure embedded within the 1933 canvas can be seen as made possible only by the limited choices provided by a core-periphery model. A decade later, however, Kahlo's self-presentation is radically different, and this is because it has broken out of core-periphery conceptualizations to include a realization of the zemiperiphery as a space of unique possibility rather than one simply as one in-between, moving from the periphery to the core.

Fig. 4: Nickolas Muray, Frida on the Rooftop, New York (1946)

In *Frida on the Rooftop, New York*, a stylized photograph of Kahlo taken by Hungarian-American Nickolas Muray, Kahlo wears indigenous Tehuana clothes, which are displayed in order to form a visual contrast and confrontation to Manhattan's skyscraper glorification of capitalist power.[23] The blouse's patterns both repeat the blackened windows of the towers while also being distinguished by their florid colors. Yet this binary difference is literally grounded on a zemiperipheral space, the rooftop of a "bohemian" Greenwich Village building, a zemi space that situates Kahlo as neither between rural

---

23   Brooklyn Museum, "Frida in New York," *Brooklyn Museum*, https://www.brooklynmuseum.org/opencollection/objects/197205.

Mexico, represented by the clothes, not the urban core, represented by the background's commercial, Midtown towers, but in a location that grounds her. The rooftop's tiles, cemented at a 45-degree angle create a formal diagonal "z" that cuts between the rectilinearity of Kahlo's dress and Midtown's erections. While the 1932 canvas used a binary core-periphery model that produces Kahlo's defensiveness by Kahlo, seen with her crossed, self-protective arms that guard her body against the viewer, Muray's photograph captures a different tone entirely. Kahlo's arms are open, and her slanted head and semi-enclosed eyes imply a greater sense of empowered autonomy that is comfortable with risking the vulnerability of semi-sleep.

The self-control represented in this image suggests a new approach to issues of culture, migration, and revolutionary desires as it highlights the zemiperiphery as a place of creativity and connection to other zemiperipheries. Here, this space represents a location within the capitalist world-system that allows for different possibilities than either the path of the core's development or the periphery's experience of the underdevelopment of development.

By over-idealizing the core's emancipatory potential in the 1932 painting, Kahlo sets up the fall and despair over its failed promise in the 1933 one. Yet by Muray's 1946 photograph, neither the euphoria of mechanical modernity, nor the degradation of its cultural industry is given the final word. Here a zemiperipheral non-space, a liminal rooftop becomes a way to stage the intersection of a feminized Mexican dress in the bohemian North in ways separate from either the peripheral countryside or the financial core. Questions of transit, origin, and trajectory are not even asked as the zemiperipheral time and space has its own substantive status.

Here, Muray's photograph solves a problem that Petzold's cinema did not. Petzold's work presents the zemiperiphery as an aimless void, since its vision continues to rely on a binary model of time and space. On one side lies a self-congratulatory and amnesiac bourgeoisie. On the other float those who have been shunted to the margins because of their inability or refusal to be submerged within the wake of contemporary German history. No third place is conceptualized, so that the female zemiproletarian is left without community, without vibrancy, without direction. Like the ghosts of the movie's title, Petzold's cinema presents the liminal as rarely able to disturb the everyday norm. Kahlo's 1930s paintings are similarly caught in the nowhereness of this binary. Muray's later photograph, however, depicts the zemiperiphery as a site lacking the core's power, but not one empty of resilience and creative possibility. While Kahlo is alone in the image's frame, the setting implies the possibility of others soon joining her for an impromptu fiesta, perhaps one that talks about revolution.

Conclusion

My juxtaposition of Petzold's movie and the images of Kahlo is meant to highlight three larger points about migration and the zemiperipheries. First, each zemiperiphery can formally register its particularity as well as linkages to other zemiperipheries. Second, migration to the zemiperipheries needs to be considered as structurally linked to the core and peripheries, but they must also be seen as spaces capable of realizing social and cultural aspects that neither the core nor the peripheries can see or present. Lastly, migration to the zemiperiphery is a rich resource for tapping into the experience of the subjects within it, of those people who may suffer but are also able to forge radical alternatives. When considering the energies of political change in the present moment, it will be the linked zemiperipheries that may stand as domains requiring our attention. Zemiperipheries matter, then, for any anti-developmental and socially emancipatory Cultural Studies.

Works Cited

Augé, Marc. *Non-places: Introduction to an Anthropology of Supermodernity*. London: Verso, 1995.
Brooklyn Museum. "Frida in New York." Brooklyn Museum. https://www.brooklynmuseum.org/opencollection/objects/197205.
Chase-Dunn, Christopher. "Comparing World Systems: Toward a Theory of Semipheral Development." *Comparative Civilizations Review* 19, no. 19 (1988): 29–66.
Chase-Dunn, Christopher. *Global Formation: Structures of the World-Economy*. London: Basil Blackwell, 1989.
Davis, Mike. *Planet of Slums*. London: Verso, 2006.
Detroit Institute of Arts. "Self-Portrait on the Borderline Between Mexico and the United States, Frida Kahlo, 1932." Google Arts & Culture. https://artsandculture.google.com/asset/self-portrait-on-the-borderline-between-mexico-and-the-united-states-frida-kahlo/JwHDw-_2L73Nzw.

Dunaway, Wilma A. "Revisionist with a Cause: Interview with Wilma Dunaway." *Appalachian Journal* 31, no. 2 (2004): 166–191.
Fridakahlo.org. "My Dress Hangs There, 1933 by Frida Kahlo." fridakahlo.org. httpv://www.fridakahlo.org/my-dress-hangs-there.jsp.
Goldfrank, Walter L. "Paradigm Regained? The Rules of Wallerstein's World-System Method." *Journal of World-Systems Research* 6, no. 2 (2000): 150–195.
Hoffmann, E.T.A. *The Golden Pot and Other Tales*. Oxford: Oxford University Press, 1992.
Marx, Karl. "On the Jewish Question." In Karl Marx, *Early Writings*, 211–241. New York: Vintage, 1975.
Petzold, Christian, dir. *Die Innere Sicherheit*. Berlin: Schramm Film, Hessischer Rundfunk, and ARTE, 2000.
Petzold, Christian, dir. *Gespenster*. Berlin: Schramm Film Koerner & Weber, 2005.
Shapiro, Stephen. *The Culture and Commerce of the Early American Novel: Reading the Atlantic World-System*. University Park, PA: Pennsylvania State University Press, 2008.
Wallerstein, Immannuel. "Citizens All? Citizens Some! The Making of the Citizen." *Comparative Studies in Society and History* 45, no. 4 (2003): 650–679.
Wallerstein, Immanuel. *Geopolitics and Geoculture: Essays on the Changing World-System*. Cambridge: Cambridge University Press, 1991.
Wallerstein, Immanuel. *Unthinking Social Science: Limits of Nineteenth-Century Paradigms*. Philadelphia: Temple University Press, 2001.
Wallerstein, Immanuel. "World-System Analysis as a Knowledge Movement." In *Routledge Handbook of World-Systems Analysis*, edited by Christopher Chase-Dunn and Salvatore Babones, 515–521. London: Routledge, 2012.
Wallerstein, Immanuel. *World-Systems Analysis: An Introduction*. Durham, NC: Duke University Press, 2004.

4. Semiosphere and World-System
A Semiotic Reflection on Migration and Nationalism within the World-System

Giuditta Bassano

In 2002, commenting on his previous article on the relevance of the *Communist Manifesto*,[1] Umberto Eco argues that the document "astonishingly witnessed the birth, 150 years ahead of its time, of the era of globalization." He goes on to say: "[I]t almost suggests that globalization is not an accident that happens during the course of capitalist expansion ... but rather the inevitable pattern that the emergent class could not fail to follow, even though at the time, through the expansion of markets, the most convenient (though also the most bloody) means to this end was called colonization." Eco concludes with a strategic comment: "It is also worth dwelling again (and that is advisable not for the bourgeoisie but for all classes) on the warning that every force opposing the march of globalization is initially divided and confused, tends toward mere Luddism, and can be used by its enemy to fight its own battles."[2] Thus, one of the leading figures of semiotic studies presents with ease how

---

1 On January 8, 1998, Eco wrote an editorial for the Italian newspaper *L'Espresso* advocating the efficacy and currency of the *Communist Manifesto* of 1848. It was re-published in Umberto Eco, *On Literature*, trans. Martin McLaughlin (Orlando, FL: Harcourt, 2004), 23–27. The remarks added in a new Italian edition from 2002 address this passage: "One sees [...] this unstoppable force [the bourgeoisie], which, urged on by the need for new markets for its goods, pervades the whole world on land and sea [...], overturns and transforms distant countries because the low prices of products are its heavy artillery, which allows it to batter down any Chinese wall and force surrender on even the barbarians who are most hardened in their hatred for the foreigner; it sets up and develops cities as a symbol and as the foundation of its own power; and it becomes multinational, globalised, and even invents a literature that is no longer national but international." Ibid., 24.
2 Ibid.

a political perspective – or, more explicitly, a Marxist one – is vital when studying contemporary culture. This is no surprise since semiotics – at least in France and Italy – began to become a major approach to media theory in the late 1960s and considered itself a *critical method*, including through the notion of "semiotic guerrilla warfare" coined by Eco to claim the construction of counterhegemonic meanings for media texts.³ Moreover, another point of convergence should be noted.⁴ In a 1981 interview, Immanuel Wallerstein endorsed the spread of a shared language based on the Marxist perspective:

> [W]e are moving toward a world in which everyone will use Marxist terminology. It'll take another fifty or one hundred years, but we'll get there. And I think that this will create a very favorable situation. On the one hand, if you use a certain terminology, you are compelled to accept certain presuppositions implicit within it, and in this case, these are presuppositions which I don't mind at all. But on the other hand, it is also true that when a terminology becomes universal, each person is intellectually free to think within it, internally.⁵

Not very unlike Wallerstein, Eco was committed to conveying the relevance of a widespread awareness of Marxism as far back as 1976. He claimed, taking a rather over-optimistic view, in hindsight, that Marxist values had become everyone's values, as the "set of so-called Marxist principles and political strategies" was eventually accepted and seen as undeniable.⁶ In the present day, it is quite ironic that such is the charge brought by many New Right movements

---

3   Umberto Eco, *Travels in Hyperreality*, trans. William Weaver (Boston, MA: Mariner Books, 1990), 165.
4   We may also add a strictly philosophical aspect according to Prigogine and Stengers, who assume that both semiotics and world-systems theory are based on the refusal of the human subjectivity as a core theoretical notion. Ilya Prigogine and Isabel Stengers, *La nouvelle alliance: Métamorphose de la science* (Paris: Gallimard, 1979), 16. It is also quite obvious that both world-systems and semiotics are structural models, in an extended sense. However, such a statement would open up a number of problems concerning different concepts of "structure," and this is not the place to address them.
5   Immanuel Wallerstein, "Immanuel Wallerstein's Thousand Marxisms," interview by Nicolette Stame and Luca Meldolesi, trans. David Broder, *Jacobin*, November 11, 2019, https://www.jacobinmag.com/2019/09/immanuel-wallerstein-marxism-world-systems-theory-capitalism.
6   Umberto Eco, "Scusate qualche testo," *Corriere della Sera*, February 27, 1976. Despite his normal clarity, it is not clear, here, if Eco's motion is addressed to Italy, to the West, or even universally.

and populist movements, which mostly count Marxism among the forces endangering local people's rights, interests, and earnings.

Conversely, there are some reasons making the connection between the world-system and semiotics problematic. We will briefly examine two of them. As Wallerstein stated on many occasions, the first feature of the world-system is of being a totality, a capitalist system encompassing the economy of the whole world. The perspective is then enriched by the introduction of six kinds of institutions collected by the capitalist world economy: "the markets; the firms that compete in the markets; the multiple states …; the households; the classes; and the status groups (to use Weber's term, which some people in recent years have renamed the 'identities')."[7] Subsequently comes a spatial model interrelating economic core areas, economic periphery areas, and economic semi-periphery areas where the institutions act and exist as products of the capitalist system. The world-system as such works within an admirable socioeconomic analysis of the system's stages and the proposal of a final ongoing transition from the capitalist system to an uncertain future[8] that will occur from about 2025.[9] One can notice three more meta-theoretical features resulting from the foregoing: the inclination for simple tools, which is, according to Wallerstein, also the key element setting an open, flexible and general theory; the virtual but complex possibility of relating migration phenomena with different institutions among those mentioned (see further on this below); and the focus on economics and historical studies, which, as stated by Stephen Shapiro, shows how it "does not immediately or easily offer them to application for cultural studies and the reading of texts."[10]

The first friction hence involves the theoretical framework, chiefly since semiotics is largely committed more to microanalysis than macroanalysis, assuming a complex, stratified, and heterogenous set of models. All these models depend on an essential analytical prerequisite: the analytical outcomes logically follow the analysis and could never be predicted within its theoretical foundations. In other terms, the friction is between a method and a theory.

---

7   Immanuel Wallerstein, *World-Systems Analysis: An Introduction* (Durham, NC: Duke University Press, 2004), 24.

8   See also Giovanni Arrighi, *Long Twentieth Century: Money, Power and the Origins of Our Time*, rev. ed. (London: Verso, 2010), 247–386.

9   Terence Hopkins and Immanuel Wallerstein, eds., *The Age of Transition: Trajectory of the World-System, 1945–2025* (London: Zed Books, 1996), 200–233.

10   Stephen Shapiro, "What is World-systems for Cultural Studies?" chapter draft provided by the author, 2020.

Semiotics is a *method*[11] developed by collecting tools, mainly from linguistics and anthropology (but with a political basis, as stated), to empower the *analytical description* of practices, discourses, strategies, images, as well as verbal texts considered as communicative phenomena.[12] World-systems is a *theory*, albeit a very solid one, built on general economic assumptions on the way the whole reality we experience works, and its theorists seek to refine it almost independently from empirical data or, more precisely, to work out empirical data illustrating its validity.[13] Succinctly, we are dealing with a triple divergence: while the world-system is a theory focused on macro-economic and self-validating problems, semiotics is an analytical method to be applied to empirical

---

11   For this issue as the main topic, see Algirdas Julien Greimas and Joseph Courtés, *Sémiotique: Dictionnaire raisonné de la théorie du langage I* (Paris: Hachette, 1979); Algirdas Julien Greimas and Joseph Courtés, *Sémiotique: Dictionnaire raisonné de la théorie du langage II: Compléments, débats, propositions* (Paris: Hachette, 1986); Algirdas Julien Greimas, *The Social Sciences: A Semiotic View*, trans. Paul Perron and Frank H. Collins (Minneapolis, MN: University of Minnesota Press, 1990); Bronwen Martin and Felizitas Ringham, *Key Terms in Semiotics* (London: Continuum, 2000); Gianfranco Marrone, *The Invention of the Text*, trans. Sara Anselmi, Dario Mangano and Peter Carne (Milan: Mimesis, 2014).

12   At times, semiotics and Louis Althusser's semio-political thought are confused. For a precise account on the reception of Althusser's thought through Gramsci's in the field of *cultural studies*, see Miguel Mellino, "Note sul metodo di Stuart Hall: Althusser, Gramsci e la questione della razza," *Décalage* 2, no. 1 (2016): 12, https://core.ac.uk/reader/733 45870. Another possible confusion with Chomsky's perspective, very much far from the contemporary semiotic perspective, is settled by Greimas, *The Social Sciences*. In light of this clarification, semiotic studies are related to two fundamental theoretical bases: an antidealistic approach to phenomena – so that the idea of *one* migration does not make much sense in semiotics – and the assumption that Marx's idea of superstructure can be somehow overturned, since any speculation and/or action is interpreted by the framing of human languages.

13   In his fairly well-known critique of Wallerstein's theory, Aronowitz disputed, among other points, the assumption of "expansion" as an universal feature: "Take the proposition that expansion is a property of all social systems or they must die. Critical theory would refuse this formulation as ahistorical and would argue that societies are not understood by cyclical theories that purport to explain contraction by means of 'natural' causes. Nor is 'growth' an invariant property of social formations. These disputes cannot be settled empirically but must be argued on the basis of metatheoretical assumptions that underlie research. To be sure, Wallerstein does not argue his starting points either, but tries to account for well-known events such as feudalism's decline by means of them." Stanley Aronowitz, "A Metatheoretical Critique of Immanuel Wallerstein's The Modern World System," *Theory and Society* 10 (1981): 511.

discourses and practices and which refuses any general correspondence of research questions and research outcomes.

The second friction is the more interesting. The semiotic model developed by the Russian scholar and semiotician Yuri Lotman,[14] which has spread widely and somehow independently from semiotics as a whole field of studies,[15] features a spatial pattern partially overlapping with Wallerstein's one. It is only partial, however, since it seems possible to enable a first exchange between semiotics and world-system precisely because of such overlays.

Lotman's Semiosphere

Yuri Lotman studies culture as a living, evolving, and complex system and introduces the notion of the "semiosphere" by analogy with Vladimir Vernadsky's concepts of the noosphere and, particularly, the "biosphere."[16]

> The semiotic universe may be regarded as the totality of individual texts and isolated languages as they relate to each other. In this case, all structures will look as if they are constructed out of individual bricks. However, it is more useful to establish a contrasting view: all semiotic space may be regarded as a unified mechanism (if not organism). In this case, primacy does not lie in one or another sign, but in the "greater system," namely the semiosphere. The semiosphere is that same semiotic space, outside of which semiosis cannot exist.[17]

A semiosphere consists of a nested link of subsystems, each organized by the presence of a core-periphery hierarchal structure. The core (or the center) is occupied by normative (familiar) elements, and the periphery with irregular,

---

14   For a general introduction, see Aleksei Semenenko, *The Texture of Culture: An Introduction to Yuri Lotman's Semiotic Theory* (New York: Palgrave MacMillan, 2012).
15   See Andreas Schönle, ed., *Lotman and Cultural Studies: Encounters and Extensions* (Madison, WI: University of Wisconsin Press, 2006); Andreas Ventsel and Peeter Selg, "Towards a Semiotic Theory of Hegemony: Naming as Hegemonic Operation in Lotman and Laclau," *Sign Systems Studies* 36, no. 1 (2008): 167–183; John Hartley, Indrek Ibrus, and Maarja Ojamaa, *On the Digital Semiosphere: Culture, Media and Science for the Anthropocene* (New York: Bloomsbury, 2020).
16   Vladimir Vernadsky, *The Biosphere* (New York: Copernicus, 1998).
17   Jurij Lotman, "On the Semiosphere," *Sign System Studies* 33, no. 1 (2005): 208.

innovative, and/or foreign elements. It is noteworthy in this regard how Lotman states that all levels of the semiosphere – at various levels of culture – are "semiospheres inserted into one another," like matryoshka dolls.[18]

Therefore, there are two caveats. The first is about the minimum and maximum extensions of a semiosphere; the second concerns whether the semiosphere is to be considered an objective (material) substance or an abstract concept. Even though Lotman described individuals as logically framed by the notion, this does not seem particularly productive; a better example is that of a museum as a space where different levels interact, such as those of the exhibition, usually including objects of different ages, verbal texts in different languages, booklets by curators, museum maps, rules of conduct, safety regulations, etc. Regarding the problem of a maximum extension, the answer is simpler. Since Lotman's model is based on a dialogical principle, any semiosphere needs at least one partner: in isolation, it cannot mean anything, nor can it produce any information.

Therefore, if a global model such as world-systems is inconceivable, this does not prevent the semiosphere model from being applied in the case of small towns or transnational institutions.[19] Further, the extension of a semiosphere depends on the existence of micro and microcultural boundaries, so it is not difficult to conceive human groups (geographically, linguistically, politically, or religiously speaking) as semiospheres, nor transnational institutions, such as maritime law, voluntary or compulsory teams and crews, such as academic research groups or the ensemble of the prisoners of a detention camp, or even cultural practices and rituals, such as microelectronics, carpet manufacture, or funerals.[20]

---

18   Semenenko, *Texture of Culture*, 115.
19   According to Kull and Torop, the semiosphere is a metaconcept, a "construct of semiotic method" that takes an holistic approach to culture, and as an object it refers to a given semiotic space that is studied in the analysis. Somewhat paradoxally, it is possible to say that the "semiosphere is studied by the means of [the] semiosphere." Kalevi Kull, "Semiosphere and a Dual Ecology: Paradoxes of Communication," *Sign Systems Studies* 33, no. 1 (2005): 184; Peeter Torop, "Tartuskaia shkola kak shkola," in *Lotmanovskii sbornik* 1, eds. Evgenii Permiakov and Roman Leibov (Moscow: IC-Garant), 231. For that reason, one might distinguish between *the* semiosphere, the precondition of semiosis, and *a* semiosphere, a specific semiotic space that is described or reconstructed in the analysis. Semenenko, *Texture of Culture*, 120.
20   "The semiosphere as a multidimensional space that produces equally multidimensional messages always emphasizes the situation of dialogue between different 'dialects' of culture. The national context is a traditional delimiter of a given culture,

However, the key issues of Lotman's model lie elsewhere with regard to its focus on the dynamic change of cultural systems. Firstly, the semiosphere model comes with a pattern of boundaries. This issue is so striking that some see the whole theoretical framework as a model of boundaries. The division between the center and the periphery is a manifestation of the fact that the semiotic space of culture is permeated with boundaries. The periphery is not "the end" of a system but a transition point between different systems and structures. Here, Lotman seems to take the system as a medium-large scale notion, approaching the world-system foundations. He argues that the boundaries between systems are not exact but quite vague, subject to constant fluctuations, and resemble not an impenetrable wall but rather a filter or membrane. The function of boundaries "is to control, filter and adapt the external into the internal," and they also serve as catalysts of communication. "Because the semiotic space is transected by numerous boundaries, each element that moves across it must be many times translated and transformed, and the process of generating new information thereby snowballs."[21]

The dialogic principle presupposes a constant dynamic tension on the boundaries not only of different systems but also between different levels of any semiotic system. If there is no tension on the border, no translation occurs, and therefore no new meaning can occur either. The tension is thus essential for the culture's sustainability and is created by two tendencies: the given incomplete mutual translatability and the need for full translatability. The immanent development of culture and the production of new culture cannot be realized without the inflow of external elements. "The outside" can be represented by any element that is extrinsic to the normative frame of a given structure, whether it is genre, tradition, or culture as a whole:

> Thus, from the position of an outside observer, culture will represent not an immobile, synchronically balanced mechanism, but a dichotomous system,

---

but it is quite a crude criterion because national boundaries often presuppose cultural monoglotism and therefore may neglect other phenomena that do not fit the culture's self-description. Apart from that, semiosphere transcend national borders (e.g., film noir, or art nouveau architecture) as well as 'microcultures' of various groups or even 'individual cultures.' From the methodological point of view, such a flexible concept turns out to be more accurate than the historically and politically laden concepts of 'national culture,' 'subculture,' or 'mass culture.'" Semenenko, *Texture of Culture*, 124.

21 Jurij Lotman, *Culture and Explosion*, trans. Wilma Clark (Berlin: Mouton de Gruyter, 2009), 140.

the "work" of which will be realized as the aggression of regularity against the sphere of the unregulated and, in the opposite direction, as the intrusion of the unregulated into the sphere of organization. At different moments of historical development either tendency may prevail. The incorporation into the cultural sphere of texts which have come from outside sometimes proves to be a powerful stimulating factor for cultural development.[22]

It follows that a semiosphere is essentially polyglot and consists of a diversity of semiotic systems that are not equivalent to one another but, at the same time, are mutually interprojected and have various degrees of translatability.

Secondly, Lotman claims that the tendency toward isolation is quite frequent in cultures. Accordingly, cultures' boundaries are intrinsically associated with ideology, the metalevel of culture, which, as we will see below, is oriented primarily toward the delineation of borders.

Neo Nazi groups, totalitarian sects, football hooligans, and many others are oriented toward maintaining rigid and explicit boundaries. … The oppressive regimes and ideologies always attempt to introduce a specific discourse that from a semiotic point of view defines the dialogic principle of communication: repressive ideological discourses adopt ontological categories of own and alien, right and wrong. Thus, most texts here become reaffirmation of the established hierarchies.[23]

Some further specifications frame the opposite case, which frequently occurs, of an active reception of foreign material. Lotman sees gradual processes as complementary to what he calls "explosions," and both are required for the dynamic development of culture. Cultural explosions coexist with gradual processes because different layers and elements of culture develop at different rates (for example, language, chemistry, and fashion all move at various "speeds").[24] An explosion may remain local, influencing only a specific cultural process, but other explosions may affect all levels of culture. The gradual and explosive tendencies can be presented in terms of continuity and discontinuity: the former represents "a perceived predictability," and the latter is perceived as an abrupt change, an explosion. A cultural explosion is defined

---

22 Jurij Lotman, Boris Uspenskij, Viacheslav Ivanov, Vladimir Toropov, and Alexander Pjatigorskij, "Thesis on the Semiotic Study of Culture," in *The Tell-Tale Sign: A Survey of Semiotics*, ed. Thomas A. Sebeok (Lisse: Peter de Ridder Press), 60.
23 Semenenko, *Texture of Culture*, 62–63.
24 Lotman, *Culture and Explosion*, 12.

as a moment of drastic change in the state of a system when its conventional balance is disturbed. For example, Lotman employs the notion of the explosion as a social cataclysm to deal with the history of Russia, seen as a model of evolutionary processes marked by continuous revolutionary jolts.

In terms of the core-periphery dichotomy, the explosive moment can be imagined as a gravitational collapse: centripetal forces make peripheral elements burst into the core and virtually destroy the balance of the system. The normative core becomes vague and "shaky," ceasing to be the tentative point of departure in texts' comprehension, interpretation, and/or creation. At the moment of explosion, the information load of the system drastically increases, and unpredictably increases proportionally. Like a virus that provokes the immune system to respond, the new elements occupy a significant part of the system and make it deploy counter mechanisms in order to accommodate the system to a new, changed state. The difference is that for the organism's survival, the virus should be destroyed, whereas culture transforms (changes in structure) every time it receives something foreign, slowly and gradually or rapidly and radically. "The metaphor of explosion should not be understood literally, as something that happens very quickly with an immediate effect; it may last several months or decades."[25] Furthermore, explosions inevitably provoke dampening processes, which are especially evident in technological revolutions (e.g., the invention of printing, the technology of travel and air travel, new weaponry, and the Internet). "Every abrupt change in human history releases new forces. The paradox is that movement forward may stimulate the regeneration of archaic cultural and psychological modes, may give rise both to scientific blessings and to epidemics of mass fear."[26] Fear and disorientation often follow cultural explosions because explosions break the chain of causality, violating temporal boundaries and creating a field of unpredictability:

> Each time we speak of unpredictability we have in mind a specific collection of equally probable possibilities from which only one may be realized. In this way, each structural position represents a cluster of variant possibilities. Up to a certain point they appear as indistinguishable synonyms. However, movement from the point of explosion causes them to become more and

---

25 Ibid., 46, n. 8.
26 Jurij Lotman, "Technological Progress as a Problem in the Study of Culture," *Poetics Today* 12, no. 4 (1991): 798.

more dispersed in semantic space. Finally, the moment arrives when they become carriers of semantic difference.[27]

This thesis of an outset of any explosion where probabilities are equally probable brings to mind the concept of "bifurcation" coined by Ilya Prigogine in his works on reversible processes in thermodynamics. This same "bifurcation" inspired Wallerstein's theory. Bifurcation is a point of development of the system when it reaches the point of "choice" between two possible scenarios; this is a random process that can be compared with a coin toss. So, effectively, Lotman refers to Prigogine's theory, but he also mentions Isabelle Stengers and Ross Ashby as congenial to his antideterministic view of history and emphasizes the role of unpredictability at the moment of instability.[28] After remarking that Lotman's notion of the semiosphere as a cultural system is not integrative, unlike Wallerstein's world-system since "capitalism was always a world system based on the primacy of the economic over the political and cultural,"[29] a last crux is provided within the notion of metalevel of culture. The highest form of the structural organization of a culture is the point of self-description, which any developed culture inevitably reaches.[30]

> Self-description demands the creation of a metalanguage for the given culture. On the basis of the metalanguage there arises the metalevel on which the culture constructs its ideal self-portrait. [...] The appearance of an image of culture on the metalevel signifies the secondary structuration of this very culture. It becomes more rigidly organized, certain aspects of it are declared to be non-structural, i.e. "non-existent."[31]

---

27 Lotman, *Culture and Explosion*, 123. See also Jurij Lotman, *Universe of the Mind: A Semiotic Theory of Culture*, trans. Ann Shukman (London: I. B. Tauris, 1990), 231.
28 Lotman, *Culture and Explosion*, 14. The way Lotman refers to Prigogine is radical compared to Wallerstein. While the former assumes entropy and unpredictability as fundamental within the notion of the semiosphere, the latter is ultimately grounded on a general determinism, partly later corrected by Prigogine's bifurcation. However, the relevance of unpredictability also involves the issue that capitalism can take advance of explosions; we need only think about COVID-19 in this respect.
29 Aronowitz, "A Metatheoretical Critique," 505.
30 Lotman, *Universe of the Mind*, 128.
31 Jurij Lotman, "Culture as Collect Intellect and The Problems of Artificial Intelligence," in *Dramatic Structure: Poetic and Cognitive Semantics*, eds. L. M. O'Toole and Ann Shukman (Colchester: University of Essex), 92.

Encyclopedias, dictionaries, grammars, chronicles, criticism, and research, among which are Lotman's works and this paper, are all manifestations of culture's self-awareness and its attempt to comprehend itself as a whole. The metalevel of culture, together with the norm, is located in the center. That is why, on the metalevel, culture always describes itself as more logical and organized than it is in reality. Moreover, culture may proclaim some of its elements nonexistent if they do not fit its ideal self-portrait.[32]

The Role of the Semiotic Boundary and its Connection with Migration

Wallerstein explored the problem of self-description on many occasions,[33] and this stands at the basis of his criticism of universalism as a moral value disclosing universalistic criteria as operative in legitimating capitalist cadres of the world-system. On further examination, however, a closer connection between the two models can be seen, albeit with several important discrepancies. Therefore, a possible merge of the two in relation to the issues of immigration and nationalism can be distinguished.

Some have proposed that Lotman's vocabulary can be used to replace the vocabulary of another leading figure of Marxist studies within a cultural

---

32   Paolo Fabbri points out how, until 1930, Italian pedagogy fought hard to discourage the use of sign language in deaf-mute children learning in favor of lip reading. This was because even though sign language is an actual language, with its own syntax and full chance of abstraction, it is based on gesticulation. Consequently, as gesticulation was linked at the time to apes' communication, sign language simply could not exist as a human language. Paolo Fabbri, "Tra scritto e immagine," lecture given at the University of Siena, November 14, 2007, https://www.radiopapesse.org/frontend/index.php?pat h=it/archivio/lectures/paolo-fabbri-tra-scritto-e-immagine.
33   For a focus on universalism in international law, see Helen Stacy, "The Legal System of International Human Rights," In *Immanuel Wallerstein and the Problem of the World: System, Scale, Culture*, eds. David Palombo-Liu, Bruce Robbins, and Nirvana Tanoukhi (Durham, NC: Duke University Press, 2011), 187–201. Furthermore, Wallerstein argues how the "invention of the housewives" and traineeships was a powerful means by which capitalism turned women's and young people's work into "non-work". Immanuel Wallerstein, *Historical Capitalism with Capitalist Civilization* (London: Verso, 1995), 23; Étienne Balibar and Immanuel Wallerstein, *Race, Nation, Class. Ambiguous Identities*, trans. Chris Turner (London: Verso, 2010), 35.

frame, Ernesto Laclau;[34] however, we suggest, following Schönle, Steedman, and Restaneo,[35] that there is an opportunity to compare the world-systems theory and Lotman's model, hitherto considered solid and unitary paradigms.

Going back to an earlier consistent connection, let us recall Lotman's idea of semiospheres inserted into one another, like matryoshka dolls. That is precisely the figure Chase-Dunn uses to explore the micro-structure of the world-system in detail. "The core/periphery hierarchy is a system-wide dimension of structured inequality, but at the same time it is also a regionally nested hierarchy." As such, far from being an ideal homogeneity of national state or international market interests, "many of the developments which we study at the level of the world-system also occur within countries."[36] In much the same way, Shapiro applies and extends an idea of Wallerstein, who considers the factor of multilayered hierarchies within identities:

> For each kind of identity, there is a social ranking. It can be a crude ranking, with two categories, or elaborate, with a whole ladder. But there is always a group on top in the ranking, and one or several groups at the bottom. There rankings are both worldwide and more local, and both kinds of ranking have enormous consequences in the lives and in the operation of the capitalist world-economy. ... Ethnic rankings are more local, but in every country, there is a dominant ethnicity and then the others. ... Nationalism often takes the form of constructing links between one side of each of the antinomies into fused categories, so that, for example, one might create the norm that adult

---

34 "[I]f we substitute the vocabulary of 'logic of equivalence' in Laclau with Lotman's idea of 'continuous coding', we will not lose the point that Laclau is making by his theory. And the reason is that these two notions bear the same functional role in each theory." Ventsel and Selg, "Towards a Semiotic Theory of Hegemony," 168.

35 Schönle argues that Lotman's "analysis of the relations between center and periphery echoes the infatuation with the margins of culture in cultural studies. They shared a concern with ways that people acquire their 'conception of the world' in relation to dominant groups." Steedman underlines that "in similar ways, Lotman's work parallels Gramsci's." Andreas Schönle, "Lotman and Cultural Studies: The Case for Cross-Fertilization," *Sign System Studies* 30, no. 2 (2002): 431; Marek D. Steedman, "State, Power, Hegemony, and Memory: Lotman and Gramsci," *Poroi* 3, no. 1 (2004): 83; Pietro Restaneo, "Il concetto di potere nel pensiero di Ju. M. Lotman," *Studi filosofici* 34 (2013): 209–234.

36 Christopher Chase-Dunn, *Global Formation: Structures of the World-Economy* (Oxford: Blackwell, 1989), 209.

white heterosexual males of particular ethnicities and religions are the only ones who would be considered "true" nationals.[37]

Shapiro seems to cross the input of Chase-Dunn (about the nested structure of core-periphery) and that of Wallerstein (of identity social ranking), projecting both on an urban dimension.

> Individual nation-states have their own internal corelike and peripheral zones (north/south and urban/agrarian divisions), and they often have a "city-system," where some cities dominate others. Cities likewise have their own "Manchester-effect" of class-differentiated regions, such as the core sectors where elites live and work and the peripheral slums housing the manual labor force.[38]

Since the notion of the core differs from the world-system and Lotman's semiosphere because it corresponds to a number of geographical places in the former and has the status of a methodological position in the latter, we argue that just as the world-system lacks the provision of a pattern of boundaries, Lotman's model discloses a possible solution. His idea of the periphery as a filter, together with the claim that, in many cases, the periphery is oriented toward the center,[39] allows us to describe migration as a phenomenon with some consequences and a general pattern. Migration, mainly mass migration, occurs at the boundaries of each of the micro-systems described by Chase-Dunn and Shapiro: what takes place is a filtering process by which new human groups are embedded in the cultural space. But it does not have any natural course, and this is where world-system and semiosphere match again. Migration (a) thickens the boundary, since the filtering process is conflictual and articulated, (b) usually reinforces the center, increasing the distance between the core and periphery, and (c) can also redouble the periphery, creating new zones close to the boundary, graduated in terms of extension and orientation (toward the center or the boundary).

Seeking to display some possible different structures of such a "live boundary," able to generate other new peripheries, let us look at four kinds of cultural

---

37   Wallerstein, *World-Systems Analysis*, 39.
38   Stephen Shapiro, *The Culture and Commerce of the Early American Novel: Reading the Atlantic World-System* (University Park, PA: Penn State University Press, 2009), 33.
39   Lotman, *Culture and Explosion*, 41.

mergers that a semiosphere can enact: assimilation, exclusion, segregation, and admission.[40]

In the case of assimilation, the semiosphere is centered on a centripetal force, and the attraction towards the core prevails in the creation of further interstitial spaces. Leaving aside some self-evident historical cases – like the British Raj or the Australian policy concerning Indigenous Australians in the first half of the 20th century – assimilation processes are those where, in a Lotmanian sense, the center attracts the periphery to create a sort of "skating corridor" to the core values, interests and way of life. In these terms, we agree with the analysis by which Benedict Anderson compares Chulalongkorn's kingdom in Siam during the late 19th century to the contemporary situation of South Arabia.[41]

Exclusion is the way in which the boundary itself is reinforced: because of the complete denial by the core of the existence of something external that has penetrated the inner space, here exists the maximum distance between the periphery and the core, and everything happens close to the boundary. In terms of economic issues, exclusion favors the creation of the underworlds of illegal hiring, drug microtrafficking, and prostitution. It is also where phenomena of expulsion are at work, sometimes through the activation of other boundaries, external to the system, that create more places to be crossed to reach the inner periphery. The agreement signed between Italy and Libya in 2017 on the management of migrant flows is one such example.

Segregation is where, unlike the previous cases, the periphery grows and eventually redoubles itself. An extreme example of a contemporary periphery that in western Europe is placed somehow inside the center (also in a Wallerstein sense) is that of the Sinti and Roma. The fact that "antiziganism is one of the most acute problems for many European societies"[42] is hardly in doubt. Cervelli argues that the contemporary segregation phenomena in the center of Europe could also be described by the use of time rather than space. More precisely, there are countless strategies by which systems create inner peripheries as temporary spaces of indefinite duration. Such vague, often multiple

---

40 Eric Landowski, *Présences de l'autre: Essais de socio-sémiotique II* (Paris: PUF, 1997), 78. See also Pierluigi Cervelli, *La frontiera interna: Il problema dell'altro dal fascismo alle migrazioni internazionali* (Bologna: Esculapio, 2020).
41 Benedict Anderson, *Imagined Communities: Reflections on the Origin and Spread of Nationalism* (London: Verso, 1983), 95–96.
42 Cervelli, *La frontiera interna*, 165–196.

dimensions are usually subject to bland and fitful control by the center so that, in some cases, they may re-organize themselves in new micro-systems with a center-periphery structure.

Admission is probably the trickiest case of cultural merging. It is the most productive process in terms of results, but it is also the most varied. The acceptance is conditional, and the conditions, regularly expressed in legal terms, differ from one semiosphere to another. In their study on contemporary European legal norms on migration, Rebecca Hemlin and Hillary Mellinger argue: "Perhaps the largest lesson gained from a focus on the relationship between courts and migration in Europe is that it is difficult, even unhelpful, to make sweeping generalizations about the role of courts in migration. Ultimately, the impact of courts can depend on the type of non-citizen, the place, and the moment."[43] However, it seems possible to interpret such processes as those where the core is seen by those on the periphery as the most attractive since the embedding unfolds with the promise of achievable, full inclusion.

From a Lotmanian perspective, the case of more than one structure operating at the same time cannot be excluded, neither when the basis for a cultural self-description is very different to the reality, nor where a potential series of structures successively alternate.[44] Moreover, since Lotman's model does not

---

43 Rebecca Hemlin and Hillary Mellinger, "The Role of Courts and Legal Norms," in *The Routledge Handbook of the Politics of Migration in Europe*, eds. Agniezska Weinar, Saskia Bonjour, and Lyubov Zhyznomirska (New York: Routledge, 2019), chap. 8, Kindle.

44 This proposal is not an overall framework. With respect to migration, Eco traces another distinction between immigration and migration that would require to consider a fifth structure to describe his view of a massive change of a semiosphere driven by a penetration from the boundary. Eco argues that immigration occurs when a group of individuals, "even many individuals, but in numbers that are statistically insignificant with respect to the indigenous stock," move from one country to another. Such a movement may be controlled politically, limited, or encouraged according to the needs of the receiving country. Migration, on the other hand, is comparable to those found in nature: "They occur, and no one can control them. We have migration when an entire people, little by little, moves from one territory to another, and what matters is not how many remain in the original territory, but to what extent migrants change the culture of the territory to which they migrate." Eco gives the examples of some great past migrations: that of the people who moved from East to West, "as a result of which the peoples of the Caucasus changed the culture and biological heritage of the natives"; those of the so-called "barbarian" peoples who invaded the Roman Empire, creating new kingdoms and new cultures; and that of Europeans to the American continent. This too is considered a migration "because European whites did not adopt the customs and the culture of the natives, but rather founded a new civilization to which even the

separate economic features from cultural ones, it presents itself as a way to accomplish Wallerstein's task of "abolishing the lines between economic, political, and sociocultural modes of analysis."[45] It also highlights the risks involved in the deployment of some theoretical shortcuts: if, in a preliminary discussion on the interrelationship between nationalism, world-systems, and migration, we found it useful to investigate the notion of a "world migration system," a thorough consideration discloses its uncertain theoretical validity. Because of its traits as a theory, including its being a totality and being provided by a set of crucial and fundamental actors, it is implausible to conceive it as a model available to be applied, recursively, to specific phenomena.

From Migration to Nationalism: An Overview of the Matter of Self-Description and Semiosphere Structure

It may be noticed that Wallerstein occasionally seems to understate the matter of migration or take it for granted. In a 2010 article, while deconstructing the commonsense assumption that capital would benefit from free circulation, he

---

natives (those who survived) have adapted … It is immigration only when immigrants (admitted according to political decisions) largely accept the customs of the country to which they immigrate, and it is migration when migrants (whom no one can stop at the borders) transform the culture of the territory to which they migrate. As long as it is a matter of immigration … people can hope to contain the immigrants, so that they don't mix with the native population. When it is migration, containment is no longer possible, and the métissage becomes uncontrollable." In his view, the movements that Europe has attempted – and continues – to manage as immigration are actually cases of migration. "The Third World is knocking at the doors of Europe, and it will enter even if Europe does not consent. The problem is no longer to decide, as politicians pretend to believe, whether female students will be admitted to the universities of Paris if they wear the chador, or how many mosques may be erected in Rome. The problem is that in the next millennium – and since I am not a prophet, I cannot specify the exact date – Europe will be a multiracial continent or, if you prefer, a 'brown' continent. Whether you like it or not will not change the outcome." Umberto Eco, *Five Moral Pieces*, trans. Alastair McEwen (London: Verso, 2001), ch. 5.

45 Wallerstein, *World-Systems Analysis*, 21. We must stress that he seems to think that there is simultaneously, on the one hand, a "cultural base" compared to which, on the other, is an "economic base" that is to be preferred, and here we discuss such an approach critically: "In their insistence on total history and unidisciplinarity, world-systems analysts refuse to substitute a so-called cultural base for an economic base." Ibid.

highlights how, conversely, the "protector state" plays a key role in the protection of the market's interests and links the circulation of people to the circulation of commodities and capital:

> The free flow of labor is in some ways the most interesting issue in the long history of *laissez-faire* as an ideology. Few of the strong advocates of laissez-faire normally are enthusiastic about the free flow of labor. A truly free flow of labor would mean no rules whatsoever about individuals crossing state borders, and those who cross might then choose to remain in the state into which they have moved either temporarily or permanently. Formal barriers to movement (requiring passports and visas) are a relatively recent phenomenon, scarcely known until the twentieth century. And people have always moved. But the advance of transport technology has made it easier as time went forward. The basic starting point for any analysis is to recognize that states vary in (a) wealth and standard of living, (b) demographic density, (c) environmental attractiveness, and (d) political structures. Any of the four may provide an explanation of why individuals choose to migrate to particular countries. [...] Still, economic difficulties or ambitions as well as political difficulties in the birth state lead many to seek to migrate. Actually, migration seems often to be a ladder phenomenon – rural persons moving to urban areas in their birth state, urban persons moving to a relatively stronger and/or wealthier state, and then to a further, still stronger, still wealthier state. The basic political issues surrounding migration are well known. The receiving state has various motives for welcoming migrants. [...] In times of higher unemployment, however, unemployed workers and potentially unemployed ones may see migrants as competitors for jobs or as persons who will undercut wage levels. [...] In addition, whereas open frontiers for migration from poorer/weaker states to richer/stronger states may seem desirable from the point of view of the poorer/weaker states, they may hesitate to endorse a general principle of open frontiers, for fear that migration in the other direction may hurt them. If wealthier individuals move to poorer states – as settlers, or even as persons in search of retirement homes in warmer climates and lower costs of living – the net effect can be negative for the receiving states, which might see thereby a loss of land rights by indigenous persons and/or an inflation in home prices, making it more difficult for indigenous persons to retain and/or obtain housing they need. Let me thus resume what I have been arguing. Capitalists need states to protect them. Workers need states to protect them. Consumers need states to pro-

tect them. But what is protection for some is often harm for others. If one wants to argue against the harm that is being done to you by the protection offered to others, one can invoke the ideology of *laissez-faire*.[46]

This long quote showcases how, while entirely acceptable as a critical hypothesis against *laissez-faire* ideology, the analytical frame is somehow unbalanced. Indeed, the economic level of the description presents a magnetized character, displaying a force field with attraction and repulsion, while any other issue concerning migration turns out to be neutralized.[47]

---

[46] Immanuel Wallerstein, "Free Flows and Real Obstacles: Who Wants Laissez Faire?," in *Mass Migration in the World-system: Past, Present, and Future*, eds. Terry-Ann Jones and Eric Mielants (New York: Routledge, 2016), chap. 1, Kindle. However, it must not be forgotten that some specific kind of migration falls within such a perspective. Jones and Mielants deal for example with the traffic in girls and woman for sex work: "As noted by many authors in *Global Woman* these migrations are driven by global inequality [...]. Women in poorer peripheral countries, even women with a substantial education, find they can make more money taking menial jobs in core countries." Terry-Ann Jones and Eric Mielants, eds., *Mass Migration in the World-system: Past, Present, and Future* (New York: Routledge, 2016), chap. 2, Kindle. See also Saskia Sassen, "Global Cities and Survival Circuits," in *Global Woman: Nannies, Maids, and Sex Workers in the New Economy*, eds. Barbara Ehrenreich and Arlie Russell Hochschild (New York: Metropolitan Books, 2003), 254–274. This is precisely the case that was linked with the semiotic processes of exclusion before.

[47] Aronowitz states: "Since in *The World System* there is no concrete examination of daily life within core or periphery societies, but merely an account of various economic, climatic, geographic and demographic factors that operated on a fairly high level of abstraction, Wallerstein could not explore the specificity of politics and culture within the underclasses to find how and why they acted, or whether their actions severely modified or constituted an aspect of the determination of the direction of history." Aronowitz, "A Metatheoretical Critique," 515–516. We do not agree with every aspect of Aronowitz's critique. For instance, he challenges Wallerstein's theory on the grounds of social history and Marx's core concept of social division, stating that Wallerstein substitutes it with a "technical division". Conversely, the fundamental issue here is not to oppose the cultural and economic levels, but rather to fine-tune world-systems. We are in this sense closer to Étienne Balibar's critique discussed below. However, Aronowitz also argues smartly that "it may be asserted that the dominant tendencies of all twentieth century science, including the social sciences, has been to resolve the apparent indeterminacy of social and natural phenomena by positing a higher level of abstraction in which the historicity of things is explained by their failure to fulfill determinate goals." Ibid., 506.

Five years later, Wallerstein dealt with the European debate around the massive population outflow from Syria, as well as with immigration into Europe from Iraq and Eritrea, arguing that the issue calls to trace a clear distinction between the consequences of migrants for 1) the global and national economies, 2) local and regional cultural identities, and 3) the national and global political arenas. His conclusions about the first aspect are that "for the world-economy as a whole, migration merely shifts the location of individuals and probably changes very little."[48] Conversely, cultural and political problems are seen as inextricable and a cause of insoluble problems. Wallerstein highlights the close connection between political issues and those about identities to conclude, tautologically, that political decisions are driven by intensive attempts to reach popular consensus. It is "an absolute impasse" since European debate is contended between Merkel's perspective, in favor of open access to Germany and firstly to Europe, and Orban's perspective, which challenges the idea of an invasion of "Christian Europe." Since "[institutional] actors have to maneuver in a national, regional, and world political arena," Wallerstein concludes, the outcome is uncertain.[49] We state that such a vision somehow makes it quite difficult to deepen the relationship between migration, the world-system, and nationalist/populist movements.

In substance, we face a double contradiction. On the one side, migration is considered a phenomenon caused by the expansion of capitalism – and is thus irrelevant to its own development as a driving force of the world-system – but able to generate international/global strategies enacted by capitalist institutions. This leaves, as emphasized above, the question of how migration matches the theoretical notion of "identities" and/or "households." The problem seems as crucial as avoided by the theory. On the other side, contemporary nationalist/populist movements are seen as an answer from the center to migration – an attempt to reaffirm core national interests – but are also discussed for their nature as anti-systemic movements, namely, as the main obstacle to world-system structure and ideology.[50] Étienne Balibar broadly reflects upon these topics in his preface to *Race, Nation, Class*.[51] He questions whether Wallerstein's thesis does not impose on the multiplicity of social conflicts a formal –

---

48 Immanuel Wallerstein, "Passions About Migrants," *Immanuel Wallerstein*, September 15, 2015, https://iwallerstein.com
49 Ibid.
50 Hopkins and Wallerstein, *Age of Transition*, 216.
51 Balibar and Wallerstein, *Race, Nation, Class*, 6–7.

or at least unilateral – uniformity and globalism and argues how contemporary nationalist movements are not simply transnational but grounded on "local forms of social conflict (whether these be economic, religious, or politico-cultural), the 'sum' of which is not immediately totalizable. ... By the same token, I would suggest that the overall movement of the world-economy is the random *result* of the movement of its social units rather than its cause."[52]

In other words, Balibar seeks to prevent us from being the "victim of a gigantic illusion regarding the meaning" of our own analysis, which is at risk of being, "in large part, inherited from liberal economic ideology (and its implicit anthropology)."[53] From this perspective, which seems entirely acceptable, Lotman's model shall become a tool both for theoretical clarity and analytical depth. Once established that it does not make much sense to talk about nationalism/populism as a single abstract phenomenon, the issue, in a Lotmanian sense, is not *what* such movements are but rather *where* they are within the space of the semiosphere.

Paolo Demuru and Franciscu Sedda[54] argue that contemporary populist and nationalist rhetorics[55] are different from one another in terms of their articulation/assembly[56] in two aspects: an inner challenge to a dominant group and an external challenge to an Other (immigrant/stranger/foreigner). The first challenge may relate to a conservative party that excludes most folk

---

52 Ibid., 6.
53 Ibid., 7.
54 Paolo Demuru and Franciscu Sedda, "Da cosa si riconosce il populismo. Ipotesi semiopolitiche," *Actes sémiotiques* 121 (2018), https://doi.org/10.25965/as.5963. See also Franciscu Sedda, "Semiotics of Culture(s). Basic Questions and Concepts," in *International Handbook of Semiotics*, ed. Peter Pericles Trifonas (Berlin: Springer, 2015), 675–696.
55 For more detailed insights, see, e.g., Marco Revelli, *The New Populism: Democracy Stares into the Abyss*, trans. David Broder (London: Reverso, 2019); Frank Jacob and Adam Luedtke, eds., *Migration and the Crisis of the Modern Nation State?* (Wilmington, DE: Vernon Press, 2018).
56 On the topic of articulation/assembly as a political framework, see Stuart Hall, "On Postmodernism and Articulation," *Journal of Communication Inquiry* 10, no. 2 (1986): 45–60; James Clifford, "Taking Identity Politics Seriously: 'The Contradictory, Stony Ground...,'" in *Without Guarantees: In Honor of Stuart Hall*, eds. Paul Gilroy, Lawrence Grossberg, and Angela McRobbie (London, Verso, 2000), 94–112; James Clifford, *On the Edges of Anthropology* (Chicago: Prickly Paradigm Press, 2006); Saskia Sassen, *Territory, Authority, Rights: From Medieval to Global Assemblages* (Princeton, NJ: Princeton University Press, 2006); Judith Butler, *Notes Toward a Performative Theory of Assembly* (Cambridge, MA: Harvard University Press, 2015).

from prospects of opportunities, rights, and redistribution of wealth or, on the contrary, may relate to a technocracy making collective decisions for its own gain, indifferent to the concrete needs of the population. In other cases, the dominant group can be identified with a government promoting inclusive policies against racial boundaries, in favor of same-sex civil unions and a human rights framework for the end of life, etc. The second challenge is about an entity that varies from Mexican and African immigrants to Sinti, Roma, and Muslims: from Trump to the French Front National and the Italian Lega, it is only with such an articulation of alterity that populist movements bring out new identities to be defended (America, France, Italy). In a Lotmanian sense, we might say that contemporary populisms often seem to be based on a semiotic spatial rearrangement wherein populist forces place themselves as constricted on both sides: internally (by the core) and externally (by the peripheries). This is not without consequences: not only would it open up the possibility of distinguishing between such populist antisystem movements – where nationalism movements are at the core and many other cases of populist/nationalist movements are on the boundary (notably, many separatist ones) – but also, according to Lotman, it would provide an analytical base for the assumption that the reorganization of the cultural space inevitably goes together with the behavior of the system. The idea of a deflection of the world-system trend here meets the crucial matter of cultural self-description.

Conclusion

This paper attempted to bring together Lotman's semiosphere and Wallerstein's world-systems, with due caution, in order to fine-tune the latter with the support of some notions of the former. The indisputable value of world-systems as *theory* is worthy of providing it with articulated analytical means, and Lotman's semiosphere has turned out to be a powerful intake.

Very briefly, Lotman's semiosphere frames social change in a strongly dynamic perspective in which the concept of the boundary is linked on one side to the idea of a filter and on the other to that of tension. Its contribution to strengthening world-systems, in this regard, is threefold: (a) it enables a theoretical conception of social space that partially overcomes the geopolitical one; (b) for the issue of migration, it displays different structures of "live boundaries" (assimilation, exclusion, segregation, admission), allowing contemporary global migration processes to be framed in more depth; and (c) for the issue of nationalism, it makes it possible to arrange various phenomena and grasp their differences in various positional configurations within the space of the semiosphere.

Works Cited

Anderson, Benedict. *Imagined Communities: Reflections on the Origin and Spread of Nationalism*. London: Verso, 1983.

Aronowitz, Stanley. "A Metatheoretical Critique of Immanuel Wallerstein's The Modern World System." *Theory and Society* 10 (1981): 503–520. https://doi.org/10.1007/BF00182156.

Arrighi, Giovanni. *Long Twentieth Century: Money, Power and the Origins of Our Time*. Revised edition. London: Verso, 2010.

Balibar, Étienne, and Immanuel Wallerstein. *Race, Nation, Class. Ambiguous Identities*. Translated by Chris Turner. London: Verso, 2010.

Butler, Judith. *Notes Toward a Performative Theory of Assembly*. Cambridge, MA: Harvard University Press, 2015.

Cervelli, Pierluigi. *La frontiera interna. Il problema dell'altro dal fascismo alle migrazioni internazionali*. Bologna: Esculapio, 2020.

Chase-Dunn, Christopher. *Global Formation: Structures of the World-Economy*. Oxford: Blackwell, 1989.

Clifford, James. "Taking Identity Politics Seriously: 'The Contradictory, Stony Ground...'". In *Without Guarantees: In Honor of Stuart Hall*, edited by Paul Gilroy, Lawrence Grossberg, and Angela McRobbie, 94–112. London: Verso, 2000.

Clifford, James. *On the Edges of Anthropology*. Chicago: Prickly Paradigm Press, 2006.

Demuru, Paolo, and Franciscu Sedda. "Da cosa si riconosce il populismo. Ipotesi semiopolitiche." *Actes sémiotiques* 121 (2018). https://doi.org/10.25965/as.5963.

Eco, Umberto. "Scusate qualche testo." *Corriere della Sera*, February 27, 1976.

Eco, Umberto. *Five Moral Pieces*. Translated by Alastair McEwen. London: Vintage Books, 2001. Kindle.

Eco, Umberto. *On Literature*. Translated by Martin McLaughlin. Orlando, FL: Harcourt, 2004.

Eco, Umberto. *Travels in Hyperreality*. Translated by William Weaver. Boston, MA: Mariner Books, 1990.

Fabbri, Paolo. "Tra scritto e immagine." Lecture given at the University of Siena, November 14, 2007. https://www.radiopapesse.org/frontend/index.php?path=it/archivio/lectures/paolo-fabbri-tra-scritto-e-immagine.
Greimas, Algirdas Julien, and Joseph Courtés. *Sémiotique. Dictionnaire raisonné de la théorie du langage I*. Paris: Hachette, 1979.
Greimas, Algirdas Julien, and Joseph Courtés. *Sémiotique. Dictionnaire raisonné de la théorie du langage II. Compléments, débats, propositions*. Paris: Hachette, 1986.
Greimas, Algirdas Julien. *The Social Sciences: A Semiotic View*. Translated by Paul Perron and Frank H. Collins. Minneapolis, MN: University of Minnesota Press, 1990.
Hall, Stuart. "On Postmodernism and Articulation." *Journal of Communication Inquiry* 10, no. 22 (1986): 45–60.
Hartley, John, Indrek Ibrus, and Maarja Ojamaa. *On the Digital Semiosphere: Culture, Media and Science for the Anthropocene*. New York: Bloomsbury, 2020.
Hemlin, Rebecca and Hillary Mellinger. "The role of courts and legal norms." In *The Routledge Handbook of the Politics of Migration in Europe*, edited by Agnieszka Weinar, Saskia Bonjour, and Lyubov Zhyznomirska, chap. 8. New York: Routledge, 2019. Kindle.
Hopkins, Terence, K., and Immanuel Wallerstein. eds. *The Age of Transition: Trajectory of the World-System, 1945–2025*. London: Zed Books, 1996.
Jacob, Frank, and Adam Luedtke, eds. *Migration and the Crisis of the Modern Nation State?* Wilmington, DE: Vernon Press, 2018.
Jones, Terry-Ann, and Eric Mielants. eds. *Mass Migration in the World-System: Past, Present, and Future*. New York: Routledge, 2016. Kindle.
Kull, Kalevi. "Semiosphere and a Dual Ecology: Paradoxes of Communication." *Sign Systems Studies* 33, no. 1 (2005): 175–189.
Landowski, Eric. *Présences de l'autre. Essais de socio-sémiotique II*. Paris: PUF, 1997.
Lotman, Jurij. "Technological Progress as a Problem in the Study of Culture." *Poetics Today* 12, no. 4 (1991): 781–800.
Lotman, Jurij. "On the Semiosphere." *Sign System Studies* 33, no. 1 (2005): 205–229.
Lotman, Jurij. *Culture and Explosion*. Translated by Wilma Clark. Berlin: Mouton de Gruyter, 2009.
Lotman, Jurij. "Culture as Collect Intellect and the Problems of Artificial Intelligence." In *Dramatic Structure: Poetic and Cognitive Semantics*, edited by L. M. O'Toole and Ann Shukman, 84–96. Colchester: University of Essex.

Lotman, Jurij. *Universe of the Mind. A Semiotic Theory of Culture*. Translated by Ann Shukman. London: I. B. Tauris, 1990.

Lotman, Jurij, Boris Uspenskij, Viacheslav Ivanov, Vladimir Toropov, and Alexander Pjatigorskij. "Thesis on the Semiotic Study of Culture." In *The Tell-Tale Sign: A Survey of Semiotics*, edited by Thomas A. Sebeok, 57–80. Lisse: Peter de Ridder Press, 1975.

Marrone, Gianfranco. *The Invention of the Text*. Translated by Sara Anselmi, Dario Mangano, and Peter Carne. Milan: Mimesis, 2014.

Martin, Bronwen, and Felizitas Ringham. *Key Terms in Semiotics*. London: Continuum, 2000.

Mellino, Miguel. "Note sul metodo di Stuart Hall. Althusser, Gramsci e la questione della razza." *Décalage* 2, no. 1 (2016): 12. https://core.ac.uk/reader/733 45870.

Prigogine, Ilya, and Isabel Stengers. *La nouvelle alliance. Métamorphose de la science*. Paris: Gallimard, 1979.

Revelli, Marco. *The New Populism: Democracy Stares into the Abyss*. Translated by David Broder. London: Reverso, 2019.

Restaneo, Pietro. "Il concetto di potere nel pensiero di Ju. M. Lotman." *Studi filosofici* 34 (2013): 209–234.

Sassen, Saskia. "Global Cities and Survival Circuits." In *Global Woman: Nannies, Maids, and Sex Workers in the New Economy*, edited by Barbara Ehrenreich and Arlie Russell Hochschild, 254–274. New York: Metropolitan Books, 2003.

Sassen, Saskia. *Territory, Authority, Rights: From Medieval to Global Assemblages*. Princeton, NJ: Princeton University Press, 2006.

Sedda, Franciscu. "Semiotics of Culture(s). Basic Questions and Concepts". In *International Handbook of Semiotics*, edited by Peter Pericles Trifonas, 675–696. Berlin: Springer, 2015.

Semenenko, Aleksei. *The Texture of Culture. An Introduction to Yuri Lotman's Semiotic Theory*. New York: Palgrave MacMillan, 2012.

Shapiro, Stephen. *The Culture and Commerce of the Early American Novel: Reading the Atlantic World-System*. University Park, PA: Penn State University Press, 2009.

Shapiro, Stephen. "What is World-systems for Cultural Studies?" Chapter draft provided by the author, 2020.

Schönle, Andreas. "Lotman and Cultural Studies: The Case for Cross-Fertilization." *Sign System Studies* 30, no. 2 (2002): 429–440.

Schönle, Andreas, ed. *Lotman and Cultural Studies: Encounters and Extensions*. Madison, WI: University of Wisconsin Press, 2006.

Stacy, Helen. "The Legal System of International Human Rights." In *Immanuel Wallerstein and the Problem of the World: System, Scale, Culture*, edited by David Palombo-Liu, Bruce Robbins, and Nirvana Tanoukhi. Durham, NC: Duke University Press, 2011. Kindle.

Steedman, Marek D. "State, Power, Hegemony, and Memory: Lotman and Gramsci." *Poroi* 3, no. 1 (2004): 78–102.

Torop, Peeter. "Tartuskaia shkola kak shkola." In *Lotmanovskii sbornik* 1, edited by Evgenii Permiakov and Roman Leibov, 223–239. Moscow: IC-Garant, 2016.

Ventsel, Andreas, and Peeter Selg. "Towards a Semiotic Theory of Hegemony: Naming as Hegemonic Operation in Lotman and Laclau." *Sign Systems Studies* 36, no. 1 (2008): 167–183.

Vernadsky, Vladimir. *The Biosphere*. New York: Copernicus, 1998.

Wallerstein, Immanuel. "Immanuel Wallerstein's Thousand Marxisms." Interview by Nicolette Stame and Luca Meldolesi. Translated by David Broder. Jacobin, November 11, 2019. https://www.jacobinmag.com/2019/09/immanuel-wallerstein-marxism-world-systems-theory-capitalism

Wallerstein, Immanuel. "Passions About Migrants." Immanuel Wallerstein, September 15, 2015. https://iwallerstein.com

Wallerstein, Immanuel. *Historical Capitalism with Capitalist Civilization*. London: Verso, 1995.

Wallerstein, Immanuel. *World-Systems Analysis. An Introduction*. Durham, NC: Duke University Press, 2004.

Wallerstein, Immanuel. "Free Flows and Real Obstacles: Who Wants Laissez-Faire?" In *Mass Migration in the World-system: Past, Present, and Future*, edited by Terry-Ann Jones and Eric Mielants, chap. 1. New York: Routledge, 2016. Kindle.

5. An Ongoing Paradox in the World-System of Migration
The EU's Response to the Migration Crises, Rising Nationalism, and its Treatment of Greece

James Horncastle

In 2015, Greece was a state in crisis as it found itself unable to manage the mass influx of refugees and migrants into the country. European leaders, citing the Dublin Regulation, commonly framed it as a "Greek" problem, despite the migrants seeking to exit the country for other European countries.[1] Unlike in 2015, however, when Greece found itself isolated due to the Greek Financial Crisis, the European Union (EU) actively assisted the country in the 2020 Migration Crisis. The European Commission, uncertain of Greece's ability to handle the crisis alone, dispatched Frontex to the Greek-Turkish land and maritime border to prevent a mass influx of migrants and refugees into the continent.[2] The migration crisis in 2015 disproportionately affected Greece due to its position on the European periphery in both the geographic and political sense of the word.[3] In 2020, however, European leaders referred to the country as Europe's shield.[4]

---

1 Andrew Connelly, "Europe's Failed Migration Policy Caused Greece's Latest Refugee Crisis," *Foreign Policy*, September 20, 2020, https://foreignpolicy.com/2020/09/20/europes-failed-migration-policy-caused-greeces-latest-refugee-crisis/.
2 Jon Stone, "EU chief praises Greece as 'shield' of Europe after police attack refugees at border," *The Independent*, March 3, 2020, https://www.independent.co.uk/news/world/europe/greece-refugees-border-eu-police-ursula-von-der-leyen-a9373281.html.
3 For an elaboration of the ideas of core and periphery, see Immanuel Wallerstein, *The Modern World-System*, vol. 1: *Capitalist Agriculture and the Origins of the European World-Economy in the Sixteenth Century* (Berkeley, CA: University of California Press, 2011 [1974]).
4 Stone, "EU chief praises Greece."

The differing responses by the European Union directly reflect the changing priorities of the organization in its efforts to maintain its prominent position as part of the core in global affairs. In 2015, Greece was the problem child of the European Union, with its role in the EU Financial Crisis causing European leaders to consider expelling it from the organization. By 2020, however, Brexit, as well as Turkey changing from a potential member candidate to a rival actor, caused the EU to reevaluate Greece's role on the continent. Whereas in 2015 Greece found itself isolated, in 2020, the rise of right-wing nationalism in Europe, in part sparked by the events of 2015 as well as Brexit, meant that Greece transitioned from being the problem child of the EU to Europe's border guard. The country, to apply Immanuel Wallerstein's world-systems analysis, had changed in the eyes of the EU leadership from a European peripheral space to a global semi-peripheral space due to the shift in the political setting because of international migration.

Before discussing Greece and the EU's response to the migrant crises of 2015 and 2020, it is important to define the terminology of migrant and refugee. Legally, the distinction is quite clear. The Refugee Convention of 1951 defined a refugee as an individual who,

> owing to well-founded fear of being persecuted for reasons of race, religion, nationality, membership of a particular social group or political opinion, is outside the country of his nationality and is unable, or, owing to such fear, is unwilling to avail himself of the protection of that country; or who, not having a nationality and being outside the country of his former habitual residence as a result of such events, is unable or, owing to such fear, is unwilling to return to it.[5]

Thus, states consider an individual who is not facing imminent threat to be a migrant rather than a refugee. This distinction, however, is only a legal one. Scholars of migration, starting with Everett Lee in 1966, instead view migration as a multifaceted spectrum. Migration possesses both 'pull' factors – such as the pursuit of a better life – as well as 'push' factors – ones that force an individual from their home.[6] In Lee's analysis, an individual faces both push and

---

5 *Convention Relating to the Status of Refugees* (New York, 1951).
6 Everett S. Lee, "A Theory of Migration," *Demography* 3, no. 1 (1966): 47–57.

pull factors, and neither is paramount in all circumstances. Most major theories of migration continue to draw upon Lee's seminal research.[7]

Importantly, in the case of Greece in 2015, individuals entered the country due to both the push and pull factors that Lee identified. In the case of pull factors, Europe, as one of the global cores, attracted individuals seeking economic opportunities. There were also push factors at work, such as people attempting to flee their homelands. This aspect was most evident in the case of the Syrian Civil War. Lastly, these reasons often overlap. In the case of economic migrants to Europe, Afghanistan consistently ranks in the top five countries of origin.[8] While officially considered economic migrants, Afghanistan has faced protracted warfare since 1979. There exists a link between Afghanistan's ongoing instability due to conflict and the lack of economic opportunities in the country.

It is also important to briefly explore the world-systems theory as it relates to migration. World-systems theory, first developed by Immanuel Wallerstein and subsequently expanded upon by other scholars, considers the world-system, and not nation-states, to be the primary means of analysis.[9] Where nation-states enter Wallerstein's analysis is that they are the primary means of dividing labour, with the resulting division creating core, semi-periphery, and periphery states. Core countries, like those that have come to dominate the European Union, focus on high-skilled and capital-intensive production, whereas the periphery and semi-periphery focus on low-skilled and labour-intensive enterprises as well as raw materials.[10] While Greece is in the EU, one of the global cores, its economy – focused on tourism and light industry – would result in it being classified as a periphery or semi-periphery state in most analyses.

---

7 See Paul L. Knox and Sallie A. Marston, *Human Geography* (Upper Saddle River, NJ: Prentice Hall, 1998), 127; Caroline B. Brettell and James F. Hollifield, eds., *Migration Theory: Talking across Disciplines* (New York: Routledge, 2014), passim.
8 Laura Smith-Spark, "European migrant crisis: A country-by-country glance," CNN, September 5, 2015, https://edition.cnn.com/2015/09/04/europe/migrant-crisis-country-by-country.
9 Wallerstein, *The Modern World-System*, 46–49.
10 Stephen P. Borgatti and Martin G. Everett, "Models of core/periphery structures," *Social Networks* 21, no. 4 (2000): 375–395.

Critical for the core countries in maintaining their dominance in the world system, as Karatzogianni and Robinson note, is immigration control.[11] The world-system, without the proper maintenance of diversified labour, would collapse, as it relies on a stratified work force. As such, for the European Union to maintain its position as a core region, it needs to prevent migrants from readily accessing its territory. The EU's goal of preserving its privileged position in global affairs guided its policy towards Greece between 2015 and 2020.

One cannot examine the 2015 Migrant Crisis and the European response without first mentioning the Greek Financial Crisis. The Greek Financial Crisis commenced in 2009 against the backdrop of the Great Recession, and the country found itself unable to pay its creditors. There were a multitude of reasons for the Greek Financial Crisis. One can, however, largely reduce them to three factors: excessive Greek government spending and underreporting of their debt, structural issues in the Greek economy itself, and a lack of monetary and fiscal flexibility caused by their membership in the Eurozone.[12] The end result for Greece was three separate bailout packages (2010, 2012, and 2015), severe austerity measures, and political instability. The financial crisis shattered Greece's traditional two-party system, and radicalized groups capitalized on the political instability to push for dramatic changes to the country. On the far-right, Golden Dawn, a party with neo-Nazi overtures, gained seven percent of the vote in the 2012 elections. In 2015, the Coalition of the Radical Left (SYRIZA) gained a plurality of the vote.[13] The financial crisis and the resulting austerity measures, in short, disrupted Greek political culture and norms. Populism, in many ways, became the new norm in Greek politics, and the only major traditional party to do well in the post-financial crisis political climate, the right-wing New Democracy, incorporated elements of it into their policies.

---

11   Athina Karatzogianni and Andrew Robinson, *Power, Resistance and Conflict in the Contemporary World: Social Movements, Networks, and Hierarchies* (New York: Routledge, 2009).

12   For a full list of domestic factors behind the crisis, see *Update of the Hellenic Stability and Growth Programme* (Athens, January 15, 2010), https://ec.europa.eu/economy_fina nce/economic_governance/sgp/pdf/20_scps/2009-10/01_programme/el_2010-01-15_ sp_en.pdf. For an analysis of the Euro's role in the crisis, see Gylfi Zoega, "Greece and the Western Financial Crisis," *Atlantic Economic Journal* 47, no. 2 (2019): 113–126.

13   Kevin Ovenden and Paul Mason, *Syriza: Inside the Labyrinth* (London: Pluto Press, 2015), 24–25; Michal Novoth, "The Greek Elections of 2012: The Worrisome Rise of the Golden Dawn," *Israel Journal of Foreign Affairs* 7, no. 1 (2013): 87–94.

Due to this financial crisis, Greece was completely unprepared for the wave of migration from Syria in 2015. However, it is important to note that refugees and migrants arriving in Europe was not a new development. Migrants and asylum seekers have been a regular feature of EU politics. The consistency of the issue was why the EU agreed to the Dublin Regulation as early as 1990, with it formally coming into effect in 1997 for the original 12 signatories. The goal of the Dublin Regulation was to "determine rapidly the Member State responsible [for an asylum claim]."[14] In effect, however, the Dublin Regulation, and its subsequent iterations, transferred responsibility for migrants and asylum seekers to the country of entry. When Greece signed the Dublin Regulation in 1990, the country had approximately eight and a half thousand refugees within its borders.[15] Given that Greece was on the periphery of the European Community at the time of the signing, it makes sense that its numbers were low. Migrants and refugees, quite simply, possessed greater opportunities elsewhere in Europe. Geopolitical and technological changes, however, would fundamentally alter this calculus.

While the structural issues that Greece faced from the financial crisis inhibited its ability to act, the circumstances of migration also shifted after 1990. The first major area of change was in terms of technology. The proliferation of cellphones and smart devices facilitates migration from less wealthy countries to Europe. As Gilespie and others note, for refugees seeking to reach Europe, "the digital infrastructure is as important as the physical infrastructures of roads, railways, sea crossings and the borders controlling the free movement of people."[16] Individuals undertaking migration, and thereby attempting to reach the core, can access routes, information about patrols by governments seeking to prevent their entry, as well as contact information for a variety of smuggling groups and organizations.

This simple technological innovation has fundamentally altered migration flows at a global level and poses a significant challenge to how countries in the

---

14   "Council Regulation (EC) No. 343/2003 of 18 February 2003 establishing the criteria and mechanisms for determining the Member State responsible for examining an asylum application lodged in one of the Member States by a third-country national," *Office Journal of the European Union* 50, no. 1 (2003): 1–10.

15   "Total number of refugees in host country, end of 1990," Migration Data Portal, accessed October 20, 2020, https://www.migrationdataportal.org/international-data?i=refug_host&t=1990.

16   Mary Gillespie et al., *Mapping Refugee Media Journeys: Smartphones and Social Media Networks* (Open University, 2016), 5–6.

world-system have dealt with the issue in the past. When European countries signed the Dublin Regulation in 1990, the number of individuals able to migrate was more restricted, both in terms of absolute numbers and socio-economic background. Said individuals typically migrated directly to Western European countries rather than Greece due to the greater economic opportunities afforded in the former countries. The smartphone and the internet, however, have significantly changed migratory flows. As Stevenson notes:

> Yet the same forces that have shrunk the world for people in its wealthier precincts – instantaneous, pocket-size communication, mundane air travel, globalized culture – have also been an invitation, or perhaps a taunt, to those in less fortunate circumstances. Confronted with war, persecution and poverty, the migrants are well aware that people are living far better in a not-too-distant place, and that their smartphones and social networks can help guide them there.[17]

Migration, in short, was no longer limited to those of advanced means. Whereas migration to Europe was previously primarily done by wealthy individuals who could bypass the semi-periphery, the increasingly large number of individuals from less advantaged backgrounds now had to pass through the semi-periphery to reach the core. Migrants' and refugees' awareness of better lives beyond their countries' borders, and the ability to access the means of getting there through social media connections, led to a significant increase in migrants and refugees.

The increased ability of people, regardless of socio-economic background, to migrate was further complicated by an internal EU policy: the Schengen Agreement. Originally signed in 1985 and initially implemented in 1995 by Western European countries, the Schengen Agreement largely removed passport and border controls from the member nations. Greece ascended to the agreement in early 2000.[18] Migrants and refugees, by entering Greece, would then have access to the rest of the EU.

These technological and internal EU political developments compounded the second factor regarding refugee and migrant flows to Europe in 2015: the

---

17   Richard W. Stevenson, "Stories of Hope, Courage, and Loss as Historic Journey Unfolds," *The New York Times*, November 12, 2015.
18   "Council Decision of 13 December 1999 on the full application of the Schengen acquis in Greece," *Official Journal of the European Communities* 327, no. 58 (2000).

Syrian Civil War. Scholars still debate the causes of the Syrian Civil War.[19] The results and impact on its population, however, are not up for debate. By 8 September 2015, there were 4.1 million Syrian refugees registered with the UNHCR.[20] This number, furthermore, did not include internally displaced peoples (IDPs) within Syria. Combined, the total number of refugees and IDPs comprised more than half the population of Syria.[21] Given that the Syrian Civil War showed no signs of abating – and, in fact, continues to this day – its people looked elsewhere for new opportunities.[22] Europe, with its high standard of living and relative security, appeared ideal.

By mid-2015, Greece had overtaken Italy as the primary country of entry by migrants and refugees into the European Union. As instability in Syria increased due to the Syrian Civil War and Italy became increasingly proficient at preventing migrants and refugees from entering Europe via the Central Mediterranean route, Greece's location and political troubles made it an ideal entry point.[23] Furthermore, due to the financial crisis, the Greek government lacked the means of protecting its borders, especially given the unprecedented number of migrants and refugees seeking to enter the country.

---

19   These causes include demographic imbalances, unequal wealth distribution, draught, and authoritarian governance. See Shahrzad Mohtadi, Colin P. Kelley, Mark A. Cane, Richard Seager, and Yochanan Kushnir, "Climate Change in the Fertile Crescent and Implications of the Recent Syrian Drought," *PNAS* 112, no. 11 (2015): 3241–3246; Badr Eddin Rahimahl, "The Class Oriented Rationale: Uncovering the Sources of the Syrian Civil War," *The Muslim World* 106, no. 1 (2016): 169–186; Human Rights Watch, *World Report: Events of 2009* (New York: Human Rights Watch, 2010), https://www.hrw.org/sites/default/files/world_report_download/wr2010.pdf.

20   Ariane Rummery, "Worsening conditions inside Syria and the region fuel despair, driving thousands towards Europe," United Nations High Commissioner on Refugees, September 8, 2015, https://www.unhcr.org/uk/news/latest/2015/9/55eed5d66/worsening-conditions-inside-syria-region-fuel-despair-driving-thousands.html.

21   UNHCR, *Protecting and Supporting the Displaced in Syria: UNHCR Syria End of Year Report*, https://www.unhcr.org/sy/wp-content/uploads/sites/3/2016/11/UNHCR-End-of-Year-2015-En.pdf.

22   "Seven factors behind movement of Syrian refugees to Europe," United Nations High Commissioner on Refugees, September 25, 2015, https://www.unhcr.org/news/briefing/2015/9/560523f26/seven-factors-behind-movement-syrian-refugees-europe.html.

23   "Migratory Routes: Eastern Mediterranean Route," Frontex, accessed October 20, 2020, https://frontex.europa.eu/along-eu-borders/migratory-routes/eastern-mediterranean-route/.

The recent memory of Greece threatening the very stability and raison d'etre of the European Union inhibited a pan-European response. The efforts by the Greek government in the summer of 2015 to challenge the conditions imposed by the EU through a referendum on the austerity package caused considerable ill-will to develop in European capitals towards Greece. In the lead-up to the referendum, Jean-Claude Juncker, the President of the European Commission, stated that a "no [vote] would mean that Greece is saying no to Europe."[24] The referendum passed, but it was a pyrrhic victory for the Greek government under Alexis Tsipras, who, immediately upon winning, was told by the French President that Juncker's statement was no brinksmanship, but rather fact; Greece could either accept the bailout terms or leave the EU.[25] Humiliated, Tsipras, despite organizing the referendum, was forced to accept the EU's terms.

The result of Tsipras' dangerous referendum gamble was that Greece, the country in Europe least well-equipped to deal with a major crisis, initially dealt with the migration issue largely on its own. Even when the European Union sought to intervene, they aggravated the problems. Angela Merkel, the Chancellor of Germany, declared in August 2015 that her country would ignore the Dublin Regulation and not place a cap on the number of refugees it accepted into Germany.[26] While this dealt with humanitarian concerns and alleviated the pressure on Greece, Italy, and other countries on Europe's periphery, it exacerbated the refugee crisis facing Europe. By giving migrants the opportunity to reach Germany via Europe's periphery in Greece, more migrants and refugees undertook the journey. These migrants and refugees were not only from Syria. Other groups, notably Afghan and Iraqi nationals, attempted to use Germany's newfound openness to enter Europe in greater numbers as well.

Certain EU leaders planted the seeds for the organization's future stance towards migrants and refugees in 2015. Eastern European leaders, dismayed at the increasing number of refugees and migrants entering Europe and the fact that the policy of the central European authorities seemed to be either to do nothing or to exacerbate the problem, took exception to these develop-

---

24 Ian Traynor, "Alexis Tsipras Must Be Stopped: The Underlying Message of Europe's Leaders," *The Guardian*, June 29, 2015.
25 *Inside Europe: Ten Years of Turmoil*, episode 2, "Going for Broke," 2019.
26 Samuel Osborne, "Angela Merkel Admits She Lost Control of Refugee Crisis in Germany and Would 'Turn Back Time' If She Could," *The Independent*, September 22, 2016.

ments.[27] Viktor Orban, the Prime Minister of Hungary, thought that Europe needed to take a more militant stance. On 15 October 2015, Orban, speaking to reporters, noted that "The best solution would be for Greece to honour its contractual obligations."[28] Greece, in short, should fulfil its obligations under the Dublin Regulation. Orban did seem to recognize that Greece's financial situation, as well as the exceptional nature of the 2015 Migration Crisis, meant that it might not be able to meet these demands, as he later added, "if [Greece] cannot then we should do it for her."[29] Ultimately, Orban's desire to send European forces to Greece's border with Turkey never came to pass. Nevertheless, while the EU did not approve such a plan in 2015, it remained a politically popular idea amongst certain factions of the EU on both the right and left.[30]

Internal EU policies did not solve the migrant crisis. Instead, foreign policy was crucial to its resolution. Specifically, in March 2016, the EU reached an agreement with Turkey to mitigate the number of refugees entering the continent. Critically, there were two key provisions to the agreement:

1) All new irregular migrants crossing from Turkey into Greek islands as from 20 March 2016 will be returned to Turkey. This will take place in full accordance with EU and international law, thus excluding any kind of collective expulsion. All migrants will be protected in accordance with the relevant international standards and in respect of the principle of non-refoulement. It will be a temporary and extraordinary measure which is necessary to end the human suffering and restore public order. Migrants arriving in the Greek islands will be duly registered and any application for asylum will be processed individually by the Greek authorities in accordance with the Asylum Procedures Directive, in cooperation with UNHCR. Migrants not applying for asylum or whose application has been found unfounded or inadmissible in accordance with the said directive will be returned to Turkey. Turkey and Greece, assisted by EU institutions and agencies, will take the

---

27 Justyna Segeš Frelak, "Solidarity in European Migration Policy: The Perspective of the Visegrád States," in *Solidarity in the European Union*, eds. Andreas Grimmel and Susanne My Giang (London: Springer, 2017), 81–95.
28 "Hungary PM: Shut Greek Border to Migrants," *Sky News*, October 15, 2015, https://news.sky.com/story/hungary-pm-shut-greek-border-to-stop-migrants-10342972.
29 Ibid.
30 Violeta Moreno-Lax, "The EU Humanitarian Border and the Securitization of Human Rights: The 'Rescue-Through-Interdiction/Rescue-Without-Protection'," *Journal of Common Market Strategies* 56, no. 1 (2018): 119–140.

necessary steps and agree any necessary bilateral arrangements, including the presence of Turkish officials on Greek islands and Greek officials in Turkey as from 20 March 2016, to ensure liaison and thereby facilitate the smooth functioning of these arrangements. The costs of the return operations of irregular migrants will be covered by the EU.

2) For every Syrian being returned to Turkey from Greek islands, another Syrian will be resettled from Turkey to the EU taking into account the UN Vulnerability Criteria. A mechanism will be established, with the assistance of the Commission, EU agencies and other Member States, as well as the UNHCR, to ensure that this principle will be implemented as from the same day the returns start. Priority will be given to migrants who have not previously entered or tried to enter the EU irregularly.[31]

Turkey did not reach the accord with the EU, however, out of concern for the refugees. Instead, Turkey did so under the condition that it received six billion dollars in financial support from the EU, as well as visa-free travel to the EU for its citizens if it met certain requirements.[32] Although some scholars and politicians have argued that the agreement was based on extortion, and this argument certainly can be made, it ignores the bigger issue.[33]

In the world-system, the burden of mass migration and refugees disproportionately affects states at the periphery and semi-periphery as individuals try to make their way to core states; in this case, in Central and Western Europe. Migration controls, as mentioned earlier, are one of the principal means that core countries possess for maintaining their position. Turkey, as both the entry point to Europe's periphery in Greece and a neighbour of Syria, had more official refugees within its boundaries than the entirety of Europe during the latter's 'crisis' in 2015.[34] Thus the agreement, rather than one of extortion, was instead one of core countries paying to avoid a crisis that had the potential to undermine their position in the world-system.

---

31 European Council, "EU-Turkey statement, 18 March 2016," https://www.consilium.euro pa.eu/en/press/press-releases/2016/03/18/eu-turkey-statement/.
32 Ibid.
33 Lisa Haferlach and Dilek Kurban, "Lessons Learnt from the EU-Turkey Refugee Agreement in Guiding EU Migration Partnerships with Origin and Transit Countries," *Global Policy* 8, no. 4 (2017): 85.
34 "Situation Syria Regional Refugees," United Nations High Commissioner on Refugees, accessed October 28, 2020, https://data2.unhcr.org/en/situations/syria/location/113.

Political Developments in Europe between 2016-2020

The most significant development for the EU in its history occurred soon after the EU-Turkish agreement on refugees: the 2016 United Kingdom's European Union membership referendum. Against the backdrop of the 2015 Refugee Crisis, the UK sought to renegotiate its relationship with the EU. This was not a new development; the UK, since joining the EU in 1973, had consistently chafed at regulations and policies that it perceived as infringing upon its national sovereignty.[35] Tensions subsequently escalated. Although the full scope of Britain's tumultuous relationship with the EU is beyond the scope of this paper, migration concerns were of paramount importance for those within the UK who sought to leave the EU.[36]

Indirectly linked to the United Kingdom's decision to launch a referendum was the EU's relationship with Turkey. As James Lindsay-Ker notes, "In the UK, the debate over immigration became intertwined with the free movement of workers – one of the core principles of the EU."[37] Turkey joining the European Union would significantly aggravate the perceived issue of job loss that the British public believed the free movement of workers caused for the country. British politicians favouring Brexit, in short, unconsciously used elements of world-system analysis to justify their break from the EU. Turkey, a country decidedly within the periphery by most analyses, also possessed a population approaching 80 million individuals.[38] The 2015 Refugee Crisis, and the need to appease Turkey in order to stymie the flow of refugees and migrants to Europe, caused the EU to open two new chapters in Turkey's long-stalled process of joining the organization.[39] The 'Leave' campaign, already inculcating a fear in the general British public about Eastern Europeans taking their jobs, used

---

35   Stephen Wall, *A Stranger in Europe: Britain and the EU from Thatcher to Blair* (New York: Oxford University Press, 2008), 1–17.
36   For an explanation of the United Kingdom's concerns about migrant labour in the lead-up to, and post-, Brexit, see Nicole Lindstrom, "What's Left for 'Social Europe'? Brexit and Transnational Labour Market Regulation in the UK-1 and the EU-27," *New Political Economy* 24, no. 2 (2019): 286–287.
37   James Ker-Lindsay, "Turkey's EU Accession as a Factor in the 2016 Brexit Referendum," *Turkish Studies* 19, no. 1 (2018): 1.
38   On Turkey's position, see Yukio Kawano, Benjamin D. Brewer, and Christopher Chase-Dunn, "Trade Globalization since 1795: Waves of Integration in the World-System," *American Sociological Review* 65, no. 1 (2000): 77–95.
39   Ker-Lindsay, "Turkey's EU accession," 4.

the threat of Turkey's EU ascension to magnify these fears.[40] The EU's need to stop mass migration to the core, in other words, helped push the UK out of the union. On 23 June 2016, the UK's population voted to leave the European Union. The United Kingdom's effort to fortify its position in the core and detach itself from the policies of the EU that allowed immigration from the semi-periphery countries of Eastern Europe and periphery countries elsewhere, therefore, played a key role in its decision to leave the supranational organization.

The United Kingdom's decision to leave the European Union changed the calculations of the decision-makers in Brussels towards Greece. Previously, politicians in Brussels were concerned that Greece and the other countries that faced major financial strain in the aftermath of the 2008 Financial Crisis (Spain, Portugal, and Ireland) would destabilize the Eurozone and threaten their position as a core region in the world-system.[41] Brexit, however, represented an even greater threat to the organization than Greece's ability to destabilize the financial system. The Eurozone, although an important part of the European dream of integrating the continent, was simply a part of the broader strategy. Although Greece challenged the form that European integration would take through its financial policies, the people themselves never gave up on the dream of EU integration. Even at the height of the financial crisis, a third of the country still held a favourable opinion of the EU. While individuals may argue that only a third of the people holding a favourable opinion of the EU indicates that the people gave up on the EU, given the domestic issues Greece faced due to the austerity measures imposed by the EU, this still represents a significant base of support. By 2019, once the worst elements of the austerity measures had passed, the EU's favorability rating returned to 53%.[42] Conversely, the people of the United Kingdom, by voting to leave the European Union, represented a fundamental challenge to the organization's right to exist. The EU's issues with Greece, therefore, were no longer as significant as they had been in the past.

Greece, in many ways, was the EU country that benefitted the most from the changing priorities in Brussels, as it improved its position in the world-system. Until Brexit, the debates in the European Union were not over its survival

---

40   Ibid., 7.
41   Zoega, "Greece and the Western Financial Crisis." 114.
42   Richard Wike et al., "The European Union," *Pew Research Center*, October 14, 2019, https://www.pewresearch.org/global/2019/10/14/the-european-union/.

but structural issues and optimizing the organization for its membership.[43] The UK's decision to leave the European Union, however, threw the organization's raison d'être into question and highlighted existing centrifugal forces that it faced.[44] If the EU lost additional members, this would potentially create a domino effect that would leave it either unviable or with a much-reduced role in global affairs. As an article in *Deutsche Welle* from 2017, when Grexit fears resurfaced, noted: "Who would have an interest in knocking everything off balance [by expelling Greece] just because Athens has been dragging out recent negotiations, for example, with regards to the liberalization of the job market? Surely no one."[45] While both the Greek government and EU Member States used the spectre of Grexit for domestic political consumption, the stakes for all parties were too high for anyone to contemplate the issue seriously. Greece now found itself firmly entrenched within the European Union as the core countries' shield against the periphery.

The 2020 Migrant Crisis and the European Response

It was against the backdrop of a European Union that was more concerned with preserving the integrity of the organization and its position at the core of the international system rather than punishing what it viewed as its problematic member states that the 2020 Migration Crisis emerged. The immediate causes of the 2020 crisis were not new but rather the result of the Turkish-EU agreement in 2016. Almost immediately after reaching this agreement, negotiations over Turkey's ascension stalled. European leaders viewed Erdogan's plans to transform Turkey from a parliamentary to a presidential system as potentially compromising the rule of law in the country. Germany's President, Frank-Walter Steinmeier, noted that "The way we look (at Turkey) is characterized by worry, that everything that has been built up over years and decades is

---

43   For what were seen as pressing issues immediately before Brexit, see Martijn Lak Jaap de Zwaan, Abiola Makinwa, and Piet Willems, eds., *Governance and Security Issues of the European Union: Challenges Ahead* (The Hague: Asper Press, 2016), 1–11.
44   Michelle Cini and Amy Verdun, "The Implications of Brexit for the Future of Europe," in *Brexit and Beyond: Rethinking the Futures of Europe*, eds. Benjamin Martill and Uta Staiger (London: UCL Press, 2018), 66–68.
45   Georg Matthes, "The myth of Grexit," *Deutsche Welle*, February 20, 2017, https://www.dw.com/en/opinion-the-myth-of-grexit/a-37642633.

collapsing."[46] However, the efforts of the German government, as well as those of other EU countries, to pressure Turkey were in vain. Erdogan responded by stating, "Turkey is not a country you can pull and push around, not a country whose citizens you can drag on the ground."[47] This symbolic action by the German President, and Erdogan's bellicose response, echoed his reaction to the European Parliament symbolically voting to halt Turkey's ascension talks due to the repressive measures the Turkish government introduced in the aftermath of the attempted coup d'état by elements of the Turkish military in July 2016.[48] Over the next three years, a variety of diplomatic furores would further dampen relations between Turkey and the EU.

Most problematic for Turkey, however, was that the EU continued to neglect its obligations under the 2016 agreement, according to which Turkey took on the preponderant burden of migrants and refugees for the European Union. In exchange, the EU was supposed to provide Turkey with financial support and visa-free travel for Turkish citizens to the EU.[49] Regarding the latter, the European Union was supposed to finalize the visa liberalization process by June 2016. Although it formally initiated the process on 4 May 2016, progress has since stalled on the issue, and even in the initial address, EU politicians placed the burden on Turkey. In the initial announcement, First Vice-President of the European Commission, Frans Timmermans, noted:

> Turkey has made impressive progress, particularly in recent weeks, on meeting the benchmarks of its visa liberalization roadmap. There is still work to be done as a matter of urgency but if Turkey sustains the progress made, they can meet the remaining benchmarks. This is why we are putting a proposal on the table which opens the way for the European Parliament and the Member States to decide to lift visa requirements, once the benchmarks have been met.[50]

---

46   Frank-Walter Steinmeier, cited in Ece Toksabay, "Erdogan warns Europeans 'will not walk safely' if attitude persists, as row carries on," *Reuters*, March 22, 2017, https://www.reuters.com/article/us-turkey-referendum-europe-idUSKBN16T13E.
47   Ibid.
48   "Euro MPs vote to freeze Turkey EU membership talks," *BBC*, November 24, 2016, https://www.bbc.com/news/world-europe-38090121.
49   European Council, "EU-Turkey statement."
50   "European Commission opens way for decision by June on visa-free travel for citizens of Turkey," European Commission, May 4, 2016, https://ec.europa.eu/commission/presscorner/detail/en/IP_16_1622.

5. An Ongoing Paradox in the World-System of Migration 113

In short, while the proposal promised much, it amounted to little of substance. Later, the European authorities, when questioned about the matter, noted that Turkey had not done enough to meet the requirements needed for visa-free travel.[51] The ability of Turkey's citizens to access the Schengen Zone, and therefore the core countries, without requiring visas was, and continues to be, indefinitely delayed.

Likewise, the financial support that the European Union provided Turkey, while appearing considerable, did little to resolve the migrant crisis or aid Turkey in a significant manner. Turkey continues to host 3.6 million refugees from the Syrian Civil War, and this does not include other migrants forced to remain in Turkey as they seek transportation to the core countries of the EU.[52] The root causes for mass migration to the European Union, its high standard of living, and the accessibility of information about it did not disappear in the years since the EU-Turkish agreement in March 2016. If anything, the underlying issues have become more pronounced as technological distribution to the developing world increases and continues to highlight the disparities that exist globally. Thus, not only had the financial support promised to Turkey, six billion Euros by 2018, ended, but it was also insufficient given the scale of the crisis, and, notably, had not even been fully disbursed. In an ironically self-laudatory press release on 10 December 2019, the European Commission noted, "The European Union has fully mobilised the €6 billion operational budget of the Facility for Refugees in Turkey, in line with its commitment to the implementation of the EU-Turkey Statement. Out of the total Facility budget of €6 billion, €4.3 billion has now been contracted and €2.7 billion disbursed."[53] Despite not meeting its obligations under the 2016 agreement, the European Commission still felt the need to recognize that it had disbursed less than half the agreed sum. This was almost a year after the amount in its entirety was due. With political tensions escalating due to Turkey's ascension to the EU being indefinitely delayed and the EU failing to fulfil its obligations under the 2016 agreement, Erdogan used one of the few means at his disposal

---

51 Ibid.
52 "Situation Syria Regional Refugees."
53 "EU Facility for Refugees in Turkey: €6 billion to support refugees and local communities in need fully mobilised," European Commission, December 10, 2019, https://ec.eu ropa.eu/commission/presscorner/detail/en/ip_19_6694.

to create pressure upon the EU: weaponizing the refugees and migrants.[54] Greece, as one of the EU countries that shares a border with Turkey, was at the frontline of this threat.

Greece's politics, likewise, had come into alignment with the EU consensus. In 2015, a radical left party led Greece, which was out of step with the major actors of the European Union. While Greece also experienced radicalization on the right, most notably with Golden Dawn gaining seats in parliament, New Democracy's position as an anti-austerity party allowed it to defeat this challenge from the far-right. New Democracy's success in 2019 returned Greece to its traditional two-party system.[55] The rise of a centre-right government re-oriented Greece to the types of governments gaining influence in Europe since 2015. Even within European countries where governments withstood political challenges from the right and populist organizations, such as France, groups espousing these beliefs made significant inroads.[56] While Greece shifted its government to the right much later than several European governments that would become key allies in 2020, most notably Austria and Poland, the challenges posed by the 2015 Migration Crisis brought European politics into rough alignment.

Unlike in 2015, the EU would take a hardline against migrants and refugees in 2020. The polarization that occurred in Greek politics before the 2015 Migration Crisis had spread to the rest of Europe in the intervening five years. Specifically, populism, whether in its left- or right-wing form, became a major political force in Europe.[57] The perspective of Viktor Orban in Hungary, previously considered anathema by other European states, gained resonance in the

---

54   The weaponization of refugees is not a new concept or development. For an analysis of the issue, see Kelly M. Greenhill, "Strategic Engineered Migration as a Weapon of War," *Civil Wars* 10, no. 1 (2008): 6–21.

55   For an explanation of Golden Dawn's rise, see Sofia Vasilopoulou and Daphne Halikiopoulou, *The Golden Dawn's 'Nationalist Solution': Explaining the Rise of the Far Right in Greece* (New York: Palgrave MacMillan, 2015). For coverage of the 2019 Greek election, see Lamprini Rori, "The 2019 Greek parliamentary election: retour a la normale," *West European Politics* 43, no. 4 (2019): 1023–1037.

56   See Ayhan Kaya, *Populism and Heritage in Europe: Lost in Diversity and Unity* (London: Routledge, 2019).

57   For an examination on the rise of right-wing populism in Europe, see Kaya, *Populism and Heritage in Europe*; for an examination of left-wing populism in Europe, see Giorgos Charalambous and Gregoris Ioannou, eds., *Left Radicalism and Populism in Europe* (London: Routledge, 2019).

European Union as a whole. The populism witnessed in Greece, already having fertile seeds in Europe, spread further in the aftermath of the 2015 Migration Crisis. Furthermore, the governments of Germany and France, the two core countries of the EU that opposed the more strenuous measures proposed in 2015, had faced significant challenges from the right since 2015. These developments made opposition to the more strenuous border defences proposed by Austria, Hungary, and other European states difficult, if not impossible. Thus, immediately before the global pandemic halted Turkey's attempt to weaponize the refugees against Europe, the EU stood relatively united on the issue due to its need for Greece to provide a buffer between it and the periphery.

Conclusion

The EU's need to solidify its position as one of the key cores of the international system led to different responses to the refugee crises in 2015 and 2020. In 2015, the EU, seeking to stabilize the monetary aspect of the supranational organization, initially left Greece to deal with the matter by citing the Dublin Regulation. Even when Germany and other key states of the EU intervened, they did so only to preserve their own positions within the organization. In 2020, however, the position of the EU was less stable than it had been in 2015. The decision of the United Kingdom to leave the organization, the first country to do so, caused EU leaders to reemphasize solidarity within the bloc rather than punish its members. Combined with the perceived threat of mass migration emanating from Turkey, a country on the European periphery that EU policymakers increasingly viewed as a destabilizing force and not a future member, European countries supported Greece in 2020 to a degree that they had been unwilling to do in 2015.

Works Cited

Borgatti, Stephen P. and Martin G. Everett. "Models of core/periphery structures." *Social Networks* 21, no. 4 (2000): 375–395.

Brettell, Caroline B. and James F. Hollifield, eds. *Migration Theory: Talking across Disciplines*. New York: Routledge, 2014.

Charalambous, Giorgos and Gregoris Ioannou, eds. *Left Radicalism and Populism in Europe*. London: Routledge, 2019.

Cini, Michelle and Amy Verdun. "The Implications of Brexit for the Future of Europe." In *Brexit and Beyond: Rethinking the Futures of Europe*, edited by Benjamin Martill and Uta Staiger, 63–71. London: UCL Press, 2018.

Connelly, Andrew. "Europe's Failed Migration Policy Caused Greece's Latest Refugee Crisis." *Foreign Policy*, September 20, 2020. https://foreignpolicy.com/2020/09/20/europes-failed-migration-policy-caused-greeces-latest-refugee-crisis/.

Convention Relating to the Status of Refugees. New York, 1951.

"Council Decision of 13 December 1999 on the full application of the Schengen acquis in Greece." *Official Journal of the European Communities* 327, no. 58 (2000).

"Council Regulation (EC) No. 343/2003 of 18 February 2003 establishing the criteria and mechanisms for determining the Member State responsible for examining an asylum application lodged in one of the Member States by a third-country national." *Office Journal of the European Union* 50, no. 1 (2003): 1–10.

"EU Facility for Refugees in Turkey: €6 billion to support refugees and local communities in need fully mobilised." European Commission, December 10, 2019. https://ec.europa.eu/commission/presscorner/detail/en/ip_19_6694.

"Euro MPs vote to freeze Turkey EU membership talks." *BBC*, November 24, 2016, https://www.bbc.com/news/world-europe-38090121.

"European Commission opens way for decision by June on visa-free travel for citizens of Turkey." European Commission, May 4, 2016. https://ec.europa.eu/commission/presscorner/detail/en/IP_16_1622.

European Council. "EU-Turkey statement, 18 March 2016." https://www.consilium.europa.eu/en/press/press-releases/2016/03/18/eu-turkey-statement/.

Frelak, Justyna Segeš. "Solidarity in European Migration Policy: The Perspective of the Visegrád States." In *Solidarity in the European Union*, edited by Andreas Grimmel and Susanne My Giang, 81–95. London: Springer, 2017.

Gillespie, Mary et al. *Mapping Refugee Media Journeys: Smartphones and Social Media Networks*. Open University, 2016.

Greenhill, Kelly M. "Strategic Engineered Migration as a Weapon of War." *Civil Wars* 10, no. 1 (2008): 6–21.

Haferlach, Lisa and Dilek Kurban. "Lessons Learnt from the EU-Turkey Refugee Agreement in Guiding EU Migration Partnerships with Origin and Transit Countries." *Global Policy* 8, no. 4 (2017): 85–93.

Human Rights Watch, *World Report: Events of 2009*. New York: Human Rights Watch, 2010. https://www.hrw.org/sites/default/files/world_report_download/wr2010.pdf.

"Hungary PM: Shut Greek Border to Migrants." *Sky News*, October 15, 2015. https://news.sky.com/story/hungary-pm-shut-greek-border-to-stop-migrants-10342972.

Inside Europe: Ten Years of Turmoil, episode 2, "Going for Broke." 2019.

Jaap de Zwaan, Martijn Lak, Abiola Makinwa, and Piet Willems, eds. *Governance and Security Issues of the European Union: Challenges Ahead*. The Hague: Asper Press, 2016.

Karatzogianni, Athina and Andrew Robinson. *Power, Resistance and Conflict in the Contemporary World: Social Movements, Networks, and Hierarchies*. New York: Routledge, 2009.

Kawano, Yukio, Benjamin D. Brewer, and Christopher Chase-Dunn. "Trade Globalization since 1795: Waves of Integration in the World-System." *American Sociological Review* 65, no. 1 (2000): 77–95.

Kaya, Ayhan. *Populism and Heritage in Europe: Lost in Diversity and Unity*. London: Routledge, 2019.

Ker-Lindsay, James. "Turkey's EU Accession as a Factor in the 2016 Brexit Referendum." *Turkish Studies* 19, no. 1 (2018): 1–22.

Knox, Paul L. and Sallie A. Marston. *Human Geography*. Upper Saddle River, NJ: Prentice Hall, 1998.

Lee, Everett S. "A Theory of Migration." *Demography* 3, no. 1 (1966): 47–57.

Lindstrom, Nicole. "What's Left for 'Social Europe'? Brexit and Transnational Labour Market Regulation in the UK-1 and the EU-27." *New Political Economy* 24, no. 2 (2019): 286–298.

Matthes, Georg. "The myth of Grexit." *Deutsche Welle*, February 20, 2017. https://www.dw.com/en/opinion-the-myth-of-grexit/a-37642633.

"Migratory Routes: Eastern Mediterranean Route." Frontex, accessed October 20, 2020. https://frontex.europa.eu/along-eu-borders/migratory-routes/eastern-mediterranean-route/.

Mohtadi, Shahrzad, Colin P. Kelley, Mark A. Cane, Richard Seager, and Yochanan Kushnir, "Climate Change in the Fertile Crescent and Implications of the Recent Syrian Drought." *PNAS* 112, no. 11 (2015): 3241–3246.

Moreno-Lax, Violeta. "The EU Humanitarian Border and the Securitization of Human Rights: The 'Rescue-Through-Interdiction/Rescue-Without-Protection'." *Journal of Common Market Strategies* 56, no. 1 (2018): 119–140.

Novoth, Michal. "The Greek Elections of 2012: The Worrisome Rise of the Golden Dawn." *Israel Journal of Foreign Affairs* 7, no. 1 (2013): 87–94.

Osborne, Samuel. "Angela Merkel Admits She Lost Control of Refugee Crisis in Germany and Would 'Turn Back Time' If She Could." *The Independent*, September 22, 2016.

Ovenden, Kevin and Paul Mason, *Syriza: Inside the Labyrinth*. London: Pluto Press, 2015.

Rahimahl, Badr Eddin. "The Class Oriented Rationale: Uncovering the Sources of the Syrian Civil War." *The Muslim World* 106, no. 1 (2016): 169–186.

Rori, Lamprini. "The 2019 Greek parliamentary election: retour a la normale." *West European Politics* 43, no. 4 (2019): 1023–1037.

Rummery, Ariane. "Worsening conditions inside Syria and the region fuel despair, driving thousands towards Europe." United Nations High Commissioner on Refugees, September 8, 2015. https://www.unhcr.org/uk/news/latest/2015/9/55eed5d66/worsening-conditions-inside-syria-region-fuel-despair-driving-thousands.html.

"Seven factors behind movement of Syrian refugees to Europe." United Nations High Commissioner on Refugees, September 25, 2015. https://www.unhcr.org/news/briefing/2015/9/560523f26/seven-factors-behind-movement-syrian-refugees-europe.html.

"Situation Syria Regional Refugees." United Nations High Commissioner on Refugees, accessed October 28, 2020, https://data2.unhcr.org/en/situations/syria/location/113.

Smith-Spark, Laura. "European migrant crisis: A country-by-country glance." *CNN*, September 5, 2015. https://edition.cnn.com/2015/09/04/europe/migrant-crisis-country-by-country.

Stevenson, Richard W. "Stories of Hope, Courage, and Loss as Historic Journey Unfolds." *The New York Times*, November 12, 2015.

Stone, Jon. "EU chief praises Greece as 'shield' of Europe after police attack refugees at border." *The Independent*, March 3, 2020. https://www.independent.co.uk/news/world/europe/greece-refugees-border-eu-police-ursula-von-der-leyen-a9373281.html.

Toksabay, Ece. "Erdogan warns Europeans 'will not walk safely' if attitude persists, as row carries on." *Reuters*, March 22, 2017. https://www.reuters.com/article/us-turkey-referendum-europe-idUSKBN16T13E.

"Total number of refugees in host country, end of 1990." Migration Data Portal, accessed October 20, 2020, https://www.migrationdataportal.org/international-data?i=refug_host&t=1990.

Traynor, Ian. "Alexis Tsipras Must Be Stopped: The Underlying Message of Europe's Leaders." *The Guardian*, June 29, 2015.

UNHCR. *Protecting and Supporting the Displaced in Syria: UNHCR Syria End of Year Report*. https://www.unhcr.org/sy/wp-content/uploads/sites/3/2016/11/UNHCR-End-of-Year-2015-En.pdf.

Update of the Hellenic Stability and Growth Programme. Athens, January 15, 2010. https://ec.europa.eu/economy_finance/economic_governance/sgp/pdf/20_scps/2009-10/01_programme/el_2010-01-15_sp_en.pdf.

Vasilopoulou, Sofia and Daphne Halikiopoulou. *The Golden Dawn's 'Nationalist Solution': Explaining the Rise of the Far Right in Greece*. New York: Palgrave MacMillan, 2015.

Wall, Stephen. *A Stranger in Europe: Britain and the EU from Thatcher to Blair*. New York: Oxford University Press, 2008.

Wallerstein, Immanuel. *The Modern World-System*, vol. 1: *Capitalist Agriculture and the Origins of the European World-Economy in the Sixteenth Century*. Berkeley, CA: University of California Press, 2011 [1974].

Wike, Richard et al., "The European Union." *Pew Research Center*, October 14, 2019. https://www.pewresearch.org/global/2019/10/14/the-european-union/.

Zoega, Gylfi. "Greece and the Western Financial Crisis." *Atlantic Economic Journal* 47, no. 2 (2019): 113–126.

6. Wallerstein's World-Systems Theory and the Role of Revolutions

Frank Jacob

> "Human history is progressive, and inevitably so."[1]

Introduction

Human progress is often linked to revolutionary change and is a consequence of transformative processes that seem to intensify the speed of reforms and even time itself. The first two decades of the 21st century were marked by a "rapid intensification of revolutionary situations, social revolts and rebellions on a global scale," and Karatasli argued that "[t]his is not an ordinary wave of social unrest. It belongs to one of the major world historical waves of mobilization which has the *potential* to transform political structures, economic systems and social relations."[2] The protests that have gained momentum since the beginning of the century were often perceived to have been motivated by anti-globalizing and anti-capitalist ideas that criticized the uncontrolled accumulation of capital while natural resources were exploited, the ecosystem of the planet destroyed, and human rights ignored.[3] Within revolutionary protest formation, multiple crises and different motifs or motivational factors overlapped and created a heterogenous mass of protesters whose demands for a

---

1   Immanuel Wallerstein, *The Essential Wallerstein* (New York: The New Press, 2000), 146.
2   Sahan Savas Karatasli, "The Twenty-First Century Revolutions and Internationalism: A World-Historical Perspective," *Journal of World-Systems Research* 25, no. 2 (2019): 306. Emphasis in original.
3   Ibid., 307.

socio-political discontinuum unite them.[4] Scholars interested in the study of the world-system and world-systems theory emphasized that the study of the former, following the works and ideas of Immanuel Wallerstein,[5] offers a very sophisticated and fruitful method to study revolutionary developments in general and the "global inequalities" that created the unrest of the last two decades in particular. As Manuela Boatcă highlighted, world-systems analysis offers a "more complex and differentiated terminology and a more encompassing historical perspective, anticipating many of the recent arguments and even predicting several country trajectories by a long shot."[6]

Wallerstein, who initially worked on African history, developed his theoretical approach because he "grew dissatisfied with existing tools of social science that, he believed, led to incorrect conclusions." The increasing "African nationalism" in the early Cold War period and during the decolonization of many African states in combination with the "[student] protests at Columbia [University] revealed [to Wallerstein] that social science tools of the sixties could not explain the empirical world."[7] As such, Wallerstein wanted to change the way social scientists look at and try to understand society:

> [M]y epistemological premise that the much-vaunted distinction between idiographic and nomothetic epistemologies is outdated, spurious, and harmful to sound analysis. Social reality is always and necessarily both historical (in the sense that reality inevitably changes every nanosecond) and structural (in the sense that social action is governed by constraints deriving from the historical social system within which the described activity occurs).[8]

---

4   On the motivational overlaps within revolutionary movements, see Frank Jacob, *#Revolution: Wer, warum, wann und wie viele?* (Marburg: Büchner, 2022), 21–56. For a detailed discussion of the revolutionary discontinuum, see Gunnar Hindrichs, *Philosophie der Revolution* (Berlin: Suhrkamp, 2017).

5   Immanuel Wallerstein, *The Modern World-System*, 4 vols. (New York: Academic Press, 1974–1989; Berkeley, CA: University of California Press, 2011).

6   Manuela Boatcă, "Global Inequalities *avant la lettre*: Immanuel Wallerstein's Contribution," *Socio* 15 (2021): 71–91.

7   Gregory P. Williams, *Contesting the Global Order: The Radical Political Economy of Perry Anderson and Immanuel Wallerstein* (Albany, NY: State University of New York Press, 2020), 97.

8   Immanuel Wallerstein, *The Modern World-System*, vol. 4: *Centrist Liberalism Triumphant, 1789–1914* (Berkeley, CA: University of California Press, 2011), ix.

Wallerstein was criticized for such an approach for three reasons: 1) he used world-systems as an analytical unit instead of looking at the history of nation-states; 2) he emphasized the meaning and necessity of a *longue durée* as an analytical time frame; and 3) these world-systems were supposed to be studied interdisciplinarily. It was consequently no surprise that Wallerstein's ideas and suggestions were attacked from different directions and disciplines alike, including orthodox Marxists and cultural particularists.[9] Wallerstein did not want easy answers to complex solutions but "to make all so-called simple variables more complex and to put them in a context in order to understand real social situations."[10] Together with other colleagues who worked relentlessly to understand the formation, demise, and reconfiguration of the world-system, Wallerstein attempted to provide broader and more complex explanations to better understand the complicated world in which we live.[11] Social movements and revolutionary developments are variables within this complicated story that often change the existent world-system through their reconfiguratory power.[12] They are expressions of specific groups within the world-system who wish to alter their own position or even the nature of the whole system due to protest and revolutionary acts. Considering that the world-system is capitalist in nature, one would assume that revolutions intend to overcome it as an organizational unit of a global scale and replace it with a truly equal form of coexistence. However, the historical reality seems to show that revolutions, which often seem to appear in waves that shake the world-system's founda-

---

9   Immanuel Wallerstein, *Welt-System-Analyse: Eine Einführung* (Wiesbaden: VS Verlag für Sozialwissenschaften, 2019), 25.
10 Ibid.
11 See, among others, Christopher Chase-Dunn, *Global Formation: Structures of the World-Economy* (Oxford: Blackwell, 1989); Christopher Chase-Dunn and Thomas D. Hall, *Rise and Demise: Comparing World-Systems* (Boulder, CO: Westview Press, 1997); Jennifer Blair and Marion Werner, "New Geographies of Uneven Development in Global Formation: Thinking with Chase-Dunn," *Journal of World-System Research* 23, no. 2 (2017): 604–619.
12 Terry Boswell, ed., *Revolution in the World-System* (New York: Greenwood Press, 1989); Jackie Smith and Dawn Wiest, *Social Movements in the World-System: The Politics of Crisis and Transformation* (New York: Russell Sage, 2012).

tions,[13] are only able to shatter it momentarily before it begins to reconfigure itself according to the post-revolutionary reality.

The following chapter intends to take a closer look at the relationship between world-systems and revolutionary processes, focusing on the ideas Wallerstein expressed about this connection in his different texts. After this first analysis, the role of the semiperiphery as a control instrument within an existent world-system that nevertheless seems to stimulate revolutionary developments shall be discussed.[14] Eventually, the future role of revolutions in the transformation of the capitalist world-system of the early 21st century will be taken into closer consideration. The chapter therefore offers an approach that combines theoretical suppositions that have been applied in world-system studies with the comparative analysis of revolutions.[15]

World-Systems and Revolutionary Processes

Revolutions or revolutionary movements, as Wallerstein remarked, intend "to end an oppressive situation." On the other hand, he emphasized with regard to the so-called Third World revolutions of the anticolonial period that revolutionaries act according to the "expectation that their victory at the state level will open the door at last to the real development of their country."[16] Wallerstein also understood the existent social structure within the world-system to

---

13   Manfred Kossok and Walter Markov, "Zur Methodologie der vergleichenden Revolutionsgeschichte der Neuzeit," in *Studien zur Vergleichenden Revolutionsgeschichte 1500–1917*, ed. Manfred Kossok (Berlin: Akademie Verlag, 1974), 9. Recently, similar claims have been renewed in David Motadel, ed., *Revolutionary World: Global Upheaval in the Modern Age* (Cambridge: Cambridge University Press, 2021).

14   For works with a focus on world-systems and revolution, see, among others, Terry Boswell and William J. Dixon, "Dependency and Rebellion: A Cross-National Analysis," *American Sociological Review* 55, no. 4 (1990): 540–559; Terry R. Kandal, "Revolution, Racism and Sexism: Challenges for World-System Analysis," *Studies in Comparative International Development* 25, no. 4 (1990): 86–102; Thomas Reifer, ed., *Globalization, Hegemony and Power: Antisystemic Movements and the Global System* (London: Routledge, 2015).

15   For the latter, see, in particular, Frank Jacob, "Revolutionen und Weltgeschichte," in *Revolution: Beiträge zu einem historischen Phänomen der globalen Moderne*, eds. Frank Jacob and Riccardo Altieri (Berlin: WVB, 2019), 11–40.

16   Immanuel Wallerstein, "Development: Lodestar or Illusion?" *Economic and Political Weekly* 23, no. 39 (1988): 2017.

develop according to specific stages,[17] and he seems to have understood revolutions as marking points or watersheds that lead from one stage to the next and determine the future course of development. Considering that Wallerstein formulated his world-systems analysis to address the social realities of the 1970s and provide a better understanding of the world at that time,[18] it definitely contains some revolution-related elements. Gregory P. Williams remarked in this regard that "Wallerstein announced that the capitalist world-economy had a division of labor between the powerful developed core, the underdeveloped periphery, and the in-between semiperiphery. He noted that this division of labor created a vicious cycle, with core states becoming strong and weak states becoming weak through unequal exchange."[19] This basic consideration points to the revolutionary possibilities for world-system-related developments as a consequence of historical caesuras marked by revolutions per se. If a core state or area falls while another semiperipheral region rises, this may be related to the outcome of revolutionary change and the end of old orders that are replaced – fully or partially – by new ones that contest the existent shape of a specific world-system.

Wallerstein's initial thoughts in relation to the world-system as a "unit of analysis"[20] were related to questions about the historical developments of the modern world. Referencing "Marx, who argued, if you will, that the nineteenth-century present was only an antepenultimate stage of development, that the capitalist world was to know a cataclysmic political revolution which would then lead in the fullness of time to a final societal form, in this case the classless society,"[21] Wallerstein intended to provide more complex but probably also more fitting explanations of these considerations from a global perspective. Therefore, he pointed out that

> if we are to give an explanation of both continuity and transformation, then we must logically divide the long term into segments in order to observe the structural changes from time A to time B. These segments are, however,

---

17   Immanuel Wallerstein, "The Rise and Future Demise of the World Capitalist System: Concepts for Comparative Analysis," *Comparative Studies in Society and History* 16, no. 4 (1974): 389.
18   Wallerstein, *Welt-System-Analyse*, 5.
19   Williams, *Contesting the Global Order*, 96.
20   Wallerstein, *The Essential Wallerstein*, 71.
21   Ibid.

not discrete but continuous in reality; ergo they are "stages" in the "development" of a social structure, a development which we determine however not a priori but a posteriori. That is, we cannot predict the future concretely, but we can predict the past.[22]

Especially considering the linear explanations related to historical materialism and the Marxist interpretation of all history as a history of class struggles that has to follow certain stages to develop to reach the revolution that opens the gate to a communist, i.e., classless society of the future, Wallerstein was interested in one particular question that can be tied to theoretical revolutionary debates[23] as well:

[C]an stages be skipped? This question is only logically meaningful if we have "stages" that "co-exist" within a single empirical framework. If within a capitalist world-economy, we define one state as feudal, a second as capitalist, and a third as socialist, then and only then can we pose the question: can a country "skip" from the feudal stage to the socialist stage of national development without "passing through capitalism"?[24]

Wallerstein accepted the existence of stages and demanded that these be applied as analytical units for chronological processes as well. However, he demanded these be "stages of social systems, that is, of totalities. And the only totalities that exist or have historically existed are mini-systems and world-systems, and in the nineteenth and twentieth centuries there has been only one world-system in existence, the capitalist world-economy."[25] If one considers this to be the case and revolutions to be caesuras within the developmental history of the modern world-system, it is not surprising that revolutions that might begin in either the core, the semiperiphery, or the periphery set a wave of revolutionary events in motion that soon transform the world-system at large, redistributing the roles of former core regions or renegotiating the status of

---

22 Ibid., 73.
23 One such debate occured in the aftermath of the Russian Revolution, as Russia was considered, in contrast to Marx's expectations for a revolution in industrialized Western Europe, too backward to be the country where a world revolution could start. On this and the debate about the "revolutionary potential" of Russia and its post-revolutionary leaders, i.e., the Bolsheviks, see Frank Jacob, *1917: Die korrumpierte Revolution* (Marburg: Büchner, 2020), 149–202.
24 Wallerstein, *The Essential Wallerstein*, 74.
25 Ibid.

6. Wallerstein's World-Systems Theory and the Role of Revolutions   127

core, semiperiphery, and periphery among those regions or states that advance or decline as a consequence of the revolutionary process.

The shaping of human history due to the "geographic expansion of the European world-economy to include now the whole of the globe"[26] was stimulated by the necessity to acquire raw materials while exporting manufactured goods and, later, capital to foreign markets within a more and more globalized economy. The building and enhancing of a "capitalist world-economy,"[27] a process one could also refer to as the "accumulation of capital,"[28] was achieved "by integrating a geographically vast set of production processes. We call this the establishment of a single 'division of labor.' Of course, all historical systems are based on a division of labor, but none before was as complex, as extensive, as detailed, and as cohesive as that of the capitalist world-economy."[29] Basing his considerations on the work of other economist thinkers, e.g., Nikolai Kondratiev (1892–1938),[30] Wallerstein argued that the capitalist world-economy showed a "pattern of cyclical rhythms"[31] and stated in this regard that

> [t]he most obvious, and probably the most important, of these rhythms is a seemingly regular process of expansion and contraction of the world-economy as a whole. On present evidence, this cycle tends to be 50–60 years in length, covering its two phases. The functioning of this cycle (sometimes called "long waves," sometimes Kondratieff cycles) is complex and I will not review it here. One part, however, of the process is that, periodically, the capitalist world economy has seen the need to expand the geographic boundaries of the system as a whole, creating thereby new loci of production to participate in its axial division of labor. Over 400 years, these successive expansions have transformed the capitalist world-economy from a system located primarily in Europe to one that covers the entire globe.[32]

The capitalist world-system created by European expansion was, however, not the first world-system, but absorbed other regional systems and declining em-

---

26   Ibid., 94.
27   Ibid., 243.
28   A classical text would be Rosa Luxemburg, *Die Akkumulation des Kapitals: Ein Beitrag zur ökonomischen Erklärung des Imperialismus* (Berlin: Paul Singer, 1913).
29   Wallerstein, *The Essential Wallerstein*, 268.
30   Nikolai Kondratiev, "About the Question of the Major Cycles of the Conjuncture" [in Russian], *Planovoe Khozyaystvo* 8 (1926): 167–181.
31   Wallerstein, *The Essential Wallerstein*, 269.
32   Ibid.

pires, especially in the Americas, where the Aztec and Incan empires were already in decline. These were eventually absorbed by the Eurocentered world-system, which turned former systems into peripheral or semi-peripheral regions through invasion, occupation, and exploitation.[33] The fact that positions within the world-system can be changed through an overall change of its configuration is important to note, especially in light of the revolutionary ambitions often expressed in a semi-peripheral context discussed later.

The previous stages of expansion and contraction within world history also changed due to globalization and the establishment of the modern capitalist world-system, which, as mentioned elsewhere in this book,[34] marked the transition from world to global history. According to Wallerstein,

> The modern world-system changed the rules of the game in two ways. In the first place, the operation of the rules of world-empires led to long-term geographical expansion followed by geographical contraction. The rules of the capitalist world-economy (the expanded reproduction of capital) involved expansion but no contraction – periods of relative stagnation, yes; attempts of areas at tactical withdrawal, yes; but real contraction, no. Hence, by the late nineteenth century, the capitalist world-economy included virtually the whole inhabited earth, and it is presently striving to overcome the technological limits to cultivating the remaining corners: the deserts, the jungles, the seas, and indeed the other planets of the solar system.[35]

In contrast to other "developmentalist" interpretations tied to Marx or Weber, Wallerstein further argued that the global transformation(s) from "feudalism" to the modern capitalist world-economy had to be understood according to the world-systems theory and the complexity of the processes involved instead of applying a form of historical determinism that only included Eurocentric

---

33 Ibid., 94. On the Aztec and Incan empires and their role for and relation to world-system analysis see Lawrence A. Kuznar, "Periphery-Core Relations in the Inca Empire: Carrots and Sticks in an Andean World System," *Journal of World-Systems Research* 2, no. 1 (1996): 322–349; Michael E. Smith, "The Aztec Empire and the Mesoamerican World System," in *Empires: Perspectives from Archaeology and History*, eds. Susan E. Alcock et al. (Cambridge: Cambridge University Press, 2001), 128–154.
34 See Chapter 2.
35 Immanuel Wallerstein, "Civilizations and Modes of Production: Conflicts and Convergences," *Theory and Society* 5, no. 1 (1978): 6.

perspectives.[36] Revolutions were without any doubt the triggers or catalysts for such transitions, especially with regard to a transformation that would stimulate a change of position – of a region or nation-state – within the world-system of the time. Consequently, Wallerstein was interested in Marx's and Engels's considerations about revolutionary change, although neither from an "orthodox" nor a utopian perspective.[37] It is therefore only fitting to take a closer look at several revolutions Wallerstein tied to world-systems theory in more detail.

Until the mid-18th century, the globalization of the world-economy and the steady accumulation of capital and access to resources, raw materials, and possible markets changed the relations between core and periphery and even whole demographic settings in some regions of the world.[38] The French Revolution, or, more precisely, the first revolutionary wave of modernity, i.e., the Atlantic revolutions in the United States, France, and Haiti, marked the beginning of a transitory period within the world-system.[39] Wallerstein remarked with regard to the French Revolution that it "propagated two quite revolutionary ideas. According to the first, political change was not unusual or bizarre, but normal and therefore a permanent condition. The second idea held that 'sovereignty' – the right of the state to make autonomous decisions within its borders – did not reside in (or belong to) a monarch or the legislature, but resided with the 'people,' who alone can legitimize a regime."[40]

The world's transition to modernity was consequently linked to the rise of revolutionary movements that opposed the current structure of the world-

---

36 Immanuel Wallerstein, "From Feudalism to Capitalism: Transition or Transitions?" *Social Forces* 55, no. 2 (1976): 277.
37 Immanuel Wallerstein, "Marxisms as Utopias: Evolving Ideologies," *American Journal of Sociology* 91, no. 6 (1986): 1295–1298. For Engels's view on utopian interpretations of socialism, see Friedrich Engels, *Socialism: Utopian and Scientific*, accessed November 25, 2022, https://www.marxists.org/archive/marx/works/1880/soc-utop/index.htm. On Engels's thoughts about revolution, see Frank Jacob, "Friedrich Engels and Revolution Theory: The Legacy of a Revolutionary Life," in *Engels@200: Reading Friedrich Engels in the 21st Century*, ed. Frank Jacob (Marburg: Büchner, 2020), 49–90.
38 Wallerstein, *Welt-System-Analyse*, 5. See also Immanuel Wallerstein, "American Slavery and the Capitalist World-Economy," *American Journal of Sociology* 81, no. 5 (1976): 1199–1213.
39 For a detailed discussion of this first modern revolutionary wave, see Frank Jacob, *Revolution and the Global Struggle for Modernity*, vol. 1: *The Atlantic Revolutions* (London: Anthem Press, 2023).
40 Wallerstein, *Welt-System-Analyse*, 8.

system, and the French Revolution "firmly established the ideological motifs of the modern world, the rallying cries and the rationale of the movements to come."[41] The French Revolution also challenged the uncontested existence and acceptance of the modern world-system, and therefore, as Wallerstein emphasized, it "was a crucial watershed in the ideological history of the modern world-system in that it led to the widespread acceptance of the idea that social change rather than social stasis is normal, both in the normative and in the statistical sense of the word. It thereby posed the intellectual problem of how to regulate, speed up, slow down, or otherwise affect this normal process of change and evolution."[42] While the revolution in France "presumably represent[ed] the overcoming of a mismatch,"[43] it also marked a historical moment in which the division of the world and its system's categories were challenged, maybe even more so when the revolutionary wave hit the colonial sphere, i.e., St. Domingue (later Haiti). Not only did the "bourgeois revolution" in France change the global sphere and its perception among people around the globe, but the modern world-system was tremendously changed as well "by [the] unleashing [of] two new concepts, whose impact was to transform the modern world-system. These concepts were the 'normality of change' as opposed to its exceptional and limited reality, and the 'sovereignty of the people' as opposed to that of the ruler or the aristocracy. This pair of concepts was the basis of something new, a geoculture that spread throughout the historical system and legitimated radical 'change' of the system by the 'people.'"[44]

The experience of the French Revolution changed the way the world was received, and since the ideas of the Enlightenment had caused actions that altered the historical course tremendously, the ruling elites needed to counter the existent danger. According to Wallerstein, the answer to the changing situation was the creation of "the three modern ideologies – conservatism, liberalism, and radicalism,"[45] as the "ideological turmoil" that had been caused by the

---

41 Immanuel Wallerstein, "Antisystemic Movements: History and Dilemmas," in Samir Amin et al., *Transforming the Revolution: Social Movements and the World-System* (New York: Monthly Review Press, 1990), 13.
42 Wallerstein, *The Essential Wallerstein*, 137.
43 Ibid., 144.
44 Immanuel Wallerstein, "Antisystemic Movements, Yesterday and Today," *Journal of World-Systems Research* 20, no. 2 (2014): 158.
45 Ibid. See also Immanuel Wallerstein, "Las Tres Hegemonías Sucesivas en la Historia de la Economía-Mundo," in *Capitalismo Histórico y Movimientos Antisistémicos*, ed. Immanuel Wallerstein (Madrid: Akal, 2004), 212–223.

revolutionary process needed to be addressed, for "the state represented what was and was not perfect, and society represented the force that was pushing toward the perfectibility of the state."[46] Starting from Wallerstein's consideration that "both the anti-capitalist relational matrix and the liberal matrix"[47] had been created by the French Revolution, Chilean scholar Ignacio Muñoz Cristi emphasized that this revolution "can be seen as generative of the practices of *popular self-management* and *social intervention* and the three institutions that operationalized these practices, each for their own specific ends, to wit: Ideologies, Social Sciences, and Anti-Systemic Movements."[48] The latter movements, however, could have an ambivalent influence on existent world-systems, because "the rise of anti-systemic movements ... [has] historically debilitated and simultaneously reinforced the world-system"[49] as the latter's existence usually stimulates these forms of anti-systemic protest in the first place. Muñoz Cristi consequently also argues that there was not "a bourgeois revolution, or a merely anti-authoritarian one in which a new class, the bourgeoisie, would arise between feudal lords and peasants. Rather, it is a history of how lords were forced by events to transform themselves into bourgeoisie in order to conserve their privileges as governors."[50] The revolution had simply demanded a structural change within the world-system's configuration and a visible (although not real) transition of power away from the old elites. However, the events the French Revolution triggered in peripheral and semi-peripheral parts of the world-system of the late 18th century proved tremendously transformative, especially with regard to those people who now, as active revolutionary conscious beings, considered themselves eligible to be political subjects.[51]

---

46 Immanuel Wallerstein, "The Development of the Concept of Development," *Sociological Theory* 2 (1984): 104.
47 Immanuel Wallerstein, "La Revolución Francesa Como Suceso Histórico Mundial," in *Impensar las Ciencias Sociales*, ed. Immanuel Wallerstein (México: S. XXI Editores 1998), 9–26.
48 Ignacio Muñoz Cristi, "Popular Self-Management, Social Intervention, and Utopistics in the Capitalist World-System," *Review* (Fernand Braudel Center) 38, no. 3 (2015): 219. Emphasis in the original.
49 Ibid., 222.
50 Ibid.
51 On the political ambitions of those who had been excluded from decision-making processes before, see Jacques Rancière, *Das Unvernehmen: Politik und Philosophie*, 7th ed. (Berlin: Surhkamp, 2018), 44.

Another consequence of the revolutionary events since 1789 was the creation of the "quintessential protagonist [of the modern world, i.e.] ... the bourgeois. Hero for some, villain for others, the inspiration or lure for most, he has been the shaper of the present and the destroyer of the past."[52] Since the bourgeoisie, however, was merely a replacement of old aristocratic elites by a new financial elite that naturally incorporated some of the former, the historical dialectic taught by Hegel and taken up by Marx needed, at least in the latter's interpretation,[53] a revolution to reach the final stage of the historical process. The proletarian revolution was thus supposed to open and clear the path toward it after a limited political "interregnum," i.e., the "dictatorship of the proletariat."[54] The role of the bourgeois as the new ruling elite and the shortcomings of the French and American Revolutions in particular with regard to creating a totally equal society led to the formulation of a "two-stage theory of national revolution," according to which "socialist parties have the responsibility not only to carry out the proletarian (or second-stage) revolution but also to play a very large role in carrying out the bourgeois (or first-stage) revolution. The argument is that the first stage is historically 'necessary' and that, since the national bourgeoisie in question has 'betrayed' its historic role, it becomes incumbent on the proletariat to play this role for it."[55]

Considering world-systems theory here, one would argue that the existent world-system was not sufficiently transformed. The frustration with this, in combination with the further industrialization needed due to the intensification of the capitalist accumulation process, inevitably caused further frictions within the world-system and, sooner or later, stimulated a new revolutionary attempt to transform the status quo. Wallerstein highlighted that the polarization caused by capital's further centralization in the world-system's core would have a significant effect on the continuously changing social strata within it

---

52 Wallerstein, *The Essential Wallerstein*, 324.
53 On Hegel's idea of a single historical "storyline," see Joshua Foa Dienstag, "Building the Temple of Memory: Hegel's Aesthetic Narrative of History," *The Review of Politics* 56, no. 4 (1994): 697. On the similarities between Marx and Hegel, see, among others, Peter Knapp, "Hegel's Universal in Marx, Durkheim and Weber: The Role of Hegelian Ideas in the Origin of Sociology," *Sociological Forum* 1, no. 4 (1986): 590–595.
54 Mike Schmeitzner, "Lenin und die Diktatur des Proletariats: Begriff, Konzeption, Ermöglichung," *Totalitarismus und Demokratie* 14, no. 1 (2017): 17–69.
55 Wallerstein, *The Essential Wallerstein*, 328.

and thereby increase the tension between two opposing classes, namely the bourgeoisie and the proletarian working class.[56]

The order that had been established by the French Revolution and the following events was shaken in 1848, the other pillar of Hobsbawm's "age of revolution,"[57] when, according to Wallerstein, a "world-revolution ... marked a turning-point in the relations of the three ideologies – rightwing conservatism, centrist liberalism, and leftwing radicalism."[58] The first two would forge an alliance to secure their positions against the menace of the social revolution that could have brought an end to the existent world-system.[59] The radical left elements were unable to change the fate of the revolution, the European continent's "first great proletarian insurrection,"[60] which was eventually suppressed. This led to Wallerstein's conclusion that a revolutionary change needed to be prepared somehow to be successful, especially since spontaneous eruptions of revolutionary spirit would hardly be enough to force a change upon the world-system.[61] Eventually, what "began as a threat to the world liberal regime" turned out to "bec[o]me the crucible in which the dominance of liberalism in the geoculture was ensured."[62] The experience of 1848 naturally stimulated thoughts about revolution, but the experiences of that year also further impacted those who would not represent the radical potential for change in the decades to come.[63]

What Marx and Engels had only briefly touched on in their writings, namely the "dictatorship of the proletariat," played an important role in later debates about revolution, in particular in 1917,[64] when a semi-peripheral country was shaken and transformed by a supposedly successful revolution, though

---

56   Ibid., 329–330.
57   Eric Hobsbawm, *The Age of Revolution: Europe: 1789–1848* (London: Weidenfeld & Nicolson, 1962).
58   Wallerstein, "Antisystemic Movements," 159.
59   Ibid.
60   Charles Tilly, "How Protest Modernized in France, 1845 to 1855," in *The Dimensions of Quantitative Research in History*, eds. William Aydelotte, Allan Bogue, and Robert Fogel (Princeton, NJ: Princeton University Press, 1972), 228.
61   Wallerstein, "Antisystemic Movements," 159–160.
62   Wallerstein, *The Modern World-System*, vol. 4, 96.
63   Herfried Münkler, *Marx, Wagner, Nietzsche: Welt im Umbruch*, 3rd ed. (Berlin: Rowohlt, 2021), 137–173.
64   One could mention the Mexican Revolution (1910) or the Chinese Revolution (1911) here as well.

it was corrupted and turned into a party regime instead.[65] Nevertheless, with regard to the precedent it created and its global impact throughout the 20th century,[66] 1917 was, as Karatasli correctly outlines, much more important for challenging and reconfiguring the modern world-system:

> Especially the success of the 1917 Bolshevik revolution in Russia and the rising tide of proletarian revolutions and national liberation movements went beyond the preceding historical examples of the 1871 Paris commune and 1905 revolutions by demonstrating that the exploited, the oppressed and the excluded could take power, establish their own states, invent new modes of governments and successfully defend it against the ruling classes and imperialist states. In short, despite all of their shortcomings, the revolutions that took place in the early 20th century were unprecedented world-historical achievements.[67]

In fact, the socialist revolutions of the 20th century – Wallerstein mentioned China, Cuba, and Russia in this regard – all occurred in places where revolutionary theorists would not have expected them to happen; instead, they were waiting, too close to Marx's textual legacy, for the revolution to begin in France or Germany. According to Wallerstein, the revolutions of the 20th century

> occurred in countries that, in terms of their internal economic structures in the pre-revolutionary period, had a certain minimum strength in terms of skilled personnel, some manufacturing, and other factors which made it plausible that, within the framework of a capitalist world-economy, such a country could alter its role in the world division of labor within a reasonable

---

65 Wallerstein, *The Essential Wallerstein*, 97. For a detailed analysis see Jacob, *1917*. Similar developments could be observed in relation to the Chinese Revolution. Mao himself commented on this dilemma as follows: "The class struggle is by no means over. ... It will continue to be long and tortuous, and at times will even become very acute. ... Marxists are still a minority among the entire population as well as among the intellectuals. Therefore, Marxism must still develop through struggle. ... Such struggles will never end. This is the law of development of truth and, naturally, of Marxism as well." Mao Tse-Tung, *On the Correct Handling of Contradictions Among the People*, 7th ed. (Peking: Foreign Languages Press, 1966), 37–38, cited in Wallerstein, *The Essential Wallerstein*, 80.
66 Frank Jacob and Riccardo Altieri, eds., *Die Wahrnehmung der Russischen Revolutionen 1917: Zwischen utopischen Träumen und erschütterter Ablehnung* (Berlin: Metropol, 2019).
67 Karatasli, "The Twenty-First Century Revolutions," 307.

6. Wallerstein's World-Systems Theory and the Role of Revolutions 135

period (say 30–50 years) by the use of the technique of mercantilist semi-withdrawal.[68]

This is not surprising, as the following discussion of the interrelationship between semi-periphery and revolution will show. All of the countries in question possessed an ambition to rise within the structures of the existent world-system, either by economic exploitation or through war.[69] The latter, however, triggered the revolution in its Russian context and, at least momentarily, imperiled its rise to the core. This was especially since the bipolar world after the Second World War was still far away, and communism had to negotiate its way through numerous wars and political reconfigurations before the world would be dominated by two antagonist cores during the Cold War.[70]

The events of 1968 were probably the most important to Wallerstein as they were the closest to his own experiences. For Wallerstein, who wrote from an American perspective, the "end of the Second World War marked the onset of two important cyclical shifts in the history of the modern world-system. It marked both the beginning of a Kondratieff A-phase and the moment of undisputed hegemony in the world-system of the United States."[71] For Wallerstein, 1968 was a global revolution, and although the events have been studied in national and regional contexts ever since,[72] he argued that "it was a single revolution. It was marked by demonstrations, disorder, and violence in many parts of the world over a period of at least three years. Its origins, consequences, and lessons cannot be analyzed correctly by appealing to the particular circumstances of the local manifestations of this global phenomenon, however much the local factors conditioned the details of the political and social struggles in

---

68   Wallerstein, *The Essential Wallerstein*, 100.
69   Ibid.
70   Frank Jacob and Tobias Hirschmüller, "War and Communism in the Age of Extremes: An Introduction," in *War and Communism: The Violent Consequences of Ideological Warfare in the 20th Century*, eds. Frank Jacob and Tobias Hirschmüller (Paderborn: Schöningh/ Brill, 2022), 1–58.
71   Wallerstein, "Antisystemic Movements," 161. He considered the timespan of "undisputed hegemony" to be relatively short, namely 25–50 years. Ibid., 162.
72   Works with different foci on the events and their impact include Julian Bourg, *From Revolution to Ethics: May 1968 and Contemporary French Thought* (Montreal: MQUP, 2007); George Katsiaficas, *Global Imagination of 1968: Revolution and Counterrevolution* (Oakland, CA: PM Press, 2018); A. James McAdams and Anthony P. Monta, eds., *Global 1968: Cultural Revolutions in Europe and Latin America* (Notre Dame: University of Notre Dame Press, 2021).

each locality."[73] Wallerstein emphasized the impact of this "world revolution" for his world-system analysis "as *the* crucial moment in which the hegemony of liberalism in the geoculture of the modern world-system was effectively challenged."[74] Unsurprisingly, Wallerstein tried to connect the events to his understanding of the modern world-system and therefore expressed some theses related to this assumption, primarily that "1968 was a revolution *in* and *of* the world-system."[75] Following this, all the single forms and formations of protest were part of "one of the great, formative events in the history of our modern world-system, the kind we call watershed events."[76]

Wallerstein also considered the events of 1968 to be directed first and foremost against the US hegemony within the existent world-system, while in the period of decolonization when the Cold War gained momentum, the "US leadership sought to create a united front at home by minimizing internal class conflict, through economic concessions to the skilled, unionized, working class on the one hand, and through enlisting US labor in the worldwide anti-Communist crusade on the other hand."[77] However, new social movements had formed, and apparently dead political ideas, e.g., anarchist ones,[78] were revived during the global protests in 1968, proving that the "death notice may have been premature."[79] The new protest movements "were led largely by young people who had grown up in a world where the traditional antisystemic movements in their countries were not in an early phase of mobilization but had already achieved their intermediate goal of state power."[80] Consequently,

---

73   Immanuel Wallerstein, "1968, Revolution in the World-System: Theses and Queries," ed. Sharon Zukin, *Theory and Society* 18, no. 4 (1989): 431.
74   Wallerstein, *The Essential Wallerstein*, 355. My emphasis.
75   Ibid. My emphasis.
76   Ibid.
77   Ibid., 357. The Cold War was not really "cold" for Wallerstein, especially not on the periphery. See Immanuel Wallerstein, "What Cold War in Asia? An Interpretative Essay," in *The Cold War in Asia: The Battle for Hearts and Minds*, eds. Hong Liu, Michael Szonyi, and Yangwen Zheng (Leiden/Boston: Brill, 2010), 15–24. On the "peripheries of the Cold War," see Frank Jacob, ed., *Peripheries of the Cold War* (Würzburg: K&N, 2015).
78   George Woodcock had declared anarchism to be dead in 1962. George Woodcock, *Anarchism: A History of Liberitarian Ideas and Movements* (New York: The World Publishing Company, 1962).
79   Carl Levy and Matthew S. Adams, "Introduction," in *The Palgrave Handbook of Anarchism*, eds. Carl Levy and Matthew S. Adams (Cham: Palgrave Macmillan, 2019), 3.
80   Wallerstein, *The Essential Wallerstein*, 359.

they, too, longed for a transformation of the world-system at hand. This, however, also led to internal struggles within the political left, namely between the old and new left,[81] about the course and methods of the revolutionary struggle. However, "[t]he revolution of 1968 had ... a particularly strong component of unplanned spontaneity and therefore, as the thesis says, counter-culture became part of the revolutionary euphoria."[82]

Of course, 1968, like other "[l]egacies of watershed-events," caused "complex phenomena" that are hard to grasp, but the challenges for the world-system's structure were obvious. It was not the first global protest movement,[83] and bonds and connections between radical elements of national societies had been forged much earlier,[84] but 1968 also marked a diversification of a global revolutionary interest group that was no longer divided into a leading working class and other minorities but united through their shared non-acceptance of the status quo.[85] For Wallerstein, the "triumph of the Revolution of 1968" was marked by the changes it achieved concerning "the legal situations (state policies) ... the situations within the antisystemic movements ... [and previously existent] mentalities."[86] It is debatable how "triumphant" 1968 really was, but like any other revolution, the demands had been expressed and could hardly be ignored in the future, although in many regards, the aims of the global protesters have still not been achieved. According to Wallerstein, since 1968, six different anti-systemic movements have co-existed. Although they were relatively hostile during the revolutionary events, especially since "all six varieties have some significant antisystemic heritage, some continuing antisystemic resonance, and some further antisystemic potential,"[87] most still exist and (some-

---

81   Philipp Gassert and Martin Klimke, eds., *1968: On the Edge of World Revolution* (Montréal/New York: Black Rose Books, 2018); Ingrid Gilcher-Holtey, ed., *1968: Eine Wahrnehmungsrevolution? Horizont-Verschiebungen des Politischen in den 1960er und 1970er Jahren* (Berlin: Oldenbourg, 2013); Michael Walzer, "La Nueva Izquierda: 1968 y post scriptum," *Revista Mexicana de Ciencias Políticas y Sociales* 63 (2018): 85–97.
82   Wallerstein, *The Essential Wallerstein*, 361.
83   Marcel Bois, "1916–1921: Ein globaler Aufruhr," in *Zeiten des Aufruhrs (1916–1921): Globale Proteste, Streiks und Revolutionen gegen den Ersten Weltkrieg und seine Auswirkungen*, eds. Marcel Bois and Frank Jacob (Berlin: Metropol, 2020), 13–57.
84   Frank Jacob and Mario Keßler, eds., *Transatlantic Radicalism* (Liverpool: Liverpool University Press, 2021).
85   Wallerstein, *The Essential Wallerstein*, 361–365.
86   Ibid., 364.
87   Ibid., 366.

times) intersectionally overlap today. Wallerstein categorized these six movements as follows:

(a) In the Western countries, there are "old left" movements in the form of the trade-unions and segments of the traditional left parties. [...]. (b) In the same Western countries, there is a wide variety of new social movements [...].[88] (c) In the socialist bloc, there are the traditional Communist parties in power [...]. (d) In this same socialist bloc, a network is emerging of extra-party organizations quite disparate in nature, which seem increasingly to be taking on some of the flavor of Western new social movements [...]. (e) In the [so-called] Third World, there are segments of those traditional national liberation movements still in power ... or heirs to such movements no longer in power [...]. (f) And finally, in these same ... countries, there are new movements that reject some of the "universalist" themes of previous movements (seen as "Western" themes) and put forward "indigenist" forms of protest, often in religious clothing.[89]

The revolutionary wave of 1968 was consequently very diverse, presenting a conglomerate of protest formations, but just as 1848 had failed in the 19th century, as Giovanni Arrighi, Terrence Hopkins, and Immanuel Wallerstein remarked, the 20th-century protesters were also unsuccessful because "the bubble of popular enthusiasm and radical innovations was burst within a relatively short period."[90]

Other world-system scholars do not consider the impact of 1968 as tremendous as Wallerstein did. To name just one example, Valentine M. Moghadam argued that "[i]t seems more appropriate to call 1968 a dress rehearsal for the events of the new century – the anti-globalization protests, the World Social Forum, and the Latin American pink tide starting in 2001; and in 2011, the Arab Spring, the European anti-austerity summer, and the American Occupy Wall Street encampments."[91] However, she also considered the impact on the Arab Spring(s) of some of the protest movements that, in Wallerstein's view, formed

---

88 These represented minorities of all sorts.
89 Ibid., 365.
90 Giovanni Arrighi, Terrence Hopkins, and Immanuel Wallerstein, "1968: The Great Rehearsal," in *Revolution in the World-System*, ed. Terry Boswell (New York: Greenwood Press, 1989), 19–20.
91 Valentine M. Moghadam, "The Semi-Periphery, World Revolution, and the Arab Spring: Reflections on Tunisia," *Journal of World-Systems Research* 23, no. 2 (2017): 624.

or were formally established in or after 1968.[92] The developments in the MENA region, i.e., what were called the "new Arab revolutions,"[93] among other things, were, in fact, revolutionary and related to the world-system. As a consequence of the events since 2011, this also had a tremendous impact on the world-system because it began to change or reconfigure its original realms due to immense movements within the world-system's different zones or spheres and contesting worldviews.[94] Among these, once again, was the question of the geography of revolutions.[95] Again, the revolutionary movements seemed to be particularly strong in the semi-periphery. As mentioned before, it therefore makes sense to take a closer look at the relationship between revolutions and the "buffer zone" of the world-system, which tends to separate core and periphery to avoid direct contact between the exploiter and the exploited. Consequently, the next section will try to make a point for a better understanding of the semi-periphery's revolutionary potential and its role in protest formations directed against an existent world-system.

The Semi-Periphery as Control Mechanism and Revolutionary Space

Wallerstein's semi-periphery, an intermediate between core and center that was also "theorized to be a blended mix of core and peripheral activities,"[96] seems to be a particularly lively space for revolutionary developments that intend to change the current status of a country or region within the world-system. The co-existence of peripheral and core elements within the same realm makes a clash between these two parts of the ambivalent world-system much more likely, intensifying the revolutionary potential in the intermediate sphere. Although it exists, in a way, to flatten the dichotomy between core and periphery and to avoid the peripheral regions of the world-system directly

---

92 Ibid., 625.
93 Farhad Khosrokhavar, *The New Arab Revolutions that Shook the World* (Boulder, CO: Paradigm Publishers, 2012).
94 Hamid Dabashi, *The Arab Spring: The End of Postcolonialism* (London: Zed Books, 2012); Gilbert Achcar, *The People Want: A Radical Exploration of the Arab Uprising* (Berkeley, CA: University of California Press, 2013).
95 David N. Livingstone and Charles J. Withers, eds., *Geography and Revolution* (Chicago, IL: University of Chicago Press, 2005).
96 Albert J. Bergesen, "World-System Theory after Andre Gunder Frank," *Journal of World-Systems Research* 21, no. 1 (2015): 147.

contesting the core, it is hardly surprising that revolutions very often take place in semi-peripheral regions. The following section intends to explain this interrelationship in some detail.

The modern world-system as a concept is, according to Albert J. Bergesen, "defined by a core-periphery division of labor which would include any interregional, inter-societal, or even inter-city division of labor with a dominant center and a dependent edge, e.g. with a core and periphery."[97] In the modern world, as Wallerstein argued with regard to this dichotomic divide, there exist

> symbiotic dyads of barbarian and civilized, non-Western and Western, periphery and core, proletarian and bourgeois, the dominated and the dominant, the oppressed and the oppressors. None of these pairs of terms involve two separate phenomena brought into (external) relationship with one another. Rather the terms represent positions on a continuum which are the outcome of a single process. The creation of the one was the creation of the other – both materially and ideologically.[98]

These dichotomies were emblematic of the world-system; the periphery and semi-periphery served the core's main interests and were even only created or turned into such by the expansion of the regions or states that would later determine the core by their power and wealth. This, however, also emphasizes that neither the core nor the other two spheres of the world-system were supposed to be or should be understood as static. The world-system fluctuates, and the positions within it can change through historical processes of advance or decline, technological shifts, or even the end of factors that determine its shape at a particular historical moment.

This was a natural development that nevertheless seems to have been camouflaged by traditional narratives because historical traditions were reinvented to match the self-perception of a nation, especially with regard to artificial continuities that legitimized one's own superiority, often in abstraction to other regions of the world or the world-system.[99] "Tradition," as Wallerstein highlighted, "is always a contemporary social creation. Civilizations are the way we describe our particularities in terms of millenial heritages. We are not free to be totally arbitrary. There must be some surface plausibility to the

---

97   Ibid., 148.
98   Wallerstein, "Civilizations and Modes of Production," 1.
99   Ibid., 2–4.

6. Wallerstein's World-Systems Theory and the Role of Revolutions

continuities asserted."[100] Although modernity, or whatever we tend to call it, has been dominated by one capitalist world-system, "[h]istorically, there have been countless mini-systems, a large but countable number of world-empires, a similarly large but countable number of world-economies."[101] The latter were transformed – although not exclusively[102] – by revolutions that also consolidated the modern world-system. However, the latter's existence has also been contested by revolutionary events directed against the nature and shape of this system itself. The semi-periphery was supposed to avoid such anti-systemic revolutionary eruptions between the extreme positions in the world-system, i.e., the core and the periphery, as direct contacts or exchanges between these zones might have automatically increased the revolutionary potential in a given time frame.

In the world-system, i.e., "a system of unequal exchange, the semi-peripheral country stands in between in terms of the kinds of products it exports and in terms of the wage levels and profit margins it knows."[103] In this regard, the semi-periphery prevents the exploited from being too close to their exploiters, thereby seeming to ease the process of exploitation as such. At the same time, the semi-periphery prevents too much anger about one's peripheral position because it offers a suitable and achievable dream of advance without the overwhelming effect of the core experience that would bluntly show why people in the periphery were poor. The semi-periphery exists because the world-system, according to Wallerstein, "could not function without being tri-modal."[104]

The capitalist world system needs a semi-peripheral sector for two reasons: one primarily political and one politico-econamic. The political reason is very straightforward and rather elementary. A system based on unequal

---

100 Ibid., 4.
101 Ibid., 5.
102 Wallerstein argues in this regard: "Since world-empires operated structurally in a cycle of expansion and contraction, they were continuously abolishing mini-systems by absorbing them and later 'releasing' zones within which new mini-systems could be created. World-economies were inherently much more unstable than world-empires, and were constantly either being converted into world-empires by conquest or disintegrating, allowing mini-systems to re-emerge." Ibid., 6.
103 Immanuel Wallerstein, "Dependence in an Interdependent World: The Limited Possibilities of Transformation within the Capitalist World Economy," *African Studies Review* 17, no. 1 (1974): 6.
104 Ibid., 3.

reward must constantly worry about political rebellion of oppressed elements. A polarized system with a small distinct high-status and high-income sector facing a relatively homogeneous low-status and low-income sector including the overwhelming majority of individuals in the system leads quite rapidly to the formation of classes für sich and acute, disintegrating struggle. The major political means by which such crises are averted is the creation of "middle" sectors, which tend to think of themselves primarily as better off than the lower sector rather than as worse off than the upper sector. This obvious mechanism, operative in all kinds of social structures, serves the same function in world systems."[105]

Of course, it would be too simple to generalize everything within the world according to such a tri-modal system, and Wallerstein himself pointed out that "it would be an oversimplification not to bear in the front of our mind that each structural sector contains states of varying degrees of political and economic strength."[106] However, it is precisely this complexity and co-existence of differences within the semi-periphery that makes it a hotbed for revolutionary change; because of its closeness to both the core, which turns into a supposedly achievable aim, and the periphery, which resembles a possible decline, the different elements within the semi-periphery struggle against each other. If poverty were sufficient as a reason for revolution, we could probably better predict this relatively unpredictable social phenomenon.[107] Instead, it is the simultaneous co-existence of both possibilities, poverty and social advancement, that seems to allow revolutionary movements to gain ground, especially if the chances for social change coexist with a weakness of the ruling regime, whose elites look too often to the core status they want to achieve, forgetting the peripheral elements that are still part of their own sphere.

As capitalism, and thereby the modern world-system on which it is based, "is a system based on the logic of the endless accumulation of capital,"[108] it simply cannot exist without the exploitation of many for the benefit of a few. To put it in Wallersteinian terms, the core can only exist through and by exploiting the rest of the world-system. For those in the core region, the system is supposed to remain static with regard to their own position because

---

105 Ibid., 4.
106 Ibid., 5.
107 Chalmers Johnson, *Revolutionstheorie*, trans. Karl Römer (Cologne/Berlin: Kiepenhauer & Witsch, 1971), 141; Jacob, *#Revolution*, 57–69.
108 Wallerstein, *The Essential Wallerstein*, 335.

[c]apitalists do not want competition, but monopoly. They seek to accumulate capital not via profit but via rent. They want not to be bourgeois but to be aristocrats. And since historically – that is, from the sixteenth century to the present – we have had a deepening and a widening of the capitalist logic in the capitalist world-economy, there is more not less monopoly, there is more rent and less profit, there is more aristocracy and less bourgeoisie.[109]

At the same time, however, the static continuation of the division of the spheres within the world-system must be camouflaged, as the only thing that keeps people and their possible revolutionary potential in check is hope: the hope to end their lives in the (semi-)periphery and work as part of the core. Therefore, the world-system needs the semi-periphery to provide such immediate hope for social advancement for everyone if they only work hard enough to make their way up. Of course, there are people who, due to migration and their participation in the world's exploitative system, will eventually pave the way for some to the core. Hence, some also return from the core to lead the revolutionary movement in their sphere of origin because they no longer intend to accept the given order of the world-system.

Alongside such conscience-related forms of protest formation, which were particularly important during the age of decolonization in the aftermath of the Second World War, there are other reasons why some regions of the world-system revolt against their place or rank within it. For instance, the American Revolution was triggered, at least to some extent, by the rivalry between the different interests of American colonial and British businesses.[110] While it did not involve all parts of colonial American society – which itself could be understood as a mini-system of core, semi-periphery, and periphery, with different interest groups within these spheres[111] – the eventual clash between the semi-peripheral elites of the colony and the core elites could not be prevented. This clash culminated within the American Revolution, although this was less of a social and more of an economic struggle between two spheres of the 18th-century world-system. One can consequently argue that proximity to and rivalry

---

109 Ibid., 339.
110 Immanuel Wallerstein, *The Modern World-System*, vol. 3: *The Second Era of Great Expansion of the Capitalist World-Economy, 1730s-1840s* (San Diego, CA: Academic Press, 1989), 196 and 202. See also Jonathan Leitner, "Classical World-Systems Analysis, the Historical Geography of British North America, and the Regional Politics of Colonial/Revolutionary New York," *Journal of World-Systems Research* 24, no. 2 (2018): 409.
111 Wallerstein, *The Modern World-System*, 3: 237.

with the core stimulates revolutionary developments in the semi-periphery, especially since the advance to become the core would demand a contesting approach toward the latter rather than an attempt to fuse with it. Bearing the three parts of the slogan made famous by the French Revolution in mind, i.e., "liberty, equality, fraternity," the American Revolution was interested in "liberty in the political arena [and] equality in the economic arena," but not so much in "fraternity in the socio-cultural arena."[112] Although this made the revolutionary process in the American context rather "half-hearted,"[113] it showed which elements and competitions turned the semi-periphery into a revolutionary space.

At the same time, a revolution demanding liberty, for Wallerstein, could not exist without the concomitant equality that would be achieved through it:

> The antinomy of liberty and equality seems to be absurd. I don't really understand myself how one can be "free" if there is inequality, since those who have more always have options that are not available to those who have less, and therefore the latter are less free. And similarly I don't really understand how there can be equality without liberty since, in the absence of liberty, some have more political power than others, and hence it follows that there is inequality. I am not suggesting a verbal game here but a rejection of the distinction. Liberty-equality is a single concept.[114]

When liberty, especially in the semi-periphery, only exists for the small elite that exploits the majority of the sphere to keep its position on top and obtain a chance to move toward the core, the revolutionary potential almost naturally increases. The world-system's "standard systemic features of hierarchy and exploitation"[115] – in particular through unequal trade[116] – polarized the world. However, it also created such polarization in the middle of its extremes, namely in the semi-periphery, which keeps the core and the periphery from having direct contact. Underdevelopment was therefore politically intended and "a consequence of historical capitalism."[117]

---

112 Wallerstein, *The Essential Wallerstein*, 371.
113 For a more detailed debate of this evaluation, see Frank Jacob, *1776: Die halbherzige Revolution* (Marburg: Büchner, 2023).
114 Wallerstein, *The Essential Wallerstein*, 371.
115 Wallerstein, "Antisystemic Movements," 158.
116 Wallerstein, *Welt-System-Analyse*, 17.
117 Ibid., 18. On a related argument, see also Walter Rodney, *How Europe Underdeveloped Africa* (London: Bogle-L'Ouverture, 1972).

6. Wallerstein's World-Systems Theory and the Role of Revolutions 145

It was European expansion during the "long sixteenth century (1450–1640)"[118] that created the three spheres of the world-system, while capitalism, even before nation-states were established,[119] divided the world into these spheres to serve the economic purpose of accumulating capital through exploitation. The core regions gained from "the strength of the state-machinery" that allowed them to better control the periphery from afar so that "intervention of outsiders via war, subversion, and diplomacy [was usually] the lot of peripheral states."[120] In the divided world-system, it was consequently clear where and why the influence of the core had the most negative impact, but in most cases, the periphery was not the stage for revolutionary attempts to change the existent system. The semi-periphery, on the other hand, seems to have had more revolutionary potential, although its natural role in the world-system was supposed to achieve the opposite. According to Wallerstein,

> The semi-periphery is needed to make a capitalist world-economy run smoothly. Both kinds of world-system, the world-empire with a redistributive economy and the world-economy with a capitalist market economy, involve markedly unequal distribution of rewards. Thus, logically, there is immediately posed the question of how it is possible politically for such a system to persist. [...] The semi-periphery is then assigned as it were a specific economic role, but the reason is less economic than political. That is to say, one might make a good case that the world-economy would function every bit as well without a semi-periphery. But it would be far less *politically* stable, for it would mean a polarized world-system. The existence of the third category means precisely that the upper stratum is not faced with the *unified* opposition of all the others because the *middle* stratum is both exploited and exploiter. It follows that the specific economic role is not all that important, and has thus changed through the various historical stages of the modern world-system.[121]

However, from a revolution-oriented analysis, this middle stratum stimulates the particular danger of the semi-periphery as a revolutionary space. Nowhere else in the world system is an advance to the core and a decline to the periphery as close as in the semi-periphery. Nowhere else do the core and the periphery

---

118 Wallerstein, *The Essential Wallerstein*, 93.
119 Ibid., 87.
120 Ibid., 89.
121 Ibid., 89 and 91. Emphasis in original.

coexist as close as in this sphere. This is why the social and political conflicts related to this dichotomy are particularly strong and intensify the revolutionary potential for a violent change of or within the world-system. For Moghadam, the "theorization of the semi-periphery is one of the most significant conceptual contributions to our understanding of both the global economy and cycles of contention."[122] I would add that only a closer analysis of the semi-periphery will allow a better understanding of the development of revolutions as a consequence of global exploitation and further explain the interrelation of anti-globalizing social movements in the semi-periphery.[123]

Conclusion: Revolutions of the Future and the Role of the World-System

When the three-layered structure of the world-system that Wallerstein established is contested or changed, the whole system begins to disintegrate and transform.[124] In this regard, the world-system seems to be flexible, and the semi-periphery is where this flexibility is supposedly the most visible. Since capitalism is based on the exploitation of labor and its value, as a system, it "requires movement and change, at least formal change. The maximal accumulation of capital requires not only goods and capital to circulate but manpower as well. It requires in addition a constant evolution in the organization of production in terms both of the nature of the leading sectors and of the sites of production."[125] While these changes constantly happen, capitalism also creates a strong polarization, especially with regard to the core and the periphery as the extremes within the world-system. Next to the spheral polarization, there is also a strong social polarization, with the exploited poor majority of the world on the one hand and the exploiting rich minority on the other. These polarizations are particularly felt in the semi-periphery, which is why the forces contesting this systematic polarized exploitation often begin to move there. What

---

122   Moghadam, "The Semi-Periphery," 620.
123   Moghadam emphasized this relation as well: "What I find especially interesting is the correlation of semi-peripheral development with both the evolution of capitalism and the emergence of revolutions and rebellions." Ibid. See also Valentine M. Moghadam, *Globalization and Social Movements: Islamism, Feminism, and the Global Justice Movement*, 2nd ed. (Lanham, MD: Rowman & Littlefield, 2013), 72–73.
124   Wallerstein, *The Essential Wallerstein*, 90.
125   Ibid., 270.

6. Wallerstein's World-Systems Theory and the Role of Revolutions 147

we consider revolutionary movements directed against globalization are, in fact, anti-capitalist and anti-world-system movements that intend to dissolve the capitalist system of control within the particular sphere where the revolutionary fire is sparked, i.e., the semi-periphery. The world-system as such, including its shape and structure, can be contested because, as Wallerstein remarked,

> the capitalist world-economy is an historical system. And being historical, it has a life cycle and, as any other such system, must at some point cease to function as the consequence of the aggregated results of its eventually paralyzing contradictions. But it is also a system which is based on a particular logic, that of the ceaseless accumulation of capital. Such a system therefore must preach the possibility of limitless expansion.[126]

When the accumulation of capital can no longer be achieved through new resources and the exploitation of them and a global labor force, the system will have to be rearranged. This can be done through revolution, as often occurs in the semi-periphery. On the other hand, it can also be contested by war, especially those waged for the control of access to resources to be exploited in the future.

When the ideological explanation of Western superiority is challenged, a politically and economically motivated underdevelopment will be made visible. This in itself stimulates revolutions against Western control and capitalist exploitation, as in the age of decolonization after the Second World War. Given what has been discussed in this chapter, one could argue that revolutions are as modern as the world-system because they are a by-product of the latter's existence. The waves of revolution express the wish to contest the structure of the world-system and one's position within it, yet at the same time, they pose a threat to its very existence. That these revolutions often start within the semi-periphery is hardly surprising, even though this sphere was supposed to stabilize the world-system. In reality, its existence often triggers social and political conflicts that turn into dangerous revolutionary processes, within which the counter-revolutionary forces intend to keep the world-system unchallenged and unchanged. The revolution of 1968, according to Wallerstein, contested the status quo in different ways, as it not only questioned the role of scientists in

---

126 Ibid., 271.

maintaining the existent situation but also highlighted the position of those minorities who were particularly exploited through and by the system.[127]

Revolutions consequently must continue to exist as long as the foundation of the world-system is exploitation. This means that capitalism is a root for revolutionary change, and although this has been interpreted and contested differently in the past,[128] revolutions' success was rather limited: "Reformers and revolutionaries have been trying to shore up socialist principles and practices for over a century, and though millions of people have been dragged out of poverty and hunger in some parts of the world, arguably the global situation today is as bad as it has ever been."[129] Regardless of the failures of the past, revolutions, and in particular worldwide revolutionary movements, i.e., "time-bound clusters of local, national, and transnational struggles,"[130] will continue to challenge the world-system's existence. Wallerstein himself hoped that humanity would at one point achieve a "socialist world-government,"[131] which has evidently not yet been achieved. The rejection of the Enlightenment and the necessity to overcome capitalist exploitation through revolution by the "harbingers of doom"[132] has been successful. However, it remains to be seen if the revolutionary dream can overcome the modern world-system, opening the door to a post-modern, post-world-system, free, and equal future society that is no longer a utopian dream but a social and democratic reality for all.

Works Cited

Achcar, Gilbert. *The People Want: A Radical Exploration of the Arab Uprising*. Berkeley, CA: University of California Press, 2013.

Arrighi, Giovanni, Terrence Hopkins and Immanuel Wallerstein. "1968: The Great Rehearsal." In *Revolution in the World-System*, edited by Terry Boswell, 19–31. New York: Greenwood Press, 1989.

Bergesen, Albert J. "World-System Theory after Andre Gunder Frank." *Journal of World-Systems Research* 21, no. 1 (2015): 147–161.

---

127 Wallerstein, *Welt-System-Analyse*, 22.
128 Leslie Sklair, "World Revolution or Socialism, Community by Community, in the Anthropocene?" *Journal of World-Systems Research* 25, no. 2 (2019): 298.
129 Ibid., 300.
130 Moghadam, "The Semi-Periphery," 623.
131 Wallerstein, "Civilizations and Modes of Production," 5.
132 Ibid., 9.

Blair, Jennifer, and Marion Werner. "New Geographies of Uneven Development in Global Formation: Thinking with Chase-Dunn." *Journal of World-System Research* 23, no. 2 (2017): 604–619.

Boatcă, Manuela. "Global Inequalities *avant la lettre*: Immanuel Wallerstein's Contribution." *Socio* 15 (2021): 71–91.

Bois, Marcel. "1916–1921: Ein globaler Aufruhr." In *Zeiten des Aufruhrs (1916–1921): Globale Proteste, Streiks und Revolutionen gegen den Ersten Weltkrieg und seine Auswirkungen*, edited by Marcel Bois and Frank Jacob, 13–57. Berlin: Metropol, 2020.

Boswell, Terry and William J. Dixon. "Dependency and Rebellion: A Cross-National Analysis." *American Sociological Review* 55, no. 4 (1990): 540–559.

Boswell, Terry ed. *Revolution in the World-System*. New York: Greenwood Press, 1989.

Bourg, Julian. *From Revolution to Ethics: May 1968 and Contemporary French Thought*. Montreal: MQUP, 2007.

Chase-Dunn, Christopher. *Global Formation: Structures of the World-Economy*. Oxford: Blackwell, 1989.

Chase-Dunn, Christopher and Thomas D. Hall. *Rise and Demise: Comparing World-Systems*. Boulder, CO: Westview Press, 1997.

Dabashi, Hamid. *The Arab Spring: The End of Postcolonialism*. London: Zed Books, 2012.

Engels, Friedrich. *Socialism: Utopian and Scientific*. Accessed November 25, 2022. https://www.marxists.org/archive/marx/works/1880/soc-utop/index.htm.

Gassert, Philipp and Martin Klimke, eds. *1968: On the Edge of World Revolution*. Montréal/New York: Black Rose Books, 2018.

Gilcher-Holtey, Ingrid, ed. *1968: Eine Wahrnehmungsrevolution? Horizont-Verschiebungen des Politischen in den 1960er und 1970er Jahren*. Berlin: Oldenbourg, 2013.

Hindrichs, Gunnar. *Philosophie der Revolution*. Berlin: Suhrkamp, 2017.

Hobsbawm, Eric. *The Age of Revolution: Europe: 1789–1848*. London: Weidenfeld & Nicolson, 1962.

Jacob, Frank. *1776: Die halbherzige Revolution*. Marburg: Büchner, 2023.

Jacob, Frank. *1917: Die korrumpierte Revolution*. Marburg: Büchner, 2020.

Jacob, Frank. *#Revolution: Wer, warum, wann und wie viele?* Marburg: Büchner, 2022.

Jacob, Frank. "Friedrich Engels and Revolution Theory: The Legacy of a Revolutionary Life." In *Engels@200: Reading Friedrich Engels in the 21st Century*, edited by Frank Jacob, 49–90. Marburg: Büchner, 2020.
Jacob, Frank, ed. *Peripheries of the Cold War*. Würzburg: K&N, 2015.
Jacob, Frank. *Revolution and the Global Struggle for Modernity*, vol. 1: *The Atlantic Revolutions*. London: Anthem Press, 2023.
Jacob, Frank. "Revolutionen und Weltgeschichte." In *Revolution: Beiträge zu einem historischen Phänomen der globalen Moderne*, edited by Frank Jacob and Riccardo Altieri, 11–40. Berlin: WVB, 2019.
Jacob, Frank and Mario Keßler, eds. *Transatlantic Radicalism*. Liverpool: Liverpool University Press, 2021.
Johnson, Chalmers. *Revolutionstheorie*. Translated by Karl Römer. Cologne/Berlin: Kiepenhauer & Witsch, 1971.
Kandal, Terry R. "Revolution, Racism and Sexism: Challenges for World-System Analysis." *Studies in Comparative International Development* 25, no. 4 (1990): 86–102.
Karatasli, Sahan Savas. "The Twenty-First Century Revolutions and Internationalism: A World-Historical Perspective." *Journal of World-Systems Research* 25, no. 2 (2019): 306–320.
Katsiaficas, George. *Global Imagination of 1968: Revolution and Counterrevolution*. Oakland, CA: PM Press, 2018.
Khosrokhavar, Farhad. *The New Arab Revolutions that Shook the World*. Boulder, CO: Paradigm Publishers, 2012.
Kondratiev, Nikolai. "About the Question of the Major Cycles of the Conjuncture." [In Russian.] *Planovoe Khozyaystvo* 8 (1926): 167–181.
Kossok, Manfred and Walter Markov. "Zur Methodologie der vergleichenden Revolutionsgeschichte der Neuzeit." In *Studien zur Vergleichenden Revolutionsgeschichte 1500–1917*, edited by Manfred Kossok, 1–28. Berlin: Akademie Verlag, 1974.
Kuznar, Lawrence A. "Periphery-Core Relations in the Inca Empire: Carrots and Sticks in an Andean World System." *Journal of World-Systems Research* 2, no. 1 (1996): 322–349.
Levy, Carl and Matthew S. Adams. "Introduction." In *The Palgrave Handbook of Anarchism*, edited by Carl Levy and Matthew S. Adams, 1–23. Cham: Palgrave Macmillan, 2019.
Leitner, Jonathan. "Classical World-Systems Analysis, the Historical Geography of British North America, and the Regional Politics of Colonial/

Revolutionary New York." *Journal of World-Systems Research* 24, no. 2 (2018): 404–434.

Livingstone, David N. and Charles J. Withers, eds. *Geography and Revolution*. Chicago, IL: University of Chicago Press, 2005.

Luxemburg, Rosa. *Die Akkumulation des Kapitals: Ein Beitrag zur ökonomischen Erklärung des Imperialismus*. Berlin: Paul Singer, 1913.

Mao Tse-Tung. *On the Correct Handling of Contradictions Among the People*. 7th ed. Peking: Foreign Languages Press, 1966.

McAdams, A. James and Anthony P. Monta, eds. *Global 1968: Cultural Revolutions in Europe and Latin America*. Notre Dame: University of Notre Dame Press, 2021.

Moghadam, Valentine M. *Globalization and Social Movements: Islamism, Feminism, and the Global Justice Movement*. 2nd ed. Lanham, MD: Rowman & Littlefield, 2013.

Moghadam, Valentine M. "The Semi-Periphery, World Revolution, and the Arab Spring: Reflections on Tunisia." *Journal of World-Systems Research* 23, no. 2 (2017): 620–636.

Motadel, David, ed. *Revolutionary World: Global Upheaval in the Modern Age*. Cambridge: Cambridge University Press, 2021.

Münkler, Herfried. *Marx, Wagner, Nietzsche: Welt im Umbruch*. 3rd ed. Berlin: Rowohlt, 2021.

Muñoz Cristi, Ignacio. "Popular Self-Management, Social Intervention, and Utopistics in the Capitalist World-System." *Review* (Fernand Braudel Center) 38, no. 3 (2015): 219–252.

Reifer, Thomas, ed. *Globalization, Hegemony and Power: Antisystemic Movements and the Global System*. London: Routledge, 2015.

Rodney, Walter. *How Europe Underdeveloped Africa*. London: Bogle-L'Ouverture, 1972.

Schmeitzner, Mike. "Lenin und die Diktatur des Proletariats: Begriff, Konzeption, Ermöglichung." *Totalitarismus und Demokratie* 14, no. 1 (2017): 17–69.

Sklair, Leslie. "World Revolution or Socialism, Community by Community, in the Anthropocene?" *Journal of World-Systems Research* 25, no. 2 (2019): 297–305.

Smith, Jackie and Dawn Wiest. *Social Movements in the World-System: The Politics of Crisis and Transformation*. New York: Russell Sage, 2012.

Smith, Michael E. "The Aztec Empire and the Mesoamerican World System." In *Empires: Perspectives from Archaeology and History*, edited by Susan E. Alcock et al., 128–154. Cambridge: Cambridge University Press, 2001.

Tilly, Charles. "How Protest Modernized in France, 1845 to 1855." In *The Dimensions of Quantitative Research in History*, edited by William Aydelotte, Allan Bogue, and Robert Fogel, 192–255. Princeton, NJ: Princeton University Press, 1972.

Wallerstein, Immanuel. "1968, Revolution in the World-System: Theses and Queries." Edited by Sharon Zukin. *Theory and Society* 18, no. 4 (1989): 431–449.

Wallerstein, Immanuel. "American Slavery and the Capitalist World-Economy." *American Journal of Sociology* 81, no. 5 (1976): 1199–1213.

Wallerstein, Immanuel. "Antisystemic Movements: History and Dilemmas." In Samir Amin et al., *Transforming the Revolution: Social Movements and the World-System*, 13–53. New York: Monthly Review Press, 1990.

Wallerstein, Immanuel. "Antisystemic Movements, Yesterday and Today." *Journal of World-Systems Research* 20, no. 2 (2014): 158–172.

Wallerstein, Immanuel. "Civilizations and Modes of Production: Conflicts and Convergences." *Theory and Society* 5, no. 1 (1978): 1–10.

Wallerstein, Immanuel. "Dependence in an Interdependent World: The Limited Possibilities of Transformation within the Capitalist World Economy." *African Studies Review* 17, no. 1 (1974): 1–26.

Wallerstein, Immanuel. "Development: Lodestar or Illusion?" *Economic and Political Weekly* 23, no. 39 (1988): 2017–2019 and 2021–2023.

Wallerstein, Immanuel. "From Feudalism to Capitalism: Transition or Transitions?" *Social Forces* 55, no. 2 (1976): 273–283.

Wallerstein, Immanuel. "La Revolución Francesa Como Suceso Histórico Mundial." In *Impensar las Ciencias Sociales*, ed. Immanuel Wallerstein (México: S. XXI Editores 1998).

Wallerstein, Immanuel. "Las Tres Hegemonías Sucesivas en la Historia de la Economía-Mundo." In *Capitalismo Histórico y Movimientos Antisistémicos*, edited by Immanuel Wallerstein, 212–223. Madrid: Akal, 2004.

Wallerstein, Immanuel. "Marxisms as Utopias: Evolving Ideologies." *American Journal of Sociology* 91, no. 6 (1986): 1295–1308.

Wallerstein, Immanuel. "The Development of the Concept of Development." *Sociological Theory* 2 (1984): 102–116.

Wallerstein, Immanuel. *The Essential Wallerstein*. New York: The New Press, 2000.

Wallerstein, Immanuel. *The Modern World System*, 4 vols. New York: Academic Press, 1974–1989; Berkeley, CA: University of California Press, 2011.

Wallerstein, Immanuel. "The Rise and Future Demise of the World Capitalist System: Concepts for Comparative Analysis." *Comparative Studies in Society and History* 16, no. 4 (1974): 387–415.

Wallerstein, Immanuel. *Welt-System-Analyse: Eine Einführung*. Wiesbaden: VS Verlag für Sozialwissenschaften, 2019.

Wallerstein, Immanuel. "What Cold War in Asia? An Interpretative Essay." In *The Cold War in Asia: The Battle for Hearts and Minds*, edited by Hong Liu, Michael Szonyi, and Yangwen Zheng, 15–24. Leiden/Boston: Brill, 2010.

Walzer, Michael. "La Nueva Izquierda: 1968 y post scriptum." *Revista Mexicana de Ciencias Políticas y Sociales* 63 (2018): 85–97.

Williams, Gregory P. *Contesting the Global Order: The Radical Political Economy of Perry Anderson and Immanuel Wallerstein*. Albany, NY: State University of New York Press, 2020.

Woodcock, George. *Anarchism: A History of Libertarian Ideas and Movements*. New York: The World Publishing Company, 1962.

7. Nationalist New Education
A Wallersteinian Approach to Education in the World-System

Sebastian Engelmann

Sometimes it is worthwhile to take a second – or even a third – look at things that are known to almost every scholar involved with the history of alternative educational thought in Europe. New theoretical perspectives can help to understand long-term developments better.[1] They might also shine a new light on the peculiarities of a history of educational practices as we are used to them nowadays. Before this chapter connects history and theory, it must travel back roughly 120 years into the past. In 1896, the German educator Hermann Lietz[2] stayed at the boarding school of Cecil Reddie called Abbotsholme in the East Midlands of England. Lietz, who was a student of Wilhelm Rein[3] at the teachers' seminary at the University of Jena and a reader of the anti-Semitic and deeply racist writings of Paul de Lagarde, developed a new, supposedly better, alternative way of thinking about education based on his Protestant beliefs and

---

1 I would especially like to thank Frank Jacob, Riccardo Altieri, Stephen Shapiro, Marcus Emmerich, and all participants of the workshop "Migration, Nationalism and World System Theory" (online workshop, November 2020) for their helpful comments and fresh takes on Wallerstein.
2 Hermann Lietz (1886–1919) was a German educator. Lietz is known for being the founding figure of the *Landerziehungsheime* (country boarding schools) that gained a high degree of popularity at the beginning of the 20th century and are part of the German *Reformpädagogik*, which will be discussed in more detail in the next pages.
3 Wilhelm Rein (1847–1929) was Professor of Pedagogy at the University of Jena. Rein was responsible for the teachers' seminary that made teacher education at the university well-known internationally. Furthermore, he was one of the most prominent Herbartians – educators who read and further developed the ideas of Johann Friedrich Herbart (1776–1841).

desire to develop the German nation. After his return to Germany, Lietz published a work titled *Emlosstobba* (1897). The term *"Emlohstobba"* is an anagram of the name of his old school, Abbotsholme. In his text – fully titled "Emlohstobba: Fiction or Fact? Images from School Life of the Past, Present and Future" (*Emlohstobba: Roman oder Wirklichkeit? Bilder aus dem Schulleben*)[4] – Lietz processed his experiences in Abbotsholme in a partly belletristic, partly theoretical writing. Here, some of Lietz's first ideas for a pedagogy that emphasizes the potentiality of individual human nature while tying individual development to the development of the nation emerge at the turn from the 19th to the 20th century from the dense descriptions of the orderly coexistence in the school state. His reflections on the experienced pedagogical arrangement in which pupils were allowed to take on numerous tasks and were themselves involved in the governance of "their" school state ultimately led to further theorizing and adaptation to the circumstances in the schools later founded by Lietz in Germany.

In these schools, the values implicit in the narrative about the students of Abbotsholme are made explicit and became the foundation of the educational arrangement later called *Landerziehungsheime* (country boarding schools), the first of which was founded by Lietz near Ilsenburg. Telling the story this way, it almost seems like Lietz found a democratic way to deal with the problems of his time.[5] This, so to speak, can be understood as one of the starting points of institutionalized New Education in Germany, as it is discussed in various comprehensive publications[6] and recurring approaches to the topic with regard to specific questions.[7]

---

4   See Hermann Lietz, *Emlohstobba: Roman oder Wirklichkeit? Bilder aus dem Schulleben* (Berlin: Dümmler, 1897). In 2017, Ralf Koerrenz, Annika Blichmann, and Sebastian Engelmann provided an introduction to the ideas and biography of Lietz in their book on European concepts and models of Alternative Education. The thoughts in this chapter elaborate on and criticize these ideas while also using the ideas brought forward in Ralf Koerrenz, Annika Blichmann, and Sebastian Engelmann, *Alternative Schooling and New Education: European Concepts and Models* (Cham: Palgrave Macmillan, 2017). All quotes from German sources were translated by the author, while bibliographic information for the original sources is provided in the footnotes.
5   Sebastian Engelmann, "Konflikt als Movens," *Zeitschrift für Pädagogik und Theologie* 71, no. 2 (2019): 132.
6   Wolfgang Keim and Ulrich Schwerdt, eds., *Handbuch der Reformpädagogik in Deutschland (1890–1933)* (Frankfurt a.M.: Peter Lang, 2013).
7   Sebastian Engelmann and Mathias Dehne, "Pädagogisierung der Zeit als Antwort auf die Sündhaftigkeit der Welt – Landerziehungsheime nach Hermann Lietz," in *Lernen zwischen Zeit und Ewigkeit: Pädagogische Praxis und Tranzendenz*, eds. Alexander Maier,

How does the foundation of New Education as a vivid discussion of ideas on schooling relate to the theoretical writings by Immanuel Wallerstein? And how does the theoretical framework of Wallerstein add to the discussion in historical education studies? This chapter tentatively tries to grasp the emergence of a New Education regime – understood as a specific mode of education that aims at the universalization of itself – from the perspective of Wallerstein's writings, primarily those relating to world-systems theory.[8] Therefore, it reflects on the development of alternative modes of education around the world as a positive story of emancipation and, at the same time, as a story of the consequent transfer of specific ideas related to nationalist attitudes and capitalist production logics. New Education and the manifold alternative modes of education, nowadays still discussed under the umbrella term "Alternative Education," are by no means inherently better or more critical than other modes. However, they offer much-needed criticism of an authoritarian system of schooling without solving the problems of power dynamics and the potential abuse of educational settings at their time. Even though there is still a positive aura around these alternative concepts for education, recent research has pointed to the fact that precisely the contrary can be the case, too. Alternative models for schooling, such as the infamous Odenwaldschule in Germany, must be considered as potentially dangerous institutions that perpetuated ideas of closedness and elitist exclusion and prepared the ground for sexual violence. Understanding this ambivalence of New Education as inherent to its theory and practice – as Jürgen Oelkers and others have pointed out[9] – must be considered a promising way to engage anew with Alternative Education in a fruitful and critical manner. All in all, the chapter hints at a new reading of the emergence of New Education at the beginning of the 20th century by combining Wallerstein's perspective with ideas from the history of education, political sociology, and political science. Thereby, it tries to offer a new perspective on the relationship between New Education, the world-system approach, and the omnipresent educational demands for inclusion

---

Jean-Marie Weber, Anne Conrad, and Peter Voss (Bad Heilbrunn: Klinkhardt, 2018), 130–133.
8   In this chapter, I understand Wallerstein's writings as a perspective, not as a coherent theory. Instead of talking about a world-systems theory, I follow Stephen Shapiro's argument, reflecting on the world-system approach as a knowledge movement that proposes new ways to think about the world in which we live.
9   Jürgen Oelkers, *Eros und Herrschaft. Die dunklen Seiten der Reformpädagogik* (Weinheim: Beltz, 2011).

which, at the same time, transport nationalist narratives. To understand this ambivalence, one must not ban the ideas of educators such as Lietz from the discourse but critically examine and newly contextualize them.

To sketch out this approach and to make the argument plausible, this chapter, in a first step, engages with more recent discussions of Wallerstein in education studies. The results are not that spectacular, but they point to the need for further approaches to world-systems analysis in education studies. Even though Wallerstein's world-systems perspective was vividly discussed for a short time in the field of comparative education, his ideas are not present in the general discussion, even though working with Wallerstein's concepts might be useful to explain the relationship between the emergence of neoliberalism and education systems. Education studies seem to struggle with the work of Wallerstein, making new approaches to it an experiment in itself that engages with thinking coined as "Marxist" or "realist" in recent years. Nevertheless, various authors have already pointed to the potential of world-systems analysis.[10] In a second step, this chapter offers an abridged collection of Wallerstein's thoughts on the relations between education, nation-building, and the necessary construction of exclusive dichotomies in this process. This introduction prepares the ground for using world-systems analysis to rewrite the history of Alternative Education as a history of struggle with inclusion, exclusion, and identity formation. In a third step, the chapter develops this specific reading by elaborating on the ideas of Hermann Lietz in a short case study. Here, Lietz is introduced as a German educator who used various educational ideas from around the world, which in itself must be understood as a migration of ideas that would not have been possible without the infrastructure of a capitalist world system. Moreover, he is also introduced as a nationalist thinker who tried to foster nation-state building through education and can be understood as a part of the centrist liberal regime Wallerstein saw emerging at the beginning of the 20th century. Finally, the chapter closes with a hint toward a revitalization of the world-systems perspective in edu-

---

10   I agree with them. Since at least the Covid-19 pandemic that started in 2020, we have been confronted with the nation-state and a realist, conflict-oriented understanding of society again. Leaving aside this conceptualization of the world does not solve any problems but creates new ones. Even though realist accounts of world politics are sometimes marginalized, they still offer a valid way to explain what is happening in the political arena.

cation studies in both research and the practice of education in a world still struggling with nationalist attitudes and a negative stance toward migration.

Wallerstein in Education Studies: Fragments of a Discussion

Even though direct comments by Immanuel Wallerstein on the education system are quite scarce – some scholars in education studies even suggest that there is no such thing as a Wallersteinian perspective on education[11] – one can use his ideas on world-systems to talk about the development of education systems on a broad scale. Education studies have already dabbled with Wallerstein but left his thoughts aside in recent years. Instead of referring to his ideas about the world-system, more contemporary research engages with neo-institutionalist theory as put forward by the team around the sociologist John W. Meyer.[12] World-systems analysis is nowadays still mentioned in contemporary discussions in comparative education, understood as an idiosyncratic part of the education studies discourse more concerned with criticizing policies and market-related state action than the discussion of developments throughout the history of education. More recent research in comparative education addresses, for example, the global education industry and the commodification processes that led to its emergence without reference to Wallerstein, even though an analysis motivated by – but not limited to – his approach might be useful.[13] Instead of working with world-systems theory, Wallerstein's differentiated historical and sociological work is often reduced to a mere reference without further elaborating on the influence or value of applying the perspective.[14] Nevertheless, world-systems analysis is one of many attempts that try to engage with the exploitative dynamics of class relations, whether this is understood in terms of groups stratified according to race or class within a

---

11   Christel Adick, "Globale Trends weltweiter Schulentwicklung: Empirische Befunde und theoretischer Erklärungen," *Zeitschrift für Erziehungswissenschaft* 6, no. 3 (2003): 181.
12   Robert R. Arnove, "World-Systems Analysis and Comparative Education in the Age of Globalization," in *International Handbook of Comparative Education*, eds. Robert Cowen and Andreas M. Kazamias (Dordrecht: Springer, 2009), 102.
13   Marcello Parreira do Amaral, Gita Steiner-Khamsi, and Christiane Thompson, eds., *Researching the Global Education Industry: Commodification, the Market and Business Involvement* (Cham: Palgrave, 2019), 9.
14   Marcello Parreira do Amaral, *Emergenz eines internationalen Bildungsregimes? International Educational Governance und Regimetheorie* (Münster: Waxmann, 2011), 16, 55.

single society or as similarly structured relations of exploitation on a nation-state level. This involvedness of the theory in very concrete political discussions might be a problem of its own kind, as world-systems analysis in the way Wallerstein thinks it cannot be understood without grappling with societal issues, as Karin Amos laid out in the Anglo-American debate on the reproduction of societal differences in schooling.[15] Christel Adick summarized Wallerstein's ideas when she stated that he assumed an undivided world-system, understanding its specific modernity as constituted by its shared division of labor and simultaneous absence of shared control mechanisms in the political arena.[16] The goal of the non-intentional movements in the world-system is the accumulation of more capital and the reproduction of its own hegemony. The expansion of the capitalist mode of production, cyclical rhythms, and general structures are patterns for analysis that Wallerstein's world-systems approach has to offer. Adick points to the fact that this reference to reoccurring structures in the process of commodification in particular might help historical comparative education studies to grasp changes in the structure of education systems. However, this might result in the application of a theory mainly aimed at explaining economic development to processes of educationalization while taking for granted that education is a result of the aforementioned economic process[17] and applying a perspective that is "too economistic as well as overly focused on nation-states as the principal actors in the global economy."[18]

Additionally, Adick points to the gap in the theoretical architecture, the missing micro-foundation of world-systems theory, raising new awareness of the problematic connection between structure and action present in this theory and others. However, world-systems analysis is not as monolithic as she describes. Taking into account the fact that a micro-foundation is missing and some orthodox readings of Wallerstein's ideas might lead to the impression that the whole development of a world-system is deterministic, we can still work with world-systems analysis in an innovative way. As such, studies in comparative education based on world-systems analysis are strictly linked

---

15 Karin Amos, "Aspekte der angloamerikanischen pädagogischen Differenzdebatte: Überlegungen zur Kontextualisierung," in *Unterschiedlich verschieden: Differenz in der Erziehungswissenschaft*, eds., Helma Lutz and Norbert Wenning (Wiesbaden: Springer 2001), 71.
16 Adick, "Globale Trends," 181.
17 Ibid., 183.
18 Arnove, "World-Systems Analysis," 105.

to critical inquiries of the social debates that take place elsewhere in social sciences or the humanities. Therefore, new approaches to world-systems analysis must not ignore post-Marxist readings of classical Marxist texts. In more recent texts and interviews, Wallerstein distanced himself from orthodox readings of Marx; therefore, all kinds of criticism that understand the world-systems approach as economically deterministic do not grasp the concept itself correctly.[19] Wallerstein rejected this orthodox interpretation of his own approach. Instead of favoring orthodox Marxism and a determined history, Wallerstein understood Marxist approaches to history as an open discourse with many voices. So, instead of considering world-systems analysis as a closed and deterministic system, this chapter tries to offer connections that might help to re-read world-systems analysis, critically engaging the understanding of world-systems analysis as a "model with universal applicability, purporting to explain global developments from the Neolithic Revolution to recent times."[20]

By applying the lens of world-systems analysis, scholars in education studies might gain further insights into the relations between states, education systems, and educational policy on a global scale that are also connected to 1) the historical development of education systems, and 2) the rise of educational regimes, the individual fighting for their nation's success, and capitalism. Applying this perspective can "document the systemic ways in which hegemonic powers in core countries extract surplus labour from the coerced or semi-coerced labour of the noncore regions with consequent deleterious consequences for their education systems."[21] Even though world-systems analysis does not seem to be widely considered in comparative education right now, taking it into account can help to understand phenomena such as commodification or marketization differently.[22]

---

19   Immanuel Wallerstein, "Immanuel Wallerstein's Thousand Marxisms," *Jacobin Magazine*, November 11, 2019, https://jacobinmag.com/2019/09/immanuel-wallerstein-marxism-world-systems-theory-capitalism/.
20   Andreas M. Kazamias, "Reclaiming A Lost Legacy: The Historical Humanist Vision in Comparative Education," in *International Handbook of Comparative Education*, eds. Robert Cowen and Andreas M. Kazamias (Dordrecht: Springer, 2009), 1272.
21   Arnove, "World-Systems Analysis," 105.
22   For further ideas on the application of Wallerstein's ideas in comparative education, see Thomas G. Griffiths and Lisa Knezevic, "Wallerstein's World-Systems Analysis in Comparative Education: A Case Study," *Prospects* 40, no. 4 (2010): 447–449.

Wallerstein on Education: World-Systems Analysis Operationalized

Since the so-called pedagogical 18th century, education must be understood as one of the main modes of keeping power in a state harnessed by those in economically superior positions, the ruling class. Schooling in particular is always connected to the current economic and political system, which leads to the conclusion – as brought forward by Austromarxist educator Siegfried Bernfeld – that education must be understood as conservative in its nature. It only reproduces the current structure of society.[23] The same goes, according to Wallerstein, for the relation between weak and strong states. Education – which is elaborated most intensively in the fourth volume of Wallerstein's epochal work *The Modern World-System* – must be understood, as an explicitly mentioned cultural practice, as an element of this relation. This has already been pointed out in more general remarks on the relations between core and periphery, respectively, strong and weak states. As this forms the most important element of Wallerstein's thinking in realistic dependencies between nation-states, it also serves as a starting point for understanding the role of education: "Strong states relate to weak states by pressuring them to accept cultural practices-linguistic policy; educational policy, including where university students may study; media distribution-that will reinforce the long-term linkage between them."[24]

Following this line of thought, Wallerstein leads us to the conclusion that education is important in itself when it comes to transporting ideology, i.e., to stabilizing and reproducing the present system. Therefore, world-systems analysis – like most theories and approaches in sociology, political sciences, and psychology – implicitly relies on an understanding of learning: "In general, world-system scholars contend that educational assistance provides a vehicle for the transmission of ideologies from core to and, subsequently, for the 'intellectual socialization' of periphery."[25]

Without education and the governance of learning processes in various forms, there would be no reproduction of ideologies. In consequence, there

---

23 Siegfried Bernfeld, *Sisyphos oder die Grenzen der Erziehung* (Frankfurt a.M.: Suhrkamp, 1967).
24 Immanuel Wallerstein, *World-Systems Analysis: An Introduction* (Durham, NC: Duke University Press, 2004), 55.
25 Thomas Clayton, "Beyond Mystification: Reconnecting World-System Theory for Comparative Education," *Comparative Education Review* 42, no. 4 (1988): 485.

would be no foundation for the exchange of ideas and the often-forceful expansion or diffusion of modes of production. In a nutshell, education is used as a mediator to control individuals by introducing or reproducing certain aspects of ideology. This obviously leads to the result that education itself becomes a recurrent topic of political fights. Therefore, more conservative positions were always aware that educating individuals and offering them the chance to participate in a changing society might negatively affect the hierarchy: "Conservatives thus abhorred democracy, which for them signaled the end of respect for hierarchy. They were furthermore suspicious of widespread access to education, which for them ought to be reserved for the training of elite cadres."[26]

Education is thus always understood as a mode of keeping discriminating differentiations at work to control a society. Those differences, however, were not new to the daily lives of humans: "Difference and inequalities of persons of different social origins – orders (*Stände*, Estates), class, gender, race, and education – were not invented in the nineteenth century. They had long existed and had been considered natural, inevitable, and indeed desirable."[27]

When it comes to citizenship – as we will see later in the writings of Hermann Lietz – education becomes an integral element of constructing citizens. It can be understood as essential for the dichotomous construction of inside and outside because, throughout the history of emancipation, it became necessary for the ruling elites to distinguish between those who are "worthy" of participating in society and those who are to be excluded: "The attempt to circumscribe the meaning of citizenship took many forms, all of them necessarily involving the creation of antinomies that could justify the division into passive and active citizens. Binary distinctions (of rank, of class, of gender, of race/ethnicity, of education) are ancient realities."[28]

Following this argument, educational thought must be considered a crucial element of replicating the operations of inclusion and exclusion that allow nation-states to reproduce the dominant power relations. As various authors have claimed from sociological perspectives, this kind of exclusion is necessary

---

26 Wallerstein, *World-Systems Analysis*, 62.
27 Immanuel Wallerstein, *The Modern World-System*, vol. 4: *Centrist Liberalism Triumphant 1789–1814* (Berkeley, CA: University of California Press, 2011), 217.
28 Ibid., 164.

to realize inclusion.[29] Categories such as race, class, and gender were radicalized in education to control the masses via targeted education practices or their exclusion from them. Especially in educational theory, talking about equality in pedagogical settings simultaneously creates inequality because there simply is no way to educate individuals in the same way. This structure of educational processes is only leveled out by pointing to specific aims of education or focusing on a specific group of students, as will be seen later in the writings of Hermann Lietz. As mentioned above, educational aims are derived from dominant ideologies. They are not generally "humane" or detached from certain philosophical discussions or socio-economic interests. The project of educating "good" citizens for the nation-state is described by Wallerstein as a Western project driven by the values of the middle class:

> In the nineteenth century, the so-called middle classes came to dominate the Western world, and Europe came to dominate the world. When one has achieved the top position, the problem is no longer how to get there but how to stay there. The middle classes nationally, and the Europeans globally, sought to maintain their advantage by appropriating the mantle of nature and virtue to justify privilege. They called it civilization, and this concept was a key ingredient of their effort. In the Western world, it was translated into education, and education became a way of controlling the masses.[30]

Education as a means of control, however, always came in disguise. Civilization, as mentioned above, was not presented or even understood as a potentially suppressive force established by the Europeans but as a project beneficial for all human beings. Instead of unveiling civilization as the exclusive concept that solidified borders between people at the same time as it offered them the possibility to transgress them, education took off as a project closely related to the liberal center. Offering "'republicanism, secularism, popular self-education, co-operation, land reform, internationalism,' and all these themes had by now become part of the litany of the liberal center, at least of its more progressive flank."[31] All those mechanisms are marked by Wallerstein. By describ-

---

29   For the argument, see Marcus Emmerich and Ulrike Hormel, *Heterogenität – Diversity – Intersektionalität: Zur Logik sozialer Unterscheidungen in pädagogischen Semantiken der Differenz* (Wiesbaden: Springer VS, 2012).
30   Wallerstein, *The Modern World-System*, 156.
31   Ibid., 176.

ing the rise of centrist liberalism and its matrimony with what has since been coined the "neoliberal agenda," he undoubtedly touches on the cornerstones of the history of education.

Alternative Education as a Nationalist Project: A Wallersteinian Reading

As Wallerstein points out, new perspectives are better understood if we consider them "a protest against older perspectives."[32] Thinking with the categories of conflict and oppression rather than with ideas of harmonious and non-forced travel of ideas in politically engaged and comparative historical education studies is key to further developing theory and our representation of history alike: "Understanding the world is a key to changing it for the better – a goal much in accord with scholarship in the field of comparative education and its missions of contributing to theory building, more enlightened educational policy and practice, and ultimately to international understanding and peace."[33]

If science is not only about an assumed objective representation but also about making the world a better (understood) place, theories that aim at criticizing unjust social realities, such as those of Wallerstein, have a place in historical analysis. Their theoretical frame of reference allows scholars to identify the character of their own research object as a political one. Insight into this connection between researcher and research forces individuals to act in three ways: "as an analyst, in search of truth; as a moral person, in search of the good and the beautiful; and as a political person, seeking to unify the true with the good and the beautiful."[34]

One case to apply this method with a specific focus on how the theory produced in educational thought influences the production of categories such as "citizen" or "nation" is the thorough examination of New Education in light of Wallerstein's writings.[35] Instead of grasping the alternatives offered at the turn

---

32 Wallerstein, *World-Systems Analysis*, 1.
33 Arnove, "World-Systems Analysis," 114.
34 Immanuel Wallerstein, *European Universalism: The Rhetoric of Power* (New York: The New Press, 2006), 80.
35 Tom G. Griffiths and Lisa Knezevic, "World-Systems Analysis in Comparative Education: An Alternative to Cosmopolitanism," *Current Issues in Comparative Education* 12, no. 1 (2009): 66–67.

from the 19th to the 20th century as normatively better, they can be marked as small steps in the process Wallerstein describes in his books. New Education – in Germany called *Reformpädagogik*, in Japan, e.g., *Zenjin Education* – generally aimed at establishing a child-centered education that not only addressed the children via direct instruction but also fostered their individual experiences as the privileged mode of learning. New Education criticizes the assumed "old" education as dull, repetitive, and missing individual needs. So, instead of instruction in class, experiencing and learning in other environments was preferred, thereby making real life the educator of the child. New Education is normally understood as an international movement with various lines of thought and variations that developed all over the world, even though its diversity is often reduced to some key thinkers or to a non-specified idea of a different form of education.[36] Bearing in mind, however, the implications of world-systems analysis, one can also argue that New Education emerged as a capitalist project in a Western state that tried to dominate the global pedagogical discussion. Nationalism – or at least the melioration of the nation-state's pedagogical system – served as the motor of the global movement of ideas. This is especially true for Lietz, but it can also be assumed for various other examples of Alternative Education.

Hermann Lietz's thoughts on education are all based on his deeply rooted nationalism. They manifest in a declamatory and often romanticizing way of speaking about education, as Jürgen Oelkers pointed out in his ground-breaking criticism of Alternative Education.[37] Lietz's basic idea was that people are born into a specific cultural context, which continues to influence them. Education plays a special role in this, namely, in ensuring that the specifically national religious ethics subsumed in the national context will be transmitted to the next generation as effectively as possible. Education, in Lietz's sense, was not about changing society first and foremost but about conserving what would help the German nation prosper. His ideas on schooling were about schooling in and for the German nation. As such, the arrangements for school reform needed to serve the evolution of national strengths. School reform was also required to support and advance the fight against deficiencies in one's own national cultural context. Like many of his contemporaries, Lietz

---

36   Winfried Böhm, *Die Reformpädagogik. Montessori, Waldorf und andere Lehren* (Munich: C.H. Beck, 2012).
37   Jürgen Oelkers, *Reformpädagogik: Eine kritische Dogmengeschichte* (Weinheim: Juventa, 2005).

criticized the vices of his time, especially everything related to an assumed natural human being: "All German schools have to fight the bad habits of drinking alcohol and smoking, which are harmful to health and strength."[38] This shows that, to Lietz, the context of educational thought is also defined by national traits – in contrast to a progressive position, with its vision of one single humanity, universally uniting all people. The valorization of one's own nation is inevitably connected to the depreciation of others. Resonant in this respect is the saying, "*Am deutschen Wesen soll die Welt genesen*" ("German ways will cure the whole world").

His "love" for his nation becomes evident in his description of the ideal teacher. In an appeal to the body of teachers, Lietz characterizes the role and position of teachers as follows: "Spark understanding and excitement for the character and future challenges of the nation; practice with the young people in your small community to learn civic virtues, let everyone within the community serve the whole with full force, let them carry out duties, exercise their rights."[39] He also described the teacher as "[a] priest of humanity and of God in the true meaning of the word,"[40] thereby contrasting the teacher with the "instructor or even the drill master"[41] and offering deep insights into his religion. Even though Lietz's educational thought was based on firm beliefs in the superiority of his nation and the importance of an ordered state, he also aimed at establishing a relationship between teachers and students that fostered the use of the latter's own reason: "The teacher of the past viewed the student first and foremost as someone subordinate that he could command, backed up by the authority provided to him by his office and his superior age."[42] However, when discussing the contrast between the old and the new teacher, Lietz says: "The teacher of the new school and the parents of the new family are completely different [from the old types of teacher], who rely only (!) on the natural au-

---

38 Hermann Lietz, *Die dringendsten Forderungen der deutschen Schulreform: Das fünfzehnte Jahr im DLEH. Beiträge zur Schulreform, Zweiter Teil* (Leipzig: Voigtländer 1913), 95–96.
39 Hermann Lietz, "Beiträge zu einem pädagogischen Programm für die Zwecke der DLEH-Stiftung" in *Das vierzehnte Jahr im DLEH*, ed. Hermann Lietz (Leipzig: Voigtländer, 1912), 52.
40 Hermann Lietz, *Emlohstobba: Roman oder Wirklichkeit? Bilder aus dem Schulleben der Vergangenheit, Gegenwart oder Zukunft?* (Berlin: Dieck, 1897), 53.
41 Ibid.
42 Hermann Lietz, "Art. Landerziehungsheime," in *Encyclopädisches Handbuch der Pädagogik*, ed. Wilhelm Rein (Langensalza: Beyer, 1906), 298.

thority that comes with intellectual, ethical superiority."[43] The idea of a "natural authority" is Lietz's expression of the values one needs to reform society via schooling.

Yet, next to his emphasis on German values, he also presents us with a set of quite different ideas: striving for international contacts, international understanding, and an understanding of civilization – as mentioned by Wallerstein – depicted as universal, generally humane ethics. What remains in Lietz's work is an unrelieved tension between a sense of nationality and a vision of universality. The struggle to deal with this tension is not only evident in Lietz's work but also in Wallerstein's theory when he points to the interconnection between nation-building in terms of universality while, at the same time, mechanisms of exclusion are at work. Therefore, one can argue that the development of New Education in the 19th and early 20th centuries parallels the development of capitalist hegemony pointed to by Wallerstein.

According to Ralf Koerrenz, it is possible to understand the work of Hermann Lietz in two entirely different ways.[44] One very plausible view is that Lietz was politically right-wing; this is supported by his critique of urban culture mixed with his prejudices against and religiously motivated hatred of Judaism and socialism. Taking this position into account, Lietz's educational thought seems to be, on the one hand, irrelevant to today's discussions. However, on the other hand, Koerrenz points to the systematic aspects of Lietz's work that perfectly align with Wallerstein's ideas about the triumph of centrist liberalism and the neoliberal agenda. This creates turmoil in the categories ascribed to Lietz. When applying the perspective of Wallerstein's world-systems analysis, however, the categorization of Lietz as a national conservative is deconstructed. His ideas – e.g., the new relation between teachers and students or the emphasis on universally applicable ethics that tries to understand all humans as equal – are similar to liberal motifs realized in today's schooling. They are also present in politically different educational concepts of his time and, later on, are even found in communist approaches to alternative modes of education.[45] However, those assumptions are eminently flawed when one consid-

---

43 Ibid.
44 Ralf Koerrenz, *Hermann Lietz: Einführung mit zentralen Texten* (Paderborn: Schöningh, 2011), 9.
45 Sebastian Engelmann, "Edwin Hoernle: Communist Education and Revolutionary Antimilitarism," in *War and Communism*, eds. Tobias Hirschmüller and Frank Jacob (Paderborn: Brill/Schöningh, 2021).

ers Wallerstein's ideas on differences and the role of schooling in this process. From the perspective of world-systems theory, the national-conservative curricula of Lietz or his emphasis on national values are emerging centrist liberal patterns that developed over the next 100 years into the present-day capitalist schooling system.

All in all, reading the ideas of educators in the context of New Education from the perspective of Wallerstein's world-systems approach sheds light on the precarity of categories and capitalist land-grabbing in educational practice. Lietz's ideas on New Education ultimately influenced a variety of educators in Germany and other European states. The New Education movement finally institutionalized itself in the early 1920s. The exchange – mostly restricted to the European context, although newer publications hint at Asian influences[46] – was institutionalized through the establishment of the New Education Fellowship, the oldest international organization for promoting progressive education, which, during the 1920s, became a forum for the international exchange of experience. Leading members included, among others, Beatrice Ensor (England), Elisabeth Rotten (Germany), and Adolphe Ferrière (Switzerland). It is mostly understood as an international project.[47] Nevertheless, it was based on nationalist ideas that aimed at proclaiming its educational goals and their virtues as the most humane and universal ones.

This first attempt to understand New Education from the perspective of world-systems analysis produced the insight that there might be more to the assumption that education since the 18th century – especially individualization and the appeal to individual reason in an experience-based learning environment – catered to the rise of centrist liberalism. Even though Lietz offered ideas in conflict with the capitalist mode of production in his time, his thoughts are nowadays incorporated in capitalist schooling practices that rely on individualized learning and harvesting the results of individual reason. Added to this general insight into the fragility of categorical ascriptions is the fact that Lietz's ideas were altered throughout their history in various contexts. For example, Lietz influenced the socialist thinker Minna Specht, who learned at one

---

46   Elia Horn, *Indien als Erzieher: Orientalismus in der deutschen Reformpädagogik und Jugendbewegung 1918–1933* (Bad Heilbrunn: Klinkhardt, 2018).
47   Hermann Röhrs, "Die 'New Education Fellowship' – ein Forum der internationalen Reformpädagogik," in *Die Reformpädagogik auf den Kontinenten: Ein Handbuch*, eds. Volker Lehnhart and Hermann Röhrs (Frankfurt a.M.: Peter Lang, 1994), 191.

of his country boarding schools and later opened her own school.[48] Furthermore, there are still boarding schools that use Hermann Lietz's name while also developing his ideas and integrating learning experiences that try to decrease nationalism and foster international learning.[49] It seems that the ideas of Hermann Lietz are not limited to one interpretation but instead are flexible. Therefore, they can easily be claimed by the capitalist logic of a spreading world-system. The recurrent discussions about New Education itself can be understood as the epitome of capitalist education – change is structurally incorporated, keeping them flexible until there is nothing more to resist.

World-Systems Analysis and the Emergence of a New Education Regime: A Theoretical and Practical Outlook

Even though the emergence of New Education as an international movement is nowadays mostly understood as a person-driven network phenomenon on an international scale, using the world-systems approach can help to understand the rise of New Education differently. It is most definitely not an innocent case of migrating ideas. Instead of this positive interpretation, world-systems analysis marks Alternative Education as a possible element of the ever-increasing call for more *mobile* human capital and slow-and-steady economization of the educational system.

This chapter offered a new reading of selected texts of a prominent representative of the New Education movement enriched with the theoretical perspective of Immanuel Wallerstein. It made plausible the assumption that New Education can be understood as one of the elements of Wallerstein called "centrist liberalism" in his later writings. To elucidate this argument, the chapter first introduced fragments of the discussion of world-systems analysis in German and international comparative education studies. On the one hand, it pinpointed the discussed problems and, on the other hand, it emphasized the benefits of world-systems analysis. In a second step, world-systems analysis was

---

48   For further information, see Sebastian Engelmann, *Pädagogik der Sozialen Freiheit: Eine Einführung in das Denken Minna Spechts* (Paderborn: Schöningh, 2018).

49   Sebastian Engelmann, "Sprache, Weltgesellschaft und Globale Bildung: Das Modul Sprache im Bildungsjahr des Hermann Lietz Gymnasiums Schloss Bieberstein," in *Globale Bildung auf Reisen: Das Bildungsjahr an der Hermann-Lietz Schule Schloss Bieberstein*, ed. Ralf Koerrenz (Paderborn: Schöningh, 2015), 93–97.

discussed with a focus on Wallerstein's ideas on education, using his remarks on education that correspond with the rise of mass schooling and bourgeoise educational policies in the 18th and 19th centuries. In a third step, the context of New Education and the writings of Hermann Lietz were introduced and discussed, thereby also offering insights into these mostly untranslated texts for an international audience. These texts provide the evidence for this text's central argument: Lietz's educational thought can be considered an element of the capitalist, liberal centrist project Wallerstein described in his later writings. There is scope to write a more coherent and extensive history of New Education while applying the ideas of Wallerstein's world-systems analysis. However, considering the world-systems approach in education studies (again) has more to offer than a fresh perspective on history: it helps us to understand the dominance of certain practices, ideologies, and concepts, such as the almost obsessive focus on citizenship education or the constant renewal of education for the nation-state in educational theory and practice. Further, it shines a light on the ambivalence of educational practices discussed under the umbrella term "citizenship education." Often, these endeavors mask themselves as universal and ethical. However, they can also be understood as part of the history of nation-building, and they still rely on inclusion and exclusion – as Wallerstein and others have pointed out.

As I have suggested elsewhere,[50] New Education invented and radicalized the idea of the individual learner and forced individuals to act on their own. It also supported the development of concepts such as life-long learning, which is based on the assumed plasticity of the learner, and perfectly serves the ideas of the *project polis* or the *entrepreneurial self*, which are vividly discussed in ongoing critical research following the ground-breaking work by Luc Boltanski and Eve Chiapello.[51] Without the rise of New Education, schooling nowadays would not be as it is. Various concepts such as *individualization, project learning*, or even *service learning* would not be part of the didactic repertoire of teachers and educators. Additionally, current ideas on the *mobility of learners* and the *strive to internationalization* might not be on the agenda. It is this connection between and within its core that began to move the nationalist project to the periphery,

---

50 Sebastian Engelmann, "Transhumanismus und Erziehungswissenschaft: (Un)heilsgeschichten über die Entfehlerung des Menschen," in *Transzendenz zum Transhumanismus*, eds. Sabrina Lausen, Martin Dröge, Richard Janus, and Martin Fromme (Wiesbaden: Springer VS, forthcoming).

51 Luc Boltanski and Eve Chiapello, *The New Spirit of Capitalism* (London: Verso, 2017).

was implemented there, and changed the educational landscape forever that needs to be analyzed from the perspective of world-systems theory to hint at the economic results of the emergence of a New Education regime as part of a centrist liberal project.[52]

One final point is still up for discussion. Besides the possible positive outcomes for research in the history of education, world-systems analysis might become even more interesting for dealing with recent and urgent issues in education studies, especially regarding the latter's new-found interest in postcolonial settings. More and more researchers are engaging with postcolonial writings and trying to offer decolonial options for education studies. However, it seems like the discussion still lacks a sound theoretical foundation. The perspective of world-systems analysis brought forward by Immanuel Wallerstein may be helpful to understand both the history of education and educational practices anew. It is sensitive to the driving forces of capitalism while at the same time hinting at the patterns of history. Education studies need to enter this discussion, newly addressing topics such as citizenship, nationality, and migration without falling for the rhetoric of flexibility and novelty. Applying the perspective of world-systems analysis will contribute to and help to start a new knowledge movement. Rewriting what we already know seems to be a good start to this process, which will not end with academic discussion. Accordingly, the history of education and the practice of education are inseparably entwined.

Works Cited

Adick, Christel. "Globale Trends weltweiter Schulentwicklung: Empirische Befunde und theoretischer Erklärungen." *Zeitschrift für Erziehungswissenschaft* 6, no. 3 (2003): 173–187.

Amos, Karin. "Aspekte der angloamerikanischen pädagogischen Differenzdebatte: Überlegungen zur Kontextualisierung." In *Unterschiedlich verschieden: Differenz in der Erziehungswissenschaft*, edited by Helman Lutz and Norbert Wenning, 71–92. Opladen: Leske and Budrich, 2001.

Amos, Karin. "Theorien der Vergleichenden Erziehungswissenschaft." In *Internationale und Vergleichende Erziehungswissenschaft: Geschichte, Theorie, Meth-*

---

52 Wallerstein, *World System*, 321.

ode und Forschungsfelder, edited by Marcello Parreira do Amaral and Karin Amos, 59–78. Münster: Waxmann, 2015.

Arnove, Robert F. "World-Systems Analysis and Comparative Education in the Age of Globalization." In *International Handbook of Comparative Education*, edited by Robert Cowen and Andreas M. Kazamias, 101–119. Dordrecht: Springer, 2009

Bernfeld, Siegfried. *Sisyphos oder die Grenzen der Erziehung*. Frankfurt a.M: Surhkamp, 1967.

Böhm, Winfried. *Die Reformpädagogik: Montessori, Waldorf und andere Lehren*. Munich: C.H. Beck, 2012.

Boltanski, Luc and Eve Chiapello. *The New Spirit of Capitalism*. London/New York: Verso Books, 2017.

Clayton, Thomas. "Beyond Mystification: Reconnecting World-System Theory for Comparative Education." *Comparative Education Review* 42, no. 4 (1998): 479–496.

Emmerich, Marcus and Ulrike Hormel. *Heterogenität – Diversity – Intersektionalität: Zur Logik sozialer Unterscheidungen in pädagogischen Semantiken der Differenz*. Wiesbaden: Springer VS, 2012.

Engelmann, Sebastian. "Edwin Hoernle: Communist Education and Revolutionary Antimilitarism." In *War and Communism*, edited by Tobias Hirschmüller and Frank Jacob. Paderborn: Brill/Schöningh, forthcoming.

Engelmann, Sebastian. "Konflikt als Movens – Chancen für Schule, Religion und Demokratie." *Zeitschrift für Pädagogik* 71, no. 2 (2019): 131–141.

Engelmann, Sebastian. *Pädagogik der Sozialen Freiheit: Eine Einführung in das Denken Minna Spechts*. Paderborn: Schöningh, 2018.

Engelmann, Sebastian. "Sprache, Weltgesellschaft und Globale Bildung: Das Modul Sprache im Bildungsjahr des Hermann Lietz Gymnasiums Schloss Bieberstein." In *Globale Bildung auf Reisen: Das Bildungsjahr an der Hermann-Lietz Schule Schloss Bieberstein*, edited by Ralf Koerrenz, 93–104. Paderborn: Schöningh, 2015.

Engelmann, Sebastian. "Transhumanismus und Erziehungswissenschaft: (Un)heilsgeschichten über die Entfehlerung des Menschen." In *Von Transzendenz zum Transhumanismus*, edited by Sabina Lausen, Martin Dröge, Richard Janus, and Martin Fromme. Wiesbaden: Springer VS, forthcoming.

Engelmann, Sebastian and Mathias Dehne. "Pädagogisierung der Zeit als Antwort auf die Sündhaftigkeit der Welt – Landerziehungsheime nach Hermann Lietz." In *Lernen zwischen Zeit und Ewigkeit: Pädagogische Praxis und*

Tranzendenz, edited by Alexander Maier, Jean-Marie Weber, Anne Conrad, and Peter Voss, 130–148. Klinkhardt: Bad Heilbrunn, 2018.

Griffiths, Thomas G. and Lisa Knezevic "Wallerstein's World-Systems Analysis in Comparative Education: A Case Study." *Prospects* 40, no. 4 (2010), 447–449.

Griffths, Thomas G. and Lisa Knezevic. "World-Systems Analysis in Comparative Education: An Alternative to Cosmopolitanism." *Current Issues in Comparative Education* 12, no. 1 (2009): 66–75.

Horn, Elia. *Indien als Erzieher: Orientalismus in der deutschen Reformpädagogik und Jugendbewegung 1918–1933*. Bad Heilbrunn: Klinkhardt, 2018.

Kazamias, Andreas M. "Reclaiming a Lost Legacy: The Historical Humanist Vision in Comparative Education." In *International Handbook of Comparative Education*, edited by Robert Cowen and Andreas M. Kazamias, 1267–1276. Dordrecht: Springer, 2009.

Keim, Wolfgang and Ulrich Schwerdt, eds. *Handbuch der Reformpädagogik in Deutschland (1890–1933)*. Frankfurt a.M.: Peter Lang, 2013.

Koerrenz, Ralf, Annika Blichmann, and Sebastian Engelmann. *Alternative Schooling and New Education: European Concepts and Theories*. Cham: Palgrave, 2017.

Koerrenz, Ralf. *Hermann Lietz: Einführung mit zentralen Texten*. Paderborn: Schöningh, 2011.

Lietz, Hermann. "Art. Landerziehungsheime." In *Encyclopädisches Handbuch der Pädagogik*, edited by Wilhelm Rein, 290–299. Langensalza: Beyer, 1906.

Lietz, Hermann. *Beiträge zu einem pädagogischen Programm für die Zwecke der DLEH: Das vierzehnte Jahr im DLEH*. Leipzig: Voigtländer, 1912.

Lietz, Hermann. *Die dringendsten Forderungen der deutschen Schulreform: Das fünfzehnte Jahr im DLEH. Beiträge zur Schulreform. Zweiter Teil*. Leipzig: Voigtländer, 1913.

Lietz, Hermann. *Emlohstobba: Roman oder Wirklichkeit? Bilder aus dem Schulleben*. Berlin: Dümmler, 1897.

Lietz, Hermann. *Emlohstobba: Roman oder Wirklichkeit? Bilder aus dem Schulleben der Vergangenheit, Gegenwart oder Zukunft?* Berlin: Dieck, 1897.

Oelkers, Jürgen. *Eros und Herrschaft: Die dunklen Seiten der Reformpädagogik*. Weinheim: Beltz, 2011.

Oelkers, Jürgen. *Reformpädagogik: Eine kritische Dogmengeschichte*. Weinheim: Juventa, 2005

Parreira do Amaral, Marcello. *Emergenz eines internationalen Bildungsregimes? International Educational Governance und Regimetheorie.* Münster: Waxmann, 2011.

Parreira do Amaral, Marcello, Gita Steiner-Khamsi, and Christiane Thompson, eds. *Researching the Global Education Industry: Commodification, the Market and Business Involvment.* Cham: Palgrave, 2019.

Röhrs, Herrmann. "Die 'New Education Fellowship' – ein Forum der internationalen Reformpädagogik." In *Die Reformpädagogik auf den Kontinenten: Ein Handbuch*, edited by Herrmann Röhrs and Volker Lenhart, 191–203. Frankfurt a.M.: Peter Lang, 1994.

Wallerstein, Immanuel. *European Universalism: The Rhetoric of Power.* New York: The New Press, 2006.

Wallerstein, Immanuel. "Immanuel Wallerstein's Thousand Marxisms." *Jacobin Magazine*, November 11, 2019. https://jacobinmag.com/2019/09/immanuel-wallerstein-marxism-world-systems-theory-capitalism/.

Wallerstein, Immanuel. *The Modern World-System*, vol. 4: *Centrist Liberalism Triumphant, 1789–1914*. Berkeley, CA: California University Press, 2011.

Wallerstein, Immanuel. *World-Systems Analysis: An Introduction.* Durham, NC: Duke University Press, 2004.

8. Contributors

Giuditta Bassano is Researcher in Semiotics at LUMSA, Rome. Her main research interests are Greimasian Semiotics and Semiotics of Law.

Sebastian Engelmann is Assistant Professor for the History and Theory of Education at the University of Education (PH) in Karlsruhe, Germany. His main research interests are the history and theory of education, new education and democracy education.

James Horncastle is an Assistant Professor in the Department of Global Humanities and holder of the Edward and Emily McWhinney Professorship in International Relations at Simon Fraser University, Canada. His research interests include: refugee and migration studies; international relations; and the history of modern Greece.

Frank Jacob is Professor of Global History at Nord Universitet, Norway. His main research interests are revolution theory and comparative revolutionary history.

Stephen Shapiro teaches in the Department of English and Comparative Literary Studies at the University of Warwick. His main interests are cultural materialism and the cultural end of centrist liberalism.

Social Sciences

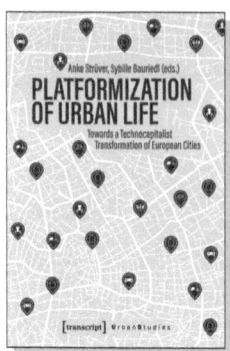

Anke Strüver, Sybille Bauriedl (eds.)
Platformization of Urban Life
Towards a Technocapitalist Transformation
of European Cities

September 2022, 304 p., pb.
29,50 € (DE), 978-3-8376-5964-1
E-Book: available as free open access publication
PDF: ISBN 978-3-8394-5964-5

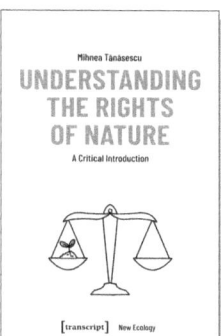

Mihnea Tanasescu
Understanding the Rights of Nature
A Critical Introduction

February 2022, 168 p., pb.
40,00 € (DE), 978-3-8376-5431-8
E-Book: available as free open access publication
PDF: ISBN 978-3-8394-5431-2

Oliver Krüger
Virtual Immortality –
God, Evolution, and the Singularity
in Post- and Transhumanism

2021, 356 p., pb., ill.
35,00 € (DE), 978-3-8376-5059-4
E-Book:
PDF: 34,99 € (DE), ISBN 978-3-8394-5059-8

**All print, e-book and open access versions of the titles in our list
are available in our online shop www.transcript-publishing.com**

Social Sciences

Dean Caivano, Sarah Naumes
The Sublime of the Political
Narrative and Autoethnography as Theory

2021, 162 p., hardcover
100,00 € (DE), 978-3-8376-4772-3
E-Book:
PDF: 99,99 € (DE), ISBN 978-3-8394-4772-7

Friederike Landau, Lucas Pohl, Nikolai Roskamm (eds.)
[Un]Grounding
Post-Foundational Geographies

2021, 348 p., pb., col. ill.
50,00 € (DE), 978-3-8376-5073-0
E-Book:
PDF: 49,99 € (DE), ISBN 978-3-8394-5073-4

Andreas de Bruin
Mindfulness and Meditation at University
10 Years of the Munich Model

2021, 216 p., pb.
25,00 € (DE), 978-3-8376-5696-1
E-Book: available as free open access publication
PDF: ISBN 978-3-8394-5696-5

All print, e-book and open access versions of the titles in our list
are available in our online shop www.transcript-publishing.com